THE BOYHOOD MEMOIRS OF

T0069274

Also by A. E. Hotchner

Dear Papa, Dear Hotch

Shameless Exploitation in Pursuit of the Common Good
(with Paul Newman)

The Day I Fired Alan Ladd

After the Storm

Louisiana Purchase

Blown Away

Hemingway and His World

Choice People

The Man Who Lived at the Ritz

Sophia, Living and Loving

Doris Day

Treasure

Papa Hemingway

The Dangerous American

Plays

The World of Nick Adams

Lovers, Lawyers and Lunatics

Welcome to the Club

Café Universe

The White House

A Short Happy Life

The Hemingway Hero

Sweet Prince

THE BOYHOOD MEMOIRS OF

A. E. Hotchner

King of the Hill

Looking for Miracles

Missouri Historical Society Press
St. Louis
distributed by University of Missouri Press

© 2007 by A. E. Hotchner
All rights reserved   13 12 11   3 4 5

The lines on page 104 are from "On the Sunny Side of the Street," by Dorothy Fields and Jimmy McHugh. Copyright 1930 by Shapiro, Bernstein & Co., Inc., 666 Fifth Avenue, New York, NY 10019. Copyright renewed and assigned. Used by permission.

The lines on page 185 are from "I Can't Give You Anything but Love," words by Dorothy Fields, music by Jimmy McHugh. Copyright 1928 by Mills Music, Inc. Copyright renewed 1956. Used by permission.

Library of Congress Cataloging-in-Publication Data

Hotchner, A. E.
[King of the hill]
The boyhood memoirs of A.E. Hotchner / A.E. Hotchner.
p. cm.
Summary: "Bound together for the first time, these two boyhood memoirs relate A. E. Hotchner's coming of age in the Midwest during the Depression"--Provided by publisher.
ISBN 978-1-883982-60-7 (pbk. : alk. paper)
1. Hotchner, A. E.--Childhood and youth. 2. Authors, American--20th century--Biography. I. Hotchner, A. E. Looking for miracles. II. Title.
PS3558.O8Z46 2007
813'.52--dc22
[B]
2007018490

Distributed by University of Missouri Press

Designed by Madonna Gauding
Cover illustration by William Low
Printed and bound by Thomson-Shore

For Virginia, with all my love,
in celebration of June 28th

Introduction

Aaron Edward Hotchner grew up in St. Louis, went to Soldan High School, and then attended Washington University, where he studied to be a lawyer. After two years in the practice of law, he left St. Louis to join the Air Force. When the war was over, he decided to forgo his legal career and pursue a career in writing. And a very successful pursuit it was. Hotchner's articles appeared in the best magazines and journals of the time, and he has also been an editor, biographer, novelist, playwright, and, with Paul Newman, entrepreneur of the rarest type. All profits from their extraordinarily successful *Newman's Own* foods and other ventures are turned over to numerous charities, including the Hole in the Wall Gang camps that they established for children with serious illnesses. A very entertaining book about their business, *Shameless Exploitation in Pursuit of the Common Good: The Madcap Business Adventure by the Truly Oddest Couple,* written by Hotchner and Newman, was published in 2003.

Hotchner's other books include the wonderful memoir *Papa Hemingway;* biographies of Doris Day and Sophia Loren; *The Man Who Lived at the Ritz,* a novel of excitement and suspense; and many more. He has written for television, the theater, and the movies. In 1993, *King of the Hill,* a memoir of his youth in St. Louis during the Depression, was made into a film directed by Steven Soderbergh. Hotchner has been a strong supporter of his alma mater, endowing the annual playwriting competition at Washington University in St. Louis and reinstating a dormant scriptwriting course, among other contributions. The university honored him with an honorary Doctorate of Letters and named the performing arts department's studio theater for him.

The most intimate legacy Hotchner has given his city is the memoirs of his life as a young St. Louisan—*King of the Hill* and *Looking for Miracles*—which we at the Missouri Historical Society Press have the privilege of reprinting. Of course he's a wonderful storyteller, and these are skillful and compelling stories. But their value, to those who live in St. Louis and to the larger community as well, is beyond entertainment. By sharing with us his story of a time past and a city much changed in seventy-plus years, Hotchner has allowed us to discover a part of our mutual history that we otherwise would not have known. This is the business the Missouri Historical Society is in, collecting and preserving the stories that have brought us to this point in time.

In the summer of 1996, Hotch sat down with me for a long interview that turned into much more of a storytelling session. It was inevitable that this conversation between a writer born and raised in St. Louis and a historian who in midlife had planted his roots here would turn to this city we both know from entirely different perspectives. Having recently reread *King of the Hill,* I was interested in what he felt for St. Louis and what role this place played, and still plays, in his life.

"It's a mother role," he mused. "I was nurtured in this city . . . the streets I was raised on were mean streets . . . in meaner times, and unforgiving times. . . . Somehow this city helped me to survive."

I knew what Hotch meant. The place we come from is imprinted on each of us, inextricably embedded in our past. I was born long after the Depression, and my youth was neither as adventurous nor as fraught with hard times as the experiences Hotch records for us in *King of the Hill,* but I easily identified with what he felt about St. Louis.

Whether you are a native of St. Louis or a longtime resident, a newcomer to the greater St. Louis metropolitan area or a stranger to this city, *King of the Hill* and *Looking for Miracles* will resonate. These are human stories, charming in their wit and innocence, genuine in their candor, universal in their appeal to what has been, and remains, young in all of us.

ROBERT R. ARCHIBALD, PH.D.
PRESIDENT, MISSOURI HISTORICAL SOCIETY

King of the Hill

Chapter One

Last summer really started May 9th, the day they put the lock on 326. You may think May is too early for summer, but let me tell you, not in St. Louis. In geography we studied about the equator running through Africa and all that, but believe me St. Louis is the equator of the U.S.A. The St. Louis sun passes through about three hundred magnifying glasses. You keep a candle on the bureau, and once that St. Louis sun really gets going the wick is right down tickling the bureau top. And that's what it does to your brain. Melts it down, and if the brain had a wick, by July it'd be tickling your eyeballs. The only good thing about the St. Louis sun is when it really gets going it melts the streets and you can just dig a finger in and scoop out a hunk and chew the black tar same as Wrigley's.

Well, it wasn't all that hot, this May 9, 1933, I'm talking about, but it was already hot enough anyplace else would think it was a heat wave. When you come out of the St. Louis sun into a dark hallway, your eyes see green for a while, which is maybe why I didn't see the lock at first. That and the fact that I was walking with my head down, watching carefully so as not to step on the black tiles which were sudden death. The black tiles were diamond-shaped in the corners of every four white tiles, and if any part of my

3

Keds touched black, I'd be struck down, ke-boom! not even time to scream. Dead in my tracks.

But I returned to the door of 326 after I passed it, and there was the lock. Yale. An old lock, used a lot, you could tell, scratched and turned color, but big and Yale. Just hanging there by its bow-legged top loop, hooked through the bracket that had been freshly screwed into the wood. Hanging there like it was Sandoz himself.

"Sandoz!" I wasn't *calling* him—I knew he couldn't be locked inside—just saying his name out loud when it dawned on me whose room it was. "Oh, no, not Sandoz!"

I raced around the turn in the corridor, second base on my way for a triple, my Keds squeaking real good against the tiles, raced down the corridor to the end, last room, 309, our room, the one with the NRA eagle on the door, and barged in.

"Mom! Listen . . ." But as I got into the room I stopped in my tracks, because there was a most unusual sight, my mother lying on the bed, the one by the window, a wet towel across her face. I had never seen my mother in bed during the day. She was always busy with a thousand things, washing things out in the basin, cooking something on the hot plate, writing things in her Windy City Hosiery book, sewing, always sewing, trying to keep things that were about worn out from giving up the ghost.

But there she was on the bed, her eyes closed, this wet cloth across her face, not moving. I tossed my schoolbooks on the table and went over and looked at her. On the wall above her head was this big blue NRA eagle, a cogged wheel in one claw and three forks of lightning in the other. My father put NRA eagles everywhere.

"Mom! You hurt or something?"

"Just a toothache," she said, keeping her eyes closed and opening her mouth just enough to say it. The whole side of her face was puffed out.

"Criminy, you're swole up—it must hurt a whole lot."

"M-m-m-m."

"Listen, Mom, guess what—there's a lock on Sandoz's door, three-twenty-six!"

She opened her eyes and raised her head a little. "What?" She put her head back. "Oh, God, wait till your father hears. They said it would never happen on the third floor."

To understand about the third floor, you have to understand about the Avalon. According to my parents, it was once, not too long ago, a pretty good hotel. Kingshighway and Delmar, right on the southwest corner. Not the greatest, like the Forest Park or the Jefferson or the Mayfair, but pretty good. A nice little restaurant, three bellhops and a captain, a pitcher of ice water on the bureau in your room when you checked in. My parents and I had stayed there for a few weeks when I was three years old. We had been living in New York City for almost a year, but things didn't go well there so they decided to return to St. Louis. Of course, I don't remember much about it, except one day a Western Union boy riding his bike on the sidewalk knocked into this woman coming out of the hotel and broke her arm. I remember that. Anyway, a year ago, when we returned from the terrible six months we spent with my grandparents in Chicago, we again came back to the Avalon, because my parents had remembered what a good hotel it had been.

But in nine years the same thing had happened to the Avalon that had happened to our family. You could tell the minute you set eyes on it. Half the bulbs were out in the Avalon sign that ran up and down along the corner of the building. The glass canopy over the entrance had several jagged holes in it, and there was a big electric sign alongside the main entrance, "GOOD TIMES DANCE," that had all *its* bulbs lighted. Below the sign was an arrow of moving lights that pointed to a door that led to the basement. There was one bellhop, no ice water, and no restaurant.

But the rent for a large double room with two full-size beds was only thirty-five dollars a month and that was a blessing, since all we had was the sixty-five dollars we got for selling our bedroom furniture before we left Chicago. The same owner, Mr. Desot, was there, and my father bragged a lot that he had given us a room with double exposure. Double exposure was a big thing with my father. In one wall was this window that looked out on the cinder parking lot in back of the hotel, and the other wall had a small window that opened on a shaftway that separated the hotel from the brick wall of the next building. But my father would say, "If you count opening the transom, it's really a triple exposure." He was very big on exposures. There wasn't enough air came through that shaftway to flicker a candle, but my father could sit in front of it with the sweat running down his temples and talk about how lucky we were that he had such pull with Desot as to get us this palace of a room with double exposure.

My parents originally took the room for a month, while they lined up something, but a year and a half had passed and they still hadn't lined up anything.

But to tell you the truth I liked the Avalon way better than living above Sorkin's delicatessen, or next to the fire station on North Union. And even in a way—but just in *a* way—better than Parker or Lawn or Art Hill. Because those places—even Concordia Lane, which was really nice—I'd come home and the place would be all empty, with my mother at work and my father out with his line, and I'd maybe eat something like a peanut-butter sandwich, and turn on the radio, but it was so *empty*. My mother always straightened up before she left for work, so when I'd come home from school it was so neat with everything put away that I felt like nobody lived there. But the Avalon—sure, everybody had a lot of troubles, but I could ride up and down in the elevator and talk to Arletta, or Danny wanted to hunk around in the turtle room, or Old Lady Heinson wanted to show me some old stuff out of her newspapers. So, even if I sat in our room and did some homework, I knew if I went out and walked down the corridor there'd be a lot of people there if I wanted to see them. Of course, I had to be awful careful not to step on the black tiles or scre-e-e! it would be all over. Sometimes I'd stomp on one on purpose; then, Ai! I'd stiffen up all over and pitch forward falling smash on my face, but I had this way of keeping my hands on my chest so my nose would wind up about an inch from the floor. Falling stiff-dead from black-tile scrunch was one of my best tricks. Sometimes, seeing me do it for the first time, people would scream. Grownups. It gave me a lot of satisfaction. I got this whole thing in me that likes to show off.

Now, about the third floor. That's where all the permanents were. The fourth floor was closed off because there wasn't enough business. Except for the Desots' suite and Danny's turtle room. The second floor was for transients. There had been a lot of lockouts on the second floor. But the third floor were the regular people. Some of them had lived there a long time. Old Lady Heinson, for example. Not only lived there for sixteen years, but hadn't left her room for twelve. Ever since they shut down the kitchen, a waiter from the Woodbine, on the other side of Delmar, brought her her meals on a tray. He'd bring the dinner menu at lunchtime, and the next day's lunch menu at dinner.

Almost everybody on the third floor was behind in rent, but they paid something in every once in a while and all the permanents believed there'd never be a lockout on their floor. But the lock on 326 changed all that. It made the third floor afraid. It caused a different kind of smell on the floor. I really mean it. I can smell when people get afraid. It has a smell to it. It really has. Kind of a putrid musty thing, like something rotting in an old, old library. Whenever I'd get in trouble with some new guy in a neighborhood we were just moving into, some bully, and I got this smell off him, I always knew I could take him easy. I've got a great nose, I really have. I never once got beat up because my nose failed me. If I didn't get the smell off some guy acting tough, I'd just yell a lot and do a little pushing and sort of get in the way of other guys standing around. I didn't get beat up very often. And for a guy who went to eleven different grammar schools, that's a pretty big compliment.

We owed $172, which is pretty good owing considering the rent was only thirty-five, so when my father came in and heard about the lock it really got to him and I could smell the fear rising off him and filling up the room. He had just been to three dentists around the neighborhood, trying to get one to take my mother, but my father owed all of them and they wanted to be paid in advance. I know about how all the dentists operate, because I had this really awful toothache and my father took me to Dr. Olvera, who had an office on the ground floor of the hotel that you entered through the back of the lobby. He had something in Spanish framed on the wall with a big gold seal and ribbons, so I guess he was an okay dentist in Cuba or Puerto Rico or somewhere.

"This boy has a cavity in his twelve-year-old molar," he said, only I'm not writing it the way he said it in broken-down Spanish-type English.

"Well, then, fix him up," my father said.

"It's a dollar for a silver filling," Dr. Olvera said.

"A dollar!" my father yelled, like Olvera had just stuck an ice pick in his gizzard. "How big can it be, a twelve-year-old boy?"

"It's a big cavity," Dr. Olvera said. "It's a dollar, in advance."

"Here's fifty cents cash," my father said, putting two quarters on the stand under the drill. Dr. Olvera looked at the quarters. My tooth hurt so bad I wanted to throw up.

"For fifty cents the tooth can be pulled," Dr. Olvera said. "Fillings are one dollar."

"Will it stop the pain to pull it?" my father asked.

"Yes."

"Well, then, if it's such a big cavity, we might as well pull it."

"It's the boy's permanent molar," Dr. Olvera said, looking at the quarters again. I was trying to sit quiet and grip the chair arms very hard to hold in the pain, but it was running through my eyes now like a hot needle going up my cheek and right through one eye

8

and across my forehead into the other, and I let out some kind of sound because of the pain. I didn't mean to. It just came out.

Dr. Olvera took the two quarters and put them in his pocket. He opened a drawer and took out a kind of pliers which he wiped off with a towel that was draped over the back of my chair. "If you'll hold his head," Dr. Olvera said to my father. "The roots aren't very deep yet." He stuck the cold pliers in my mouth and my father pressed my forehead against the chair back. The jaws of the pliers clunked onto my poor tooth and Dr. Olvera gave a mighty yank, tearing my head right out of the socket, but the tooth didn't give. It hurt like holy hell. It took about six yanks and Dr. Olvera was sweating and my father kept saying "Now you got it!" which, of course, he hadn't. I bled all over the place. Dr. Olvera gave my father the tooth.

On the way out, my father said to me, "That tooth would have given you a lot of trouble." Even now, every time the tip of my tongue plays around with that hole among my teeth, with the soft skin at the bottom, I can feel Dr. Olvera's grippers yanking me like I still had the twelve-year-old molar in my mouth.

"Did you try Dr. Olvera?" I asked my father.

"He's gone."

"Why, he was there a couple of days ago. I saw him."

"He was arrested."

Probably for pulling twelve-year-old molars.

Then my father said to my mother, "There was a room in the back of his office, where he . . . you know."

"No!" my mother said.

That's another thing about my father, always saying "you know" to my mother and giving her looks and making me feel like I was some kind of German spy. The only time I ever got to hear anything halfway decent was at night when we were all in bed, with the screen between us, and they thought I was asleep. But even then I never heard much because I'm such a quick sleeper.

So there was my poor mother dying from this toothache and

my father without five cents to pay a dentist. Also, one look at the breadbox with its lid off, getting sunned, and I knew it was another night of no food. On the days Minnie was going to come through with her fifty cents, she always did it by noon, so my mother could get things. So one look and I could always tell if there was going to be any dinner. The Avalon did not allow cooking in the rooms, so there were no iceboxes or anything. If there was anything to eat, it was right there out in the open. My father had long ago pawned everything pawnable except the radio and Skippy, and frankly I don't think Skippy was pawnable, since Lester says pawnshops won't take anything they have to feed. Skippy was our canary, who was about as old as me. He could both chop and roll, which is pretty special. Your ordinary run-of-the-mill canary only does one or the other, but old Skippy kept throwing in chops right along with his rolls. I used to talk to him a lot, and he'd talk back, sometimes, in chops.

"Aaron, we've got to get your mother some aspirin. Go ask Aunt Minnie if she has any."

I really hated asking anybody for anything. They mostly didn't have it or pretended they didn't have it. Nobody in the Avalon went around asking anybody else in the Avalon for anything. But this was an emergency if my poor mother's tooth felt anything like my twelve-year-old molar before Dr. Olvera slaughtered it. So I went across to Minnie's room, 320, an outside room facing Delmar.

Minnie was Mrs. Minnie Rosenthal, who was rich. She had her own bathroom and she had big rings on her fingers, that had not been pawned, and her rent was paid up. She was the one who gave us the hot plate, and the deal was she could eat with us whenever she wanted by paying fifty cents for her share of the food. What she didn't know was that fifty cents paid for *all* of the food. My mother shopped at the Piggly-Wiggly, which was about four blocks over, at Cabanne and Union. Eggs were about ten cents a dozen, soup meat ten cents a pound, chickens cost a quarter, and you could get two loaves of day-old bread for a nickel. So, you see, you could eat plenty okay, all of us, for fifty cents.

The one day Aunt Minnie *always* ate with us (God, I hated to call her that but she liked it and after all it didn't *kill* me, considering she was our one and only meal ticket) was Friday. Without fail. And also without fail, every Friday after supper I'd go with her to her room and play cards with her for an hour. We played rummy and I discovered the second time we played that she cheated by dropping cards in her lap.

It bothered me that she cheated, but after thinking about it I decided not to say anything, because I figured that it didn't harm anyone since I didn't care if I won or lost. (I always lost, naturally.) Also, at the end of each card game, she would announce happily, "Well, looks like I've had a lucky run tonight," and then she'd fish in her purse and find a quarter, which was for me to go to the movies. She cheated clumsily, and sometimes it was hard for me not to see the cards in her hand being exchanged for the cards in her lap.

Minnie and my father argued a lot. Once they had this big argument, yelling back and forth at each other, over whether butterflies eat anything or whether they just fly around and look beautiful for a while and then drop dead. Don't ask me how they got into that one. You should have heard some of their arguments. Plain goofy.

"Look at moths!" my father yelled. "Tell me they don't eat!"

"Moths aren't butterflies!" Minnie yelled.

"Moths aren't butterflies? What are they?"

"Moths!"

"There isn't anything that don't eat—call the *St. Louis Post-Dispatch!* Find out!" My father was always telling people to call the *Post-Dispatch.*

"I don't have to call anybody! It's been proved! Butterflies don't eat. It's a scientific fact. It's been proved!"

"Just call the *Post-Dispatch*!"

"It's been proved, I tell you, Eric."

And on and on and on and on and on and on, for about six zillion times. That's the time I almost *did* call the *Post-Dispatch*, since I was trying to study for a history test and I wanted them to shut up, but rooms behind in rent had no phone service.

Minnie came to the door and smiled at me. She was pretty ugly when she smiled. She had a big nose that got bigger when she smiled, and she had all these old teeth that were yellow from smoking so much.

"My mother was wondering if she could borrow two aspirin, Aunt Minnie."

Her smile dropped down to her socks. "You tell your mother I never allow an aspirin in my medicine chest. They cause cancer. It's been proved." She was always telling me everything'd been proved. She had this thing about flies, for instance—I mean she was really anti-fly like you can't possibly believe, with maybe forty dozen fly swatters all over the place, and this one time she gave me a big lecture about how flies caused rheumatism. We happened to be studying insects so I asked my teacher, but when I told Minnie my teacher said she was wrong, all Minnie did was get red in the face and tremble a little bit, and stomp around saying it had been proved.

Anyway, I simply told my father Minnie didn't have any aspirin, not mentioning the cancer. He told me to try the McShanes. Criminy, I barely *knew* the McShanes. They were this mother and daughter who lived two doors down in 313. They never seemed to go anywhere. Maggie, the floor maid, said the girl was fourteen but she was a little fourteen, kind of skinny with glasses. And very pale. White. Like she lived in a closet. I really *hated* to go knocking around on people's doors. But I would do anything for my mother.

The daughter answered the door. She didn't have her glasses on and her hair, which usually hung down her face, was pulled back. "Oh, sure, we've got aspirins," she said. "Just a minute." Then she closed the door while I waited in the hall. That's how it was in the Avalon. Nobody hardly ever went into anybody else's room. I guess because with two or three people living in a room it was usually pretty crowded and messed up. Also, if you had anything around that could be eaten, there was always the danger you'd have to share it if someone was sitting there drooling all over himself at the sight of it. What I hated was the way soon as people got together they trotted out all their miseries and talked about them for hours. There I'd be trying to forget I was dying of hunger, and some slob would be sitting there going on and on about not having eaten for about a week and how he tried this and that and the other place and they turned him down, and the hell with the Salvation Army and all that. There was this one friend of my father, Mr. Able, who lived around in 340, who was always coming in and giving a report on his weekly meal with his daughter. They took him out to a restaurant every Thursday, and as far as I could tell Mr. Able filled up his stomach to last the week like his stomach was the hump of a camel. So now every time he came knocking around I left, because when you were hungry and trying to do homework and the last thing you had was a teeny hamburger about a year ago, what you didn't want to hear was how Mr. Able started with chicken soup and worked his way through a hundred courses, even giving you the kind of sauce he had on his ice cream, for crying out loud.

We did have one pretty big get-together in our room when Mr. Roosevelt made his first speech last March. There must have been fifteen people from our floor. They brought chairs and sat around and listened to Mr. Roosevelt promise to do his duty and all that. As for me, I didn't like to listen to politics. Everyone said pretty much what everyone else said, how it was a great old country and things were going to get better, and then dumped everything onto God and asked Him to show us the way and all that. I don't know why everyone just doesn't vote for God and get it over with.

So while they were listening to Mr. Roosevelt, I shot marbles on the rug. That's what I always did when the radio was on. The grownups all sat there staring at that stupid box as if their eyes were glued to their ears. What in Sam Hill was there to look at? Even when the baseball games were on, which were the only things I *really* liked on the radio, and even if I was keeping box score, I shot marbles. They held on the rug pretty good.

But one thing that I really liked about Mr. Roosevelt was his voice. I mean the sound. Not the speeches so much—when he speeched, he put his voice up and got a little faky—but when he sat at his fireside and talked, the sound of his voice was just right. Like the time a couple of months ago when he said he wanted everyone to take all the gold they had and bring it back to the banks. The banks were all out of money and shut down, for Pete's sake, and here he was with this voice of his asking everyone to haul their gold out of their mattresses and stick it in these busted banks.

Well, you know something? The next morning on my way to school, where going along Kingshighway there were four banks, they all had mobs around them, all these people with satchels and packages, bringing their gold back to these busted banks. There was one geezer with a white mustache and a vest sitting there in his Pierce-Arrow while his chauffeur was up in line. I looked in the window and would you believe he had gold bars, really *bars*, stacked up all over the back seat, not wrapped or anything? What a sight that was, all those people shoving each other to give up their gold to those busted banks. I don't know what I'da done if I'd had any gold. Kept it, I think. I really like Mr. Roosevelt, even though so far we're no better off than when he took over, but I don't get along with banks, and any gold I'da had I'da kept in the fingers of my fielder's mitt.

The McShane girl gave me four aspirins, and I thanked her and brought them back to the room and my mother took two. My father was carrying on and on about Sandoz, and how he was going to give Desot a piece of his mind. My father was always giving someone a piece of his mind. There was a note on the table I hadn't seen before, from Lester, telling me to meet him in the Vampire Room at six o'clock. I really felt awful about Sandoz. All his paintings locked in there, and I guess his paints, and all those other things of his from Mexico he used to show me. On top of our dresser was this baby picture of my brother. Sandoz had painted an eggshell around the head, with the top broken, so it looked like my brother had just come into the world out of an egg. That's what Sandoz did for a living. He went around to people's houses and told them he would paint an eggshell around their baby's picture for fifty cents. He was a wonderful painter, but that's what he had to do for a living. But even so, he didn't make a lot, and out of what he made he was always sending something back to Mexico where his family was. He used to tell me about it. I was practically his only friend. He told me a lot about Mexico and about how he once tried to be a bullfighter. Some of his paintings were about bullfighting, but he never painted bulls getting stabbed. His paintings were mostly the colors that bullfighting makes. I guess that's how you'd describe it. He even painted me one day. Or I should say, one week. I came in every day and just leaned against the wall and he painted me like that. I could never understand why, since, believe me, I'm no prize that has to be painted. Just the ordinary kind of skinny kid with a zillion freckles and kind of red hair. My mother calls it auburn, but auburn's for girls. It was me, all right, leaning there against Sandoz's wall and he wanted to give me the painting, but in that small room of ours if I had had to look at myself hanging on the wall all the time, I'd have puked. I'm pretty homely, actually.

There were two hours to kill before I'd meet Lester and I was already bored of my father's droning on about what was going to be in the piece of mind he was going to give to Mr. Desot, so I got my Feltie and went out. My mother was too sick to ask me where I was going. That's one of the things that gnawed me about my mother. Every time I went out of the door, she asked me where I was going, did I have a handkerchief, and to be careful crossing the street. Criminy, I was going to be graduated from the Admiral Dewey Elementary School in about a month, but you'd have thought I was on my way to kindergarten. Oh, yes, and nine times out of ten she asked me if I had to put that dirty thing on my head. That dirty thing happened to be the best old Feltie in the neighborhood. My father called it a skullcap. I found this really great fedora in a trash can in the park, and cut out the crown and cut designs in it, and I had some really nifty buttons stuck all over it, especially this one of Mr. Herbert Hoover smiling, which, believe me, was some rare button.

I checked to see if Danny Desot was around but he wasn't, so I started down Delmar to look for cigar bands. I hadn't gone more than a block when I found a Petit Bouquet, which was on my most-wanted list. I once spotted a man who was smoking one and followed him for blocks and blocks, but when it went out he just kept chewing on the end and I knew he'd never throw it away. But here it was, right at my feet, on a cigar that was teetering right on the edge of the sewer opening, so I picked it up carefully. It was wet, so I had to go very easy taking it off: "Petit" on top, "Bouquet" on bottom, two gold coins on each side, and some kind of gold medal hanging between the "Petit" and the "Bouquet." In that St. Louis sun, the gold on the band looked real. I took out the two pieces of blotting paper I always carried in my pocket, and laid the band flat between them. It was like when Hoot Gibson or somebody was panhandling out there in the West and suddenly there was this shiny nugget in the pan. That's how it was walking the gutters looking for cigar bands. Sometimes you could walk all day and find nothing but Cremos and Dutch Masters and junk like that, and other days you went out for thirty minutes and struck gold.

Chapter Two

The Vampire Room was what me and Lester called it because you could just feel them sitting up there in the gloom staring at your veins and licking their chops. It was the kind of room Bela Lugosi would have put on his slippers in and lit up his pipe. Cobwebs all around and this old piano with a busted leg, and when you said something your voice whanged all around the walls and you could hear yourself like you were on the Victrola. And there was this giant chandelier that hung down the center of the room, with maybe a trillion hunks of glass on it, that must have weighed about the same as a Mack truck, and sometimes I'd be Quasimodo and horse around underneath it all hunched over and goopy until it would come crashing down and get me A-I-I-I! Boy, how a yell bounced around that room!

I had read almost all the French books, which are way and gone my favorites. Mr. Dumas and Mr. Hugo and especially Mr. Jules Verne. Sometimes on the way to school, when I found a good old branch to brandish, I was D'Artagnan. Once I forgot and kept right on being D'Artagnan into Miss Butler's math class. I brandished some flowers off her desk and she made me stay late and clean erasers. After I read a really good book, I couldn't help being the guy in the book. Sometimes I never got him out of my system, like I guess I'll always be Captain Nemo.

The other thing I was was Pepper Martin. I mean I could suddenly slide into second on my belly anywhere, just beating the throw, safe as good old Pepper. I was always knocking down grounders with my chest or arms or legs like Pepper did, and then I pounced on them catlike and winged them to first just in time.

Sometimes people stared at me like I was goofy, sliding into a fire hydrant or taking a cut at the old apple while I was waiting for the traffic to change, but mostly I didn't care, because it was better to be a Musketeer or rounding the old bases and doffing my Feltie for a home run than being Aaron in 309.

Lester came in carrying this big bag full of golf clubs. He dragged two chairs over to the light.

"You know anything about golf, A?" Only my mother and Lester called me A.

"No."

"You don't know what a mashie is?"

"No."

"Shit."

Lester cussed a lot. He was fifteen, but a big fifteen, like you could take him for seventeen. He shaved every day and all he ever wore were these T-shirts and he had chest hair that poked over the top. When he made a muscle it came to a huge hump, not a golf ball like mine.

"Doesn't it cost a lot of money to play?"

"You're not gonna play, dummy, you're gonna caddie. I talked to the caddie master. The only thing is the first couple of times you got to split your fee with him. You get fifty cents for nine holes so he gets two bits, but at least it gets you started. You should see the number of guys who show up Saturday and Sunday. All right, you know *any* of the clubs?"

"I know the putter," I said, pulling it out. It had "putter" stamped right on it. Besides, I knew about putters from the time I worked at the miniature golf course.

"That's stupendous," Lester said. He said stupendous a lot

when he didn't mean stupendous. He took out the clubs one by one and showed me how they were used and how one slanted a little more than another, and then he put them back in the bag and quizzed me like he was Mr. Richbucks on the links asking for this and that, and I had to pluck the right club out of the bag, but I kept getting the mashie and the niblick mixed up.

"Listen, can I keep them tonight and study them?"

"No, I gotta put them back. Ben would have a shit-fit if he knew they were out."

Ben was the bellhop. He was in charge of the lockouts and he kept all the locked-out junk in a storeroom in the basement on the other side of the dance hall.

"But how'd you get into the storeroom to get them?"

Lester just took out his pearl-handled penknife and jounced it up and down in his hand and smiled. It really was a great knife. Sometimes he'd let me whittle a tippy-tin peg with it. But I had no idea that he could pick a lock with it. That's the thing about Lester that really *got* me, that he was always *doing* things, not sitting back like everyone else and rolling his eyes up to heaven and hoping for somebody to throw him a golden ladder.

"Don't worry about the clubs. I'll get you out with me on a foursome. You eating tonight?"

"No, my mom has a toothache."

"Well, give me a coupla minutes to put these back and we'll go to Bushmeyer's."

The way I met Lester was when I was Dizzy Dean pitching in the ninth inning to Mel Ott with the bases full, really zinging 'em in there, and he was watching me although I didn't know it. I had seen him around the hotel a lot and I knew he lived on my floor, but he never paid the slightest bit of attention to me. I once said hello to him but I don't think he heard me.

"Hey, Dizzy," he said, "I'm coming up to pinch-hit." He knew I was Dizzy Dean because I was announcing the game on the radio, which was something I always did. He picked up this dilapidated broom and busted off the broom part and scratched a home plate onto the cinders. The parking lot was all black cinders which the janitor spread after he took them from the furnace. That way Mr. Desot didn't have to pay to have them carted away. There wasn't a kid in the Avalon didn't have permanent black knees from skidding on those cinders and getting them ground into their knees. Including me. Anyway, when I was pitching a big game I'd go around and collect a boxful of walnut-size cinders. Then I'd draw a chalk circle on the wall that I'd have to pitch into for a strike.

So Lester, whose name at that time I didn't know was Lester, stepped up to the plate and I reared back like Dizzy and fired one into Gus Mancuso, and Lester whished that old broomstick at it and missed. Then I started working my stuff on him, gave him my side-arm curve, my outshoot, my Jess Haines knuckle-ball drop, and even a couple of submarines now and then, and he was missing everything. You could see he couldn't believe his eyes that this skinny kid was getting him to miss all over the place. He must have missed forty or fifty pitches, and I'll bet I didn't throw more than two or three out of the strike zone.

Finally, we sat down on an empty orange-pop box to rest. "You got a great arm, kid," he said. I guess it was the best compliment I ever got. "Let's try a couple more and call it quits."

That's when it happened, that's when I learned about the law of averages, which was a law I hadn't heard about until then. The very first pitch after sitting down was a curve that didn't curve, and I heard it come clack! off the broomstick, but I never saw it and it ripped open my eye so that the eyeball was all exposed. It spurted blood and the blood covered my face so you couldn't see just where it had hit. Lester picked me up and ran me through the lobby and right through the traffic across the middle of Kingshighway and Delmar to the lobby of the Woodbine, where a doctor had his office. I couldn't see a thing out of my eye. The doctor took one look at me and called an ambulance.

For two days they really worked on my eye, but I couldn't see a thing and I knew I'd be blind. It seemed like Lester never left the hospital. He was there more than my mother and father. On the third day, a big specialist came to see me from Jewish Hospital. I was in the free ward but that didn't seem to bother him. You could tell how big he was from the way so many doctors trailed after him and stood around and watched him examine my eye. He put his hand on my cheek and smiled at me. He had a swell smile.

"Tomorrow morning, I'm going to patch up that eye a little, okay?"

"Yes, sir."

"It'll be as good as new."

"I can't see now, and I've really *got* to see." I thought I ought to explain something to him. "Doctor, I bat right-handed and without this left eye I'd never see the pitches."

"I understand."

"I could pitch all right but I'd never see a curve, and they wouldn't let me play if I couldn't see a curve."

"You'll see every pitch. I promise you."

"You're not saying that just to pep me up, are you, Doctor? Because I've got to *believe* you."

"I wouldn't be much of a doctor to do that, now would I?"

"I've tried to bat left-handed but I strike out a lot."

"I give you my word—isn't that good enough?"

"Yes, sir. I guess so. But, you see, I've been disappointed a lot." And, then, dammit, I started to cry. I never cry and I tried to hold back when I felt it coming on but I couldn't. The tears really burned my eye. The specialist took some cotton and dabbed my eye. Then he put some drops in it and covered it with squares of moist gauze and taped them on.

He put his hand on my cheek again. "You're going to see, I promise you."

That night, Lester snuck back in after my mother and father left and read me *Treasure Island* until they kicked him out. The next morning at 7 a.m. the specialist operated, and three days later I could see.

Ever since then, Lester sort of looked out for me, like lining up this caddie thing, for instance. My left eye, the one that was hit, became a little smaller than my right after it healed, but I saw out of it just as good as before. Me and Lester never mentioned my eye again after it happened.

Bushmeyer's was a big cafeteria on the corner of Union and Delmar. We got a tray, a pot of tea, a pot of hot water, and a slice of lemon. Lester paid the cashier a nickel, and at the serve-yourself dishes we got two cups and spoons. Lester carried the tray to the far end of the cafeteria. He poured a cupful of the tea, squeezed in the lemon, then he picked up the catsup bottle on the table, dumped a lot of catsup into the other cup, added some hot water from the pot, a little salt and pepper, and shoved it over to me.

"You like tomato soup?" he asked.

"Sure."

"Well, dig in." He handed me a package of soda crackers which somehow he had slipped into his pocket. He drank the tea and ate one of the crackers and I tried a spoonful of the catsup-water. It was darn good tomato soup.

Chapter Three

When there was nothing to eat, I didn't like to be in the room around dinnertime. It made my mother feel bad. I could tell. My father would just sit there with his legs crossed, wiggling his up foot a million miles a minute and carrying on about Father Coughlin or the WPA job Mr. Roosevelt was going to give him or practicing the mouthful he was going to give to Mr. Desot or how Sid Gutman was working on getting him the Elgin watch line for Missouri. (For about two years, no kidding, my father had been waiting for Sid Gutman to fix him up with the Elgin watch line.) When we didn't have food, my mother never said much, but I could tell she was watching me out of the corner of her eye with this terrible sad look on her face.

So when Lester met his two friends on the corner outside Bushmeyer's, instead of going back to 309 I just killed time for a while. The two friends were old guys, I'll bet eighteen or nineteen, but Lester was just as big. The thing about Lester was he never said hello or goodbye. I got used to it, the way he'd just leave suddenly and that was it, but the first couple of times it made me feel awful. I didn't see Lester all that often, but when I did he always had a thousand things to do. Sometimes he'd meet girls.

Once this movie-star-looking girl drove up in front of the hotel and she moved over and Lester took the wheel and zoomed off. He probably didn't have a license, but things like that didn't bother Lester. Sometimes I'd pretend I was wearing a T-shirt and kind of stand like Lester in front of the hotel and wait for Christina Sebastian to drive up in her Packard.

I walked the gutter back to Delmar, looking for cigar bands. Usually I never found much in that stretch, but when I got in front of the Walgreen's at the corner of the hotel, I practically tripped over a Flor Fina. I already had one, but this was in better condition, not wet or anything, and I knew Walter Eamons would trade me for my old one. Walter Eamons was one of those guys who never remembered what he had, so you could always trade the pants off him because every cigar band he saw he thought he was seeing for the first time. Of course, I'm not talking about White Owls or any of that slop—you know what I mean.

Usually I could duck Patrolman John L. Burns pretty good, but I was so busy peeling off that Flor Fina I forgot to pay attention. "Well, I see the little bohunk's sniping butts again!" When Patrolman John L. Burns talked to a kid, he always held on to him by the lobe of his left ear. "That's why you're such a little runt, sniping butts alla time."

He knew darn well I collected cigar bands, not butts.

"Where's that bohunk old man of yours? I never see him any more. They snatch his car yet?" With Patrolman Burns, everybody was a bohunk, wop, nigger, yid, or heinie. My father was born in Austria so he had this accent. Anybody with an accent that Patrolman John L. Burns didn't know, he called a bohunk. He was a wonderful man, all right, with a wonderful sense of humor. I once heard him say to Johnny Cafferetta, the Greek man who runs the Dew Drop Inn, "Hey, Johnny, how come they can't keep you wops on Dago Hill?" Dago Hill is this area where a lot of Italian people live.

"If they did, you'd have nothing to eat but Irish potatoes," Johnny answered, sort of laughing. But I don't think he was laughing.

Patrolman Burns pinched my ear lobe harder, pulling up my face. "How's that eye? You're lucky I was here to whistle down the traffic or that punk yid would have run you under a truck. I ever tell you that?" Only about sixty thousand times, that's all. My ear hurt like hell. "What's that yid's name?"

I noticed that his pistol was only about two inches from my nose, so suddenly I snatched it from the holster and let him have it, ke-boom, ke-boom, right in the stomach. "Lester."

"No, no, you know what I mean—his *name*."

He snapped forward, trying to hold on to me, his dying eyes pleading for mercy. Blood was already staining the belly of his uniform.

"Silverstone."

"That's it, Silverstone. Tell him I got him in my book and to watch his step. You got that?"

I flipped his gun beside him on the ground, and kicked his grasping hand loose from my ankle as I walked away. Patrolman Burns suddenly jammed his whistle in his mouth and started to blow his eyes out. Then he yelled, "What's that bastard trying to do!" and he charged out into the intersection after some guy who had turned where he wasn't supposed to. "You wait there," he yelled back at me.

I lit right out of there.

I went down Delmar toward the Uptown to look at the photos in front. It always griped me the way they'd have marvelous photos in front of the movie showing these terrific scenes, and then you'd see the movie and those scenes wouldn't be in it at all. But I liked looking at the photos anyway.

I really liked movies. The only family time I can remember—I mean, when we all did something together—was one New Year's Eve when my father got passes to the Kingshighway and we went at 7 p.m. and got out at 1 a.m. Four features, short subjects, news, and cartoons. They put "Happy New Year" on the screen at midnight, and we all sang "Auld Lang Syne" with the organ. It was the first time I ever sang at a movie, and the last. Mostly, I just puke when they put on that bouncing ball and ask you to sing the words. I like the movies, but there's a lot about them that makes me nauseous. But that New Year's Eve me and my brother sung real loud, although he couldn't read the words and wound up giggling. My mother had packed a big bagful of meatloaf sandwiches, pickles, tomatoes, apples, and sponge cake, and that's the best family time we ever had.

Although the Uptown is on the same side of Delmar as the Avalon, I crossed over so as not to get any of the cooking smells from the open door of the Dew Drop Inn. But when I got to the Uptown, wouldn't you know there was a big "HELD OVER" sign, which meant that I had seen all the photos the week before. Also, they had moved the popcorn machine next to the ticket window, and I got a big whiff of that hot buttered smell.

A lot of people who haven't been have the wrong idea about being hungry. I mean they think you go around clutching your belly all the time and moaning. There was this really goopy girl at school, Blanche something-or-other, who was always having a hemorrhage about the "poor unemployed," like they were some tribe on the moon, for crying out loud. I mean there I was with my ribs sticking together and there she was talking about those "poor unfortunates" like she was bringing me news from the front. "If I was hungry and it was dinner and I didn't have any food," I heard her saying to her friend Big-Butt Benjamin Toklen, "I mean *any* food—I would die. I really would. I would just *die*." Her father owned a loan company.

Now they're two things you've got to understand: one is I shouldn't really have been in the Admiral Dewey School, and the other is my stomach was not all that empty. The Admiral Dewey School was actually for kids who lived along Forest Park from Kingshighway to Skinker Boulevard. All those streets in there, like Pershing and DeGiverville, were lousy with private houses and big apartments, and there were front lawns and back yards with basketball backboards all over the place. It just so happened that Kingshighway and Delmar was the dividing line between the Admiral Dewey School and the Clark School, with the Avalon Hotel, which nobody figured to have school kids in it, falling on the Admiral Dewey side of the line. Actually, they should have drawn the line on the other side of Delmar, because the Admiral Dewey School had the eaters and the Clark School had the noneaters.

Not that everybody on Pershing and DeGiverville was rolling around in ten-dollar bills, but they weren't skipping meals, either. And that brings me to the point about my stomach. At the Clark School I would have probably starved to death, but at the Admiral Dewey I was the Robin Hood of the lunch period. Walkers could go home for lunch, and so could bike riders, but everybody else brought lunch boxes and could buy a carton of milk for a nickel. Also, half-vanilla, half-chocolate ice cream. Everybody ate in the basement in separate boys' and girls' lunchrooms, which became the gym when they slid back the partition that ran across the middle.

Most of the little kids ate at one end, and the middle kids in the middle, and the big kids at the other end, but if you've ever brought your lunch to a school lunchroom you know that nobody stays put very long. There were always a couple of monitors—you know, the kind of twerps who wore AAA sashes and stood at crossings with their chests out—and some teacher who sat in a corner and tried to read, but inside of ten minutes the place was always full of commotion. Especially the little kids. They took a bite out of a sandwich, then they ran all around with jelly dribbling out of their mouths trying to tag some other little monster, who maybe had his teeth glued onto an apple so he could keep his hands free. Disgusting.

I always brought my lunch box to school, so as not to be conspicuous, but a lot of the time there was nothing in it. What I discovered, though, was that empty lunch box or not, I never had to go to my afternoon classes on an empty stomach.

First of all, I discovered that little kids were complete blanks when it came to eating. Back when we lived on Art Hill Place and we could have friends to lunch and all that, my brother asked his pal Sylvester, one day, if he wanted to stay for lunch, and when Sylvester called his mother to ask permission she told him he already *had* lunch. That gives you an idea about little kids and their lunch. I'll bet if they took a poll of five hundred little kids twenty minutes after they had lunch, maybe six could tell you what they ate.

All right. Enter the Robin Hood of the Avalon Hotel, who only lifted food off the fat little boys with the oversize lunch pails. Robin Hood sized up his prey, nimbly moved beside him, pretended to be interested in other things, then as Blubber Boy waddled off to trade a marshmallow for a Tootsie Roll—whisk! half a tuna sandwich flicked off the wax paper and Robin Hood glided off to strike in another part of the forest. Lots of times I found myself eating some pretty strange sandwiches—you can't *believe* what some of those mothers stuff into those little fat kids—but the only thing that made me gag so I couldn't get it down was mushed sardines. It was amazing how many kids brought mushed sardines. Also, I wasn't wild about graham crackers, but when the pickings were thin, I got them down. The trick was never to take more than half of what the kid had, and never, for Pete's sake, take any candy. Kids who wouldn't know if they had sirloin steak or baloney counted their candies. I really liked Mary Janes, but the one time I filched one the little fatso made such a stink his mother complained to the principal. But there's no doubt about it, I slimmed down a lot of beefy kids in the Sherwood Forest in the basement of the Admiral Dewey.

Chapter Four

I went back to the hotel at seven o'clock because I knew *Amos 'n' Andy* would have my father glued to the radio and I could do some homework. My father would wait all day for the night's programs. He'd even talk about them during the day, what was going to be on that night, because that was just about all he really had to look forward to. When Andy and the Kingfish and Lightning got things going, my father would laugh out loud and really have a good time, and during the day he said things like "Oh-wah! Oh-wah!" which is what Amos said when he was in a pickle about something. It was pretty funny the way my father said, "Now doan mess wid me," and things like that with his Austrian accent.

When I came in the lobby, Danny Desot was there and I could tell he had been watching for me because it was just the right time to go up and shoot rats. Before I said yes or no, I looked around to see if Mrs. Desot was in the lobby. She was, so I said yes. It was murder to get trapped upstairs with Mrs. Desot around because she did this disgusting thing with Danny that I'd rather not talk about.

Anyway, she was safely behind the desk doing some hotel work with Mr. Desot. You'd have never in a million years thought these two were married. Mr. Desot was very tall and dark and banker-looking, with this black hair that was so slicked back it looked like it had been drawn on his head with India ink. He had a movie-father face, with these Rudolph Valentino–type nostrils. Mrs. Desot was about as high as me, with these *huge* breasts that flopped way out and a little bump in front that her corset or whatever it was couldn't keep in. She also had a long pointed nose. What you could say good about her were her eyes and some wonderful teeth that she was always smiling with. You never saw anybody smile so much in your life. I always feel creepy when I'm around someone who is flashing smiles all over the place when there's really nothing to smile about.

Arletta, who was this absolutely beautiful Negro girl who ran the elevator, took me and Danny up to the fourth floor, and she cracked her gum a few times for us on the way. We went to the turtle room, which was directly over 309 and also faced out on the parking lot. I could smell the turtles halfway down the hall. It was no worse smell than you got in the snake house at the zoo, but I wasn't crazy about it and I wished Danny kept his BB gun in some other room.

Danny turned the light on, and these two million turtles that he had all over the floor began popping their heads out and walking up each other's backs. You never saw so many turtles in your life. Danny found a lot of them in Forest Park, and also Mrs. Desot took him places where he found different kinds. There was turtle poop all over the floor, and about a ton of old lettuce leaves and chopped meat that had flies all over it. A really lot of flies. Danny wouldn't let anybody touch that room, and once when he came home early from school and found Mrs. Desot cleaning out some of the turtle poop, he got so mad he hit her in the stomach with his fist. Come to think of it, maybe that's how she got that lump there.

Danny got his BB gun out of the closet and filled it full of BBs. We turned off the light, to see better. At the far end of the parking lot where the alley was, there was a cement ashpit where the janitor burned all the papers and junk, and in front of that were the garbage cans. For a place that didn't allow cooking in the rooms, the Avalon sure had a lot of garbage. The rule about cooking was because of the fire laws. These garbage cans had been thrown around a lot, so the tops didn't fit or there weren't any tops. Beginning around this time of night, in the seven-o'clock light when we could still see them, the rats began to come. It was a pretty far distance for a BB gun, but these were *enormous* rats so you really had a big target. One time old Danny dropped one zing! right in his tracks, but when we went down to take a look at it we found it was a cat. Gives you an idea of the size of those rats.

We always bet two marbles on who would get one, but most of the time neither of us won. I could really handle that old BB gun, but a lot of times I'd pot one—you could see the BB kick into him—but he'd just sail off with the BB in him. They were *some* rats. I'd killed eight, though, and Danny only six.

But for some reason they weren't showing up. We sat there in the window for a while straining our eyeballs, but there wasn't a sign of them. "Listen," I said, "maybe Martin forgot to put out the garbage." Danny didn't say anything. He wasn't a great talker. He was exactly my age and nice enough, I guess, but he hardly ever said anything. So we just sat there some more, squinting. The band down in the dance hall started to play. They played very loud, especially this sour saxophone that was blown by some guy with lungs like a whale. Lester said there was only a piano, drum, and this saxophone maniac, but it was hard to believe three pieces could make so much racket. But I'll tell you a funny thing—after an hour or so my ears got numb and I didn't hear it any more. Not even when I did my homework.

It was really getting dark now, and still no rats. It was the first time we had gone ratless, and Danny was getting plenty griped. He was used to having things his own way. "Christ!" he said. He was itching to shoot those rats. Suddenly he pointed the barrel of the gun straight ahead. "Let's get that taxi light."

On the other side of the alley, behind a high wooden fence, was the lot where the Yellow Cab Company kept all its taxis. There was a light over the middle of the lot, hanging from a wire, with a single bulb in it. There was a hot breeze blowing and the light was jouncing around a little. We had never shot at anything but rats before. Danny smoothed back the hair from his eyes and put the BB gun into position. I had a pang of jealousy which I always got when guys smoothed back their hair from their eyes, especially when they flipped their heads a little to make the hair jump away from their eyes. I've got this really thick hair that has waves you can't straighten out, and once I comb it back it stays there even when I'm running. It's murder for a boy to have waves.

Danny was taking a long time sighting, moving the gun left and right to keep up with the swinging light, and my heart was pounding from the excitement of popping the taxi company's light. There were a couple of guys who worked there who must have had some of Patrolman John L. Burns's blood in their veins, the way they always yelled at us when we came poking around the taxis. So I really wanted to get their light.

Danny missed, then I missed, then Danny missed again. The marbles we were betting were on the sill. One of Danny's was a cleary with a red swirl, and I really wanted it. Also, I felt this rise in me that really made me *want* to win. It's this feeling I always got when I was up against something tough. Like when a pitcher got two strikes and I got this rise inside me, like I was suddenly mad as hell and I *had* to hit that ball or die. I got it when we had a really tough test at school, or my mother handed me a jar she couldn't open and I struggled around with it, getting red in the face, until finally up came this rise and ran into my muscles and plunk! the top was off.

So I jammed that old BB gun against my cheek and squinted my left eye into it, not moving the barrel, letting the bulb swing away to the right, then as it started to swing back I pulled the trigger. It was a big bulb and when that BB zinged it, it exploded like

Big Bertha. The band was resting, so you could hear the bang all over the place. I thought all it would make was a little glass tinkle but that was some bang. It was lucky we had the room light out, because right away there was a great yelling of voices and you could see men running into the alley.

Me and Danny didn't say anything but we chucked the BB gun into the closet and lit out of there fast. I stepped on a turtle and darn near broke my ankle. Danny disappeared into his room across the hall, and I ran down the stairs to the third floor. It was a fast getaway, but I hadn't forgot the marbles I'd won.

I went to the toilet, even though I didn't absolutely have to, to save me the trouble of having to go later. The toilet and the bath were way around on the other side of the elevator, so it was a real expedition when you had to go pee from our room. I looked at Danny's red-swirl cleary while I was peeing. It was beautiful, all right. I had really powdered that one-eyed monster, getting him with my all-seeing X-ray gun just before he got us.

Going down the corridor, I was Captain Nemo with these four evil eyes in my pocket to ward off the curse of the black tiles. I was announcing the whole thing on the radio when Old Lady Heinson yelled out from her room. "Aaron! That you?"

Her door was open maybe a foot. She had the greatest set of ears you can imagine. "Yes, Ma'am."

"Step in."

I told you how many years it had been since Old Lady Heinson had left her room but I didn't tell you about the room. There was a small bed, a dresser, a big soft chair with a footstool that said "God Bless This Home," a kind of low-slung table, and everything else was newspapers and books. The newspapers were in piles that ran up almost to the ceiling, and so were the books. There was just enough space between the piles to squeeze in and out, and there was this funny kind of ladder you could climb up to get things on the top of the piles. I'll bet Old Lady Heinson had more newspapers than the *Post-Dispatch*. She was always in her chair, reading, and she wore this old beat-up tennis visor to keep the light out of her eyes. She was eighty-three years old.

I was the only person I know of she let come into the room besides Maggie, who was let in once a week to clean the bathroom but not to touch anything else. Old Lady Heinson must have cleaned everything else herself, because the room was always neat and dusted. Also, the room always smelled good because she kept bags of old flower petals on top of her dresser. She was teeny and her hair was thick and white, and if you ask me she was pretty.

"Boy, have you read James Fenimore Cooper?" She knew I was batty about the French writers and she was always pushing some American at me. Or Mr. Rudyard Kipling. I really *loathed* Mr. Kipling.

"No, Ma'am, I haven't."

She handed me a book. "That'll get your mind off those Frenchies—*The Deerslayer.* You ever heard of it?"

"Yes, I think so. . . ."

"*Think* so! Why, it's a classic! A great book of literature, and you *think* so!" When anybody eighty-three years old got all excited like that, it made me nervous. "What did you think of *The House of the Seven Gables*? You finished it?"

"Not yet." I didn't want to tell her it bored me stiff. "I'm reading *The Count of Monte Cristo* right now. Have you read that?"

"Trash."

I was reading it, actually, for the second time, that's how terrific it was, but I didn't want to get into that and stir up her eighty-three-year-old heart any more than it was. Actually, I *was* the Count of Monte Cristo most of last week.

The waiter from the Woodbine appeared in the door with her dinner tray. I took *The Deerslayer* and thanked her and got out of there fast. Old Lady Heinson was very big on giving me stuff to read and telling me stories about the olden days, but she was absolutely zero on sharing food. Besides, she was a plate-wiper. That teeny little thing would sail into a mound of corned beef and cabbage, two rolls, butter, tomato salad, seven-layer chocolate cake with ice cream, tea, and when you saw the tray outside her door it was wiped so clean you'd have thought she washed the dishes. When we first moved in, I'd sit there at her feet on the "God Bless This Home" footstool while she started to eat, waiting for her to tell me to finish it up, but I wised up in a hurry when I saw how fast two huge stuffed green peppers could disappear into her dainty little mouth. She was *some* eater. I don't think anyone ever ate with her or came to see her. The only relative she ever talked about was a nephew who was in the navy. She sent books to him.

When I got to our room, I was very surprised not to hear the radio. Sure enough, my father wasn't there. I went in softly, thinking my mother might be asleep.

"A?"

"Yes, Mom. Where's Dad?" I went over and sat on the bed beside her.

"He went out for a while with the candles."

"How's your toothache?"

"Pretty bad."

"Maybe Pop will sell a couple of candles and you can get to the dentist tomorrow." Those stupid candles! He'd be better off with apples. "How about some more aspirin? I can go ask the McShanes again."

"That nice Ella McShane already brought me some." She took my hand and there were tears in her eyes, and I knew what she was thinking.

"Lester took me to Bushmeyer's for something to eat—wasn't that lucky?"

"How nice."

"He's a mighty good guy, Lester."

"I'm sorry I was so mean about him after he hurt your eye."

"I've got to do my homework. Maybe the stuff from Windy City will come tomorrow. Then you could go to the dentist."

"No, I had a letter from them. Not until next week."

"Oh. Well, I better do my homework."

I put the screen between the beds, like we always do at night, to shut out the light; then I got on my bed to study. But I couldn't get my mind on it. I thought about my father tramping around the neighborhood ringing doorbells and trying to peddle those stupid glass candles. About a year ago, he got this line of glass candles from some company that soon after went out of business. So it was okay for my father to sell the samples, but no one was ever able to sell any. I say no one because we all took turns at it. I tried going around just before last Christmas. I dirtied myself up a little and practiced looking pathetic in the mirror. Tiny Tim at your door-step, Ma'am, won't you help brighten one little lad's Christmas by buying a pair of these beautiful hand-stuffed glass candles?

One look at those candles and Tiny Tim got the door right in his mush. There was something about those candles that not only didn't make people want to buy, it made them want to kill. I admit they were pretty awful. This hollow of glass that was shaped like a candle and stuffed full of colored threads, with some of the threads coming out of the top to be the flame. That is, if you thought a bunch of colored threads looked like a flame. They came two to a box and sold for a dollar. We kept marking them down. The last time out, my father offered them for a dime but still nobody wanted them. I think if my father *gave* people a dime, he couldn't have moved any. There was something about a guy coming to the door with glass candles when the people inside were scrounging around for their next meal that rubbed people the wrong way. Shoelaces or even magazines, that was okay. But glass candles, for crying out loud!

So first I thought that was pretty stupid of my father to trot out those stupid candles and ring all those stupid bells and get pushed in the face by all those really stupid people. But then, my mother had to get to a dentist, didn't she, and those stupid glass candles were the only things he had to sell.

Chapter Five

Me and Les started out at 6 a.m. because you've got to take three streetcars to get to the St. Louis Country Club and caddie call was at seven. What I didn't understand was why, if golf was a game to have fun, anyone would want to hoist himself out of bed on Saturday to play at that ungodly hour. To *play*, for Pete's sake, golf or anything at that hour.

On the way out, Lester rehearsed me a couple of times on which clubs were which, but I was plenty nervous about making a mistake. We didn't have any clubs with us, of course, but he had this page from a magazine with about a thousand clubs on it, and he kept pointing to this one and that one and quizzing me.

The caddie shack was one of the toughest places I'd ever seen. The caddie master was this gruesome guy who was not too fat but had a balloon belly that hung over his pants. He was set up down at one end of the room in back of an old wood table. On the wall behind him was this chart that had hooks on it where he hung the caddie's name when he sent him out. The caddie master was half-sitting on the table with his arms crossed, and he always spit through his teeth before he said anything. He was one of the toughest-looking guys I ever saw. And gruesomest.

All around the room, sitting on wooden benches with their backs against the walls, were the caddies. The way they turned their eyes on me and looked at me when I followed Lester into the room, I thought they were going to make me walk the plank.

A lot of caddies yelled out nauseating things to Lester, like "Hey, Les, how's it hanging?" and then one of them said, "Where'd you find the midget?"

"He ain't no midget," another said, "he's a friggin' jockey."

Lester paid no attention to them and went over to sit beside one of his friends, leaving me standing there with all those really tough guys sneering at me. I felt like I was in front of a firing squad. I went over and leaned against the wall alongside where Lester was sitting. Practically every caddie was smoking and they were swapping filthy jokes. I mean sometimes dirty jokes are funny, like Walter Eamons knows a lot of dirty jokes that make you laugh. But these caddie jokes were just filthy, but the caddies all loved them and they'd laugh like hyenas and whack each other and spit between their teeth like the caddie master. The caddie master never laughed at anything. He just sat there looking like Scarface, if you saw *Scarface*. I don't think the caddie master *could* laugh.

I better tell you how I was about dirty words. I could *think* dirty words and I *knew* a lot of dirty words but I couldn't say them out loud. I was all right about "hell" and "dammit" but I just couldn't get myself much beyond that. I didn't know why. I wished I could get over it. You couldn't go on saying "darn" and "gosh" and "golly" for the rest of your life.

Beginning at eight o'clock, gobs of golfers began showing up and the caddie master was hanging caddie names all over the wall. There were plenty of places to sit, now that the caddies were flocking out of there. I just sat there nervous as hell. Once, when no one was paying any attention, I tried to spit between my teeth but most of it hit the tip of my nose.

We didn't get assigned until eleven o'clock, me, Lester, and the two guys he had been talking to. Lester hadn't said three words to me since we came in. The caddie master called my name in that snarly voice of his, and when I stood up I was so nervous I thought

I was going to faint. I followed Lester over to the caddie master and he tossed us all badges which said "caddie" and had a number, and we pinned them on.

I had been watching the other caddies through the open door as they went by with their golfers, and I saw that the ones who got women golfers had skinny bags with about half the clubs the men carried, so I was hoping and praying for a woman golfer. What I got was a fat guy in orange pants who smoked a cigar in an ivory holder and had a high voice. He also had a leather bag crammed with clubs that weighed about the same as a grand piano.

"What's your name, sonny?" he asked as he handed me his bag.

"Aaron."

"What the hell kind of a name's that?"

I heaved the bag onto my shoulder and I thought it would cut right through to the bone. Boy, what a monster bag that was! I gave a look at Lester and he had one that looked even bigger, with leather covers on everything and God knows what. At least I didn't have any covers.

"Don't drag the bag," orange pants said to me; then he and his friends marched up to the first tee.

I started down the hill to join Lester. The weight of the clubs pitched the bag forward and I just barely managed to clap my hand over them in time to keep them from spilling out of the bag. That was a close call. I could feel my heart knocking on my chest. I leaned back against the hill very hard to keep the bag from pushing me on my face. Lester gave me a look.

"Stop sweating," he said. "We haven't even started."

I couldn't keep as close to Lester as I had hoped, because his guy was always smacking the ball right down the middle of the fairway and old orange pants was always off in the trees somewhere. Once, for crying out loud, he almost hit his ball into the ear of an old gent who was putting on the green of a hole way off to the right. I wasn't too hot with the clubs, I admit, especially the iron ones, and I'd sort of offer him the whole bag when he asked for anything complicated, but I was darn good at locating balls. Whenever orange pants whacked one, they'd all use words like hooks and slices and all that, but all I knew was the ball was sailing into the trees or weeds or shrubbery and I found that I could follow it with my eyes right to where it plunked down and then put a good fix on the spot. We only lost one ball. Orange pants got cranky about losing that one, but criminy he had hit it into a jungle.

Old orange pants took about twice as many strokes as the other three guys put together, and he began to get very cranky with me in that soprano voice of his. "Hurry up, sonny. . . . Jesus, sonny, don't jiggle around. . . . Did you lose track of it? Pick it up, what are you waiting for?"

I kept switching the bag from one shoulder to the other, but by the sixth hole they were both worn out. It was not so bad I couldn't manage, but as it turned out the sixth hole was my last. My guy, as usual, was the last one to finish his putts. The others had already started up to the sixth green. Naturally, Lester and the other two caddies had gone ahead with them, so me and orange pants left the green by ourselves.

"Here, sonny," he said, tossing his golf ball at me, "give it a wash."

I had seen the other caddies use the white boxes with the towels under them to wash their golf balls. I noticed they pumped a wooden paddle inside the box up and down and then dried the ball with the towel underneath. So I went over to the white box down below the sixth tee, and I pulled out the wooden paddle which I noticed was attached to the inside of the box with a metal chain. Inside, the box was lined with thick bristles, like two big brushes facing each other, with just enough space between them for the ball.

I dropped the ball into the box, rammed the wooden paddle on top of it, and pumped the paddle up and down a few times the way I had seen the other caddies do it. Then I took out the paddle and looked for the ball. I couldn't see it. It was all the way down in the bottom of the box. I tried to put my hand between the bristles to get at it but there wasn't room, and besides the bristles were like needles. Orange pants was already yelling at me to throw him the ball. I was in an absolute panic. How did those other caddies do it? There must be a way. I looked all over the outside and bottom of the box but there were no openings.

"Sonny, throw me the goddam ball!"

The next set of golfers were already coming up to the tee. I was frantic. I pumped the paddle in again. I heard orange pants' friends coming in back of me. I heard the spikes of their brown-and-white shoes digging into the grass and I gave one last try, but I just couldn't find a way to get that ball out of there. Now they were all around and sort of shoving me away and looking at the brushes.

Then it dawned on orange pants. "Don't tell me you put it *in* there!" he shrieked. Lester came up beside me.

"What's the matter?" he asked.

"What's the *matter?*" orange pants shrieked. "The matter is that this stupid kid has stuffed my three-dollar Kro-Flite into those brushes."

"Didn't you put it in the paddle?" Lester asked me.

I looked at the paddle. For the first time, I saw that there was a hole in the middle of the paddle. "No," I said, "I dropped it in there."

"That's stupendous," Lester said.

"What's this kid trying to do to me?" orange pants shrieked. "Where'd they find this kid? He keeps handing me niblicks. No wonder I'm high ball. This lousy kid has ruined my game. And now my three-dollar Kro-Flite!"

While orange pants was shrieking at me, Lester had taken out his pearl-handled knife and unscrewed the white box from its stand. He turned it upside down and shook it. All the cleaning water ran out of it and finally, after he shook it really hard, the three-dollar Kro-Flite fell on the ground.

"Now, looka that," orange pants shrieked, pointing up at the tee, "they're playing through us. What did I do to deserve this kid today?"

Lester picked up orange pants' bag and slung it over his shoulder. Then he put the other bag over his other shoulder and walked me off a little, away from the others. "I'll meet you back at the caddie shack," he said to me. "Don't worry about this, A. It's nothing. We'll go out again this afternoon."

Lester moved off with the two bags and I turned and walked back in the direction we had come. I walked regular at first, till I thought they were out of sight; then I began to run. It always made me feel better to run. I ran as fast as I could back along the high grass next to the fairway. I felt like crying but I didn't. I stuck my old Feltie in my back pocket so it wouldn't pop off and I just ran, all through the grass and across the top of the first tee and on past the caddie shack right onto the road in front of the country club. I stopped there, really out of breath.

There was a big tree next to the road, and I went around to its other side where no one could see me, and leaned against it while I caught my breath. I took my Feltie out of my pocket and gave my face a good wipe with it and put it back on my head. The thing was that I intended to walk in and give my mother that caddie money to go to the dentist. She hadn't slept all night and she had a fever now, and I'd have given her that caddie money and she would have been off to the dentist. How could I know about the paddle having a hole in it? Lester should have told me. Nobody told me anything. How was I supposed to know you put the ball in a hole in the damn paddle? I'm supposed to be a genius or something. Well, I'm not! I was never on a golf course before and I never claimed to be a damn genius about putting golf balls in paddle holes. So they should just get that straight.

I didn't have carfare, so after a while I came back to the road and put up my thumb at the first car that came out of the driveway. They saw my caddie badge, so they stopped and gave me a lift. There were two very nice ladies in the front seat who talked together and didn't ask me anything. Luckily they were going right past Forest Park, so I asked them to drop me off there.

Chapter Six

They let me off not far from the tennis courts, which was where I wanted to go. I spent a lot of time around the tennis courts, which I could walk to in about half an hour from the hotel, and I knew some people there. I was suddenly hungry, tremendously hungry, so I yanked up a handful of grass and started to chew it. That was something I did when I was really starved and I was around grass. You got a lot of sweet juice out of it, and when it wadded up you could chew on it like a good old tobacco cud.

I crouched down behind the plate and flashed the sign to Tex Carleton; then I poked my cud in my cheek, the way Gus Mancuso did, and got set for the pitch. Right in there. I chewed on my cud a little as I returned the ball to Tex, then squirted some juice out between the bars of my mask, the way Gus did. I gave Tex two fingers for the curve. I wasn't broadcasting the game, just chewing my cud and steadying old Tex, who had the bases full. Actually I didn't catch very often. In fact, only when I was chewing a cud. I guess it was because when I crouched down like that I could still feel my chin getting split open that time at DeMun.

Well, I got Tex out of that jam, then last of the ninth with my cud stored in my cheek, I went for a 3-and-0 pitch and knocked it clear out of Sportsman's Park onto Grand Avenue. So Gus

Mancuso trotted around the sacks while the mob cheered him all the way to the tennis courts.

There was no one I knew at the courts. Next to baseball, tennis was my best sport. I really liked basketball a lot but you needed a backboard around to practice. If I'da had a backboard around, I'll bet I could've made the team. Not the starters, maybe, but I'll bet I could've sat on the bench.

The way I had worked it out to play tennis was I found this permit with the name Herman Willer on it and nobody ever claimed it, so Maury, who ran the courts, let me use it. Then I fixed up this racket somebody threw away because it had a big split in the frame. I took it down to Martin's workshop in the basement of the Avalon, and he really fixed it so's the split didn't make any difference. Then I bought a package of gut from the guy who strung rackets—not gut, really, but silk which cost about a hundred times less than gut but you could string it pretty tight, you really could. He gave it to me for a dollar, which is what I had saved from winning the amateur night contest at the Kingshighway. I had recited, "Sail on, O Ship of State, / Sail on, O Union, strong and great," and I got two points higher on the applause meter than a guy who played the harmonica and tap-danced at the same time.

The way I strung the racket was I got myself a piece of broom handle and pounded a nail in it. Then I strung the gut into the racket, and by wrapping an end of gut around the nail I could turn it round and round on the handle till I got it really tight. Then I had this ice pick I'd jam into the hole in the frame where the gut was, to hold it in place till I could pull through another string and tighten it the same way, moving the ice pick to the next hole. If you've never strung a racket, it probably sounds confusing but believe me it was a darn good racket, a Davis Cup, and how I learned to play was hitting balls against the practice wall all the time. It would have been better to have been able to have lessons, I guess, but you could really powder that ball against the practice wall. I used these balls I found that had turned gray and didn't have any fuzz left, but they bounced all right. Anyway, the people I played with usually had better ones.

The St. Louis sun felt like flames. I sat on the grass and watched two old guys running each other around. One old guy was dressed for ice skating. He wore a wool cap—a regular cap, with a visor and all—and long wool trousers and a sweater with a lot of old sweat rings under the arms. You could have probably counted his sweat rings like a tree and told how many times in his life he had played tennis. The other old guy, who kept yelling "Bully!" every time he missed the ball, was wearing his underwear. Really. Regular underwear. When you get right down to it, underwear shorts are not that much different than tennis shorts. But frankly underwear tops look kind of funny on a tennis court. This old guy had legs that looked like bobby pins and he hit nothing but lobs. The other old guy only hit backhands. Watching these two old guys going at each other, the ice skater running around and hitting everything with his backhand and bully boy knocking everything a mile high in the air, made me feel a little better.

I pulled a fresh cud and started back to the hotel. As I turned around the corner of court 3, a tall guy in white flannels and a white sweater like Don Budge wore came around the corner at the same time. We just about rammed each other. "Hey, Red," he said, "can you use a couple of balls?" Then he tossed me these two absolutely stupendous Spaldings with about a foot of fuzz on them and you could still read some of the name. I put one inside my shirt and played catch with the other all the way back to the Avalon.

My mother was stretched out on the bed when I came in, with a wet towel on the side of her face. She didn't stir, and I suddenly had this terrific panic I got when I thought somebody was dead. But I held my breath and watched her chest, and when I saw it move I started to breathe again. I really didn't like to be around people when they were sleeping. It gave me the creeps. I always had to keep checking on their breathing. Either everybody ought to be sleeping or everybody up. One or the other.

My father came in like he was driving a tank and it woke my mother. Before I could yell at him, he said, "Let's go! I found a dentist who will take you."

"Thank God," my mother said. She could barely open her mouth. She got out of bed and went to the closet to dress. Our room had one closet in it, and my mother would sort of scrunch in there with the door half shut to get dressed. Considering the great masses of clothes we had, she had plenty of room.

"The only drawback," my father said, "is that he's down on Jefferson and Market and we'll have to walk."

"That's all the way downtown!" I said.

"Do you think you can make it?" my father asked her.

"Don't worry, I'll make it," my mother said.

"I wish there was gas in the car," my father said.

"If Aunt Minnie was here, I'll bet she'd loan you carfare," I said. It was a stupid thing to say, since this was one of the two afternoons Minnie worked in her brother's store, and besides she hated to be asked for anything, especially money. The fifty cents for dinner and the two bits for our Friday rummy game were her limits. But I felt terrible about my mother walking all that way with her toothache. You can't imagine how far it is from Kingshighway all the way down to Jefferson. I never heard of anybody walking it.

My mother got ready in a hurry.

"Listen," I said, "it's awful hot. You both ought to drink a big glass of water before you go." They did, and then they left.

Where they were really going, I knew, was out to their country place to spend the afternoon. You can only take about so much of this sacrificing for your kids and then you've got to think of yourselves a little. So just about now they were stepping into their Pierce-Arrow and being driven out to that mammoth place they had in Kirkwood. On the way, my mother would take out that hunk of cotton she had been keeping in her cheek to fool me. It was this theory of theirs, you see, that I should live tough in the beginning so I wouldn't grow up a soft little rich kid. They would probably go on like this for a while, until they thought my steel had set, but I already knew what kind of life I'd really have. I knew the names of all their help, from the gardener to the cook, and I knew that room of mine by heart, all those jackets and pants hanging in the closet, and a rack full of nothing but shoes. Over in the corner was a leather chest full of sweaters. And they had already enrolled me in the Country Day School. I always had a good time thinking about things as they really were with my parents. They hadn't fooled me one bit when my mother, being much too showy, took off her brown diamond that time and gave it to my father and told him he could pawn it. It was the last thing to go, that brown diamond, but I knew that it was all an act and my father didn't pawn it at all but they kept it out in Kirkwood in the wall safe.

That's why I didn't mind living there in the Avalon and going through all that misery and being hungry—I mean *dying* of hunger, the way I was right then—because I knew how rich they really were and how it would be when they thought I was ready for my other life. Just like they pretended my brother was up with my aunt and uncle in Keokuk, and that they paid two dollars a week for his keep. Of course I knew he was in a pretty rooty boarding school where they wore jackets with crests on the pockets. Who did they think they were kidding? What griped me was why they thought my brother was ready to be a rich kid and I wasn't.

But like I say, I really enjoyed lying back and visiting around that room of mine out there in Kirkwood. It had its own bathroom with a stand-up shower. All around the walls were my favorite books, and just above my bed, which was in the corner, was a shelf with nothing but Mr. Dumas and Mr. Hugo and Mr. Jules Verne. And over by the window was a Victrola with about a thousand records next to it, and none of them were Rudy Vallee or Al Jolson or Harry Richman or Kate Smith or Lawrence Tibbett or Gene

Austin, who all made me sick to my stomach. Especially Rudy Vallee and *especially* "I'm Just a Vagabond Lover," with that voice of his that sounded like somebody making noises under water.

Over there on the mantel above the fireplace was my violin, which I practiced every evening. Not like now, when I only got to play when we had orchestra rehearsal at school and afterward the instruments had to be left in the music room. There was nothing like having your own violin so you could practice at home and get really good at it. The truth is I didn't like to do anything I wasn't really good at. It meant an awful lot to me when people noticed me do something. That's why I worked so hard at school. You got an E in a subject, that teacher had *noticed* you. You were not some cheesy kid living in a ratty hotel room with only one pair of pants and a crummy sweater and a pair of busted Keds; no, sir, you were the kid who got E-plus in English or pitched the three-hitter or played the funny butler in the eighth-grade play. I was really pretty good on the stage. Especially comic parts. It was this show-off thing in me I mentioned. I mean how better could you get noticed than standing up there in a butler's outfit in front of all those people and making them *laugh*, for crying out loud? And let me tell you, it wasn't as easy to make people laugh as it used to be.

It was the sound of laughing that woke me up. First I thought I was on the stage standing there with a tray and my nose up in the air being the butler, but then I realized it was my mother and father coming through the door and giggling like a couple of sixth-graders—giggling, for Pete's sake! They were both carrying two big brown paper bags, and they came over to my bed and dumped them all around me, spilling bread and apples and a chicken and butter and fresh peas and eggs and cookies, and God knows what, all over the spread and my father even tossed a package of American cheese on my stomach.

I jumped off the bed, knocking off a head of lettuce that rolled across the room. "What happened? Where'd you *get* all that stuff? What about your tooth?" My mother's jaw was just as swollen.

"Here," she said, and she handed me an Eskimo Pie, "quick, it's melting."

While I ate the Eskimo Pie, they explained that it had taken them an hour to walk downtown, but that the dentist was very nice and immediately found the trouble. My mother had developed an infection, an abscess I think they called it, inside a bridge she had, and the dentist had removed the bridge and drained away the infection and said in a couple of days the swelling would be gone. She already felt tons better, she said.

"But *then*," my father said, his face all beams, "the dentist looked at the bridge and saw there was gold in it. He drilled it out and weighed it, and after deducting what we owed him he gave us three dollars and fifty cents. So we took the streetcar home and tonight we're going to have a feast, a *feast!* What do you think of that?"

My mother was already over at the hot plate and my father was opening a bottle of beer they were going to share. President Roosevelt had given everybody beer a couple of months back, but this was their first bottle. My mother began to brown some onions to get the chicken going and I peeled off a slice of that American cheese and began to eat little bites of it. My father said "Ah-h-h" when he took his first taste of the beer, and then he handed the glass to my mother, who said "M-m-m-m."

I guess that was the best meal I ever ate. I wound up opening the top button of my pants. I had one of the breasts of the chicken and a thigh and I mixed the peas into the mashed potatoes, which is a thing I liked to do with butter all over it, and I must've had about fifty helpings. Afterward, we went downstairs and sat out in front of the hotel on the wicker chairs they kept on the sidewalk for the guests. Danny Desot came by and I gave him a purple lollipop from a bunch that was in with the groceries. I didn't like purple. Boy, but I felt wonderful!

But the next day, wouldn't you know it, I had diarrhea from chewing all that grass.

Chapter Seven

Room 317 and Room 333 were locked out on the same day. Mr. Guberly, who lived in 317, used to work for Famous-Barr in the shoe department until they laid him off last year. He was very fat and I always wondered how he could bend over far enough to work on his customers' feet. Room 333 was Miss Vincent, who was a cranky old toad who sure didn't look like a Miss. She once complained that my Keds squeaked too much when I ran down the hall.

The evening they locked her out I was in the lobby when she came in and yelled and screamed about how she didn't have a stitch to put on. They paid no attention to her. Finally she calmed down and asked politely whether at least she could have the framed photo of her mother, who was dead and it was the only picture she had. Mr. Neville, the room clerk, said they would hold her things for thirty days as required by law, and if she paid her bill she could have the photo and everything else. Otherwise not. She asked for Mr. Desot. Mr. Neville said he wasn't there. Miss Vincent stood around awhile, looking like she was going to cry; then she left.

Mr. Guberly never showed up at all.

Chapter Eight

On Monday the canary business happened. I was coming out of school after debate practice—I was on the affirmative team, Resolved: The United States Should Recognize the Soviet Union—when there was Billy Tyzzer backed against the wall by these two really snotty kids from Blewett Junior High who went to Admiral Dewey last year. I liked Billy Tyzzer, not that he was a friend or anything, I didn't have any friends at Admiral Dewey, but I liked hearing him talk; he was always so polite, and he wore suits to school. I don't want you to get the idea he was a sissy; he wasn't. What really got me was that when he wore shirts and ties he had this gold bar underneath the tie between the points of the collar to keep them in place. That gold bar was about the peachiest thing I had ever seen anyone wear.

These snotty Blewett kids were yelling that Billy had agreed to shoot for twenty marbles but now he was welshing.

"Look at the marbles they put up," Billy said, in that quiet polite voice of his, "then look at mine. I'd say theirs were inferior, wouldn't you?"

"So's your old man!" the biggest Blewett kid said.

There was no doubt about it, Billy had some real beauties compared to the ratty collection the Blewetts had, but they were bigger than us and one of them was pretty mad.

"I'll tell you what," I said, "we'll shoot partners, us against you, and I'll put up ten and Billy can pull ten of his."

They took one look at me and agreed. I told you I wasn't much to look at. But anyone who got in a marbles game with me for keeps was in for a big surprise. I played a lot on cinders, and once you got good on cinders anything else was duck soup.

I let Billy shoot first for us. I almost fainted when I saw he shot cunny-thumb. I hadn't seen anyone shoot cunny-thumb since the fourth grade. And I had never shot marbles with anyone wearing a necktie. The guy who shot second for them was pretty good and ran seven marbles out of our twenty, so I knew I'd have to fire from the hip. In marbles I was usually Tom Mix and this was my trusty old six-shooter, and every time I shot I went Pow! It was just a habit of mine. Another thing was I didn't give it that long-aim business, squinting my eye like some guys and squeezing the marble so tight my hand shook before I fired off. I just put my middle knuckle on the ground and Pow!

But now I had to figure how to take these guys with Cunny-Thumb Tyzzer as my pardner. Wal, sir, what ah did wuz ah clumsily aimed at the closest Blewett taw, missed it by a couple of miles, and wound up on the other side of the ring. This convinced the Blewett kid that I was even worse than Billy, so instead of going for me, which he should have, he went for Billy. He only got two, then Billy cunny-thumbed to the middle of the ring like I told him, and I went to work. I used my best shooter, an evil-eye agate I had won from Walter Eamons. I just went Pow! Pow! Pow! Pow! firing my old six-shooter from the hip as I went after those bad guys who were riding out there in front of me. I thought those two Blewetts would have heart attacks right there in the middle of the ring. I got back the nine they had taken from us, and then Pow! Pow! Pow! I ran off their whole twenty, taking the last one from clear across the ring and hitting it on the fly. I hit it so hard it split in two, showing you what high-class marbles they had.

They didn't say anything. They just walked away. Oh, yeah,

one of them spit in the ring before he left, but when you've just raked in twenty marbles you let the other guys spit all they wanted.

"That's the best thing that's happened to me since I came to Dewey," Billy said, smiling and happy. He'd been there less time than me. He used to go to Country Day, but I guess times got a little hard for his father. "I never played marbles before I came to Dewey." Now *there* was a big surprise! "Would you like to come by my place for a Coke or something?"

Now, what you've got to realize is that no one had ever asked me to their home before. The kids at Admiral Dewey had all gone there since they were born and they all clanned together, and anyway I wasn't such a beautiful object to be asked to anybody's home.

Billy Tyzzer lived in a house on Westminster that looked bigger than the Avalon. No kidding. When I first saw it, I thought maybe, you know, they had the first floor or something. But no, on the gate leading in there was this brass nameplate, "Raymond Tyzzer, M.D." It was no place for me. I looked up that long flight of steps past all that lawn and flowers going up to the front door and I tried to think of some reason fast why I suddenly had to go home. But Billy was already halfway up the stairs and I felt doomed.

It was a house like you can't imagine, with *two* living rooms, for crying out loud, and fireplaces everywhere, and the walls next to the stairs going up to Billy's room had *silk* wallpaper. I'm not fooling. At least it felt like silk. Billy introduced me to his mother, who was really *some* beautiful mother. She was older than my mother and I'm not saying that my mother isn't beautiful, she is, but Billy's mother belonged in the White House.

Billy showed me his brother's room, who was away at college, and then his room, and would you believe it was a spittin' image of my room in our Kirkwood house! He even had a Victrola on a table by the window and he hated Rudy Vallee worse than me.

I thought he would change his clothes and put on old play stuff like I did when I came home, but no, he just took off his jacket and threw it on his bed. I looked out of his window, which faced the back of the house, and there was a back yard as big as the entire Avalon parking lot, only instead of cinders it was all lawn and shrubbery and roses crawling up the sides of things. But I was disappointed to see he didn't have a backboard. Can you imagine with a back yard like that and not having a backboard? But then what can you expect from a kid who shoots cunny-thumb? But don't get the idea I didn't like Billy Tyzzer. I did. It's only I would have liked him more if he'd had a backboard.

"Listen, Aaron, how are you about birds?" he asked me.

"I'm in favor of them," I said.

"Well, the reason I ask is I thought you might like to see my birds. It's only that when Walter Eamons came by last week, I showed them to him and the next day a lot of kids at school razzed me about them."

"Oh, that Walter Eamons, he's just jealous, that's all. The same way he got jealous of my cigar bands. What kind of birds you got?"

"Canaries.

"Well, so do we!" It made me feel a little less inferior, him having a canary, too. "Mine'll eat a grape out of my lips, and if I let him have a fly around the room he'll come down and perch on my finger the minute I put my hand in the air."

"That's nifty. Come on down and see mine."

We went down to the basement, which really wasn't a basement except that it was down where basements were. It was a big kind of lounge-around room, with a piano and Ping-Pong table and a big radio about forty times the size of ours. Down at the far end of the room there was nothing but solid canaries.

Billy had these little cages hung all over the wall, with a couple of big cages in front of the others. I just stood there looking at those two million canaries with my mouth open.

"I breed them. That's my hobby," Billy said. "I sell them to Mr. Farley, who runs the pet shop on DeBaliviere."

"You *sell* them? How much do you get?"

"Three dollars a bird. The average female lays four eggs, so I earn twelve dollars and it only costs me about two to raise them."

"God-amighty!" I was really floored. "And Skippy is a roller and a chopper."

"Why don't you go into business? I'll arrange it for you with Mr. Farley."

"But I've only got Skippy. . . ."

"Oh, listen, I'll give you a female. They're not worth anything. They don't sing."

"You really mean it? You mean that's all I need?" I was so excited I stuttered a little.

"Well, let's see. You need a breeding cage like this big one here, but any big cage will do. Then you need a few odds and ends." He picked up a booklet and handed it to me. "Here, take this, it's put out by the Mrs. Finch Bird Seed people and it tells you everything." Billy put his hand in one of the big cages and plucked a big yellow bird off the perch. "Here's a pretty sexy-looking dish." He put the canary in a little wooden cage, more like a box, and handed her to me. "You want me to come over and get you started?"

My heart jumped up to my eyeballs. No one had ever seen how we lived or even *where* we lived, and the first person sure wasn't going to be Billy Tyzzer! In fact, I'm not so sure anyone even knew I lived at the Avalon. At least I hoped they didn't. I was pretty ashamed about living there.

We paraded upstairs, me with my pretty new moneymaker, just as Billy's father came in. He was a tall man with a mustache, and Billy told him he was putting me in the canary business. I had never been with a doctor in his house before and I couldn't quite get my voice to work. I was having trouble with it anyway. The last debate, it went up on me during rebuttal and I kept pushing it down and some of the kids started laughing. We won, anyway.

Billy told his father how me and him had creamed the Blewetts, and showed him the marbles he had won. You could tell

Dr. Tyzzer had been going through a lot of lean times with Billy's marbles, because he got all excited and kept saying "Marvelous!" and "Swell!" and "That's the way!" and putting his arm around the two of us and fracturing our shoulders. Then, for Pete's sake, he asked me if I could stay to dinner. "Elaine!" he called up the stairs. "Is it all right if Billy's friend stays to dinner?"

"Why, of course, Raymond, I'd be delighted. But have him telephone his mother."

Oh, sure, on a phone Mr. Desot cut off six months ago. "Well, sir," I said, trying to get my voice down, "I'd sure like to but I came here from school wearing these school clothes, which aren't proper for dinner." Of course, my only alternative was *no* clothes, but thank God he didn't know that.

"Oh, Billy will lend you something. The phone's right there." Right there was about six steps away. What could I do? I gave the operator the number of the Avalon and old Clara, who ran the switchboard, came on with that clothespin-on-the-nose Rudy Vallee voice of hers.

"Avalon Hotel." What was in my favor was the fact that Clara was the dumbest person in the city of St. Louis.

I talked fast. "Hello, Clara, this is Aaron. I know my mother's at her mah-jongg club, but would you please tell her I'm dining at the Tyzzers' tonight and not to lay a place for me? There's a good girl." I hung up. That's just the way Ronald Colman said it. I swear. "There's a good girl." I saw the movie three times. Ronald Colman was my idea of how I'd like to be if I wanted to be English.

"That's fine," Dr. Tyzzer said, not suspecting that any minute now he'd be called to emergency to treat Clara's heart attack. "Now why don't you boys wash up?"

Billy took a blue blazer with gold buttons and a pair of gray flannels out of his closet and put them on the bed. Then he gave me a blue shirt and a red striped tie and a pair of saddle shoes. He was just about my size. He said to take my time, dinner wasn't ready yet, and to come down to the canary room when I was dressed.

I looked at the things on the bed. The coat was all lined with silk and the gold buttons had little crowns on them. The red stripes of the necktie were kind of raised up a little and the label on the back of the tie was Scruggs-Vandervoort & Barney, which was a department store my father had always tried to sell something to but couldn't. "Sid Gutman gets me that Elgin line, I'll even sell Scruggs for their carriage trade," he had said only yesterday.

I dressed slowly and I never felt so good, I mean my *body,* in my whole life. Like someone was pinning medals all over me. What I probably haven't told you is that I had never been to a clothing store, so trying on things was something I had never done. The pants I wore to school were given to me by my Uncle David that time we were in Chicago, and my mother had made them over for me. Ditto my shirts and sweaters. I did get my Keds new, but my father bought them from a bin on the sidewalk outside a shop.

I just stood there looking at myself in Billy Tyzzer's mirror and I'd have given anything if someone had taken a picture. I couldn't get my eyes off the saddle shoes, which had dark-red rubber soles and felt like air cushions. I peeked in Billy's closet. He had six pairs of shoes. But only this one pair of saddles.

I combed my hair and tossed it back out of my eyes; then I went to call for Christina Sebastian and took her to the movies and then to Big Jack's for a shake. She kept looking at me with these goopy eyes. Christina Sebastian was this girl who sat next to me in American History who could have won the Miss America contest without putting on a bathing suit if she wanted to. I could tell she wanted to sit there at Big Jack's and moon around a little, but I had promised her mother to get her home on time. At the door, she put her face close to mine when she said good night, and I was puckering up to kiss her when I heard Billy Tyzzer coming up the stairs. I dashed to the door and into the hall just as he appeared.

"Hey, those fit you better than they do me. Maybe you better keep them." He laughed, and I laughed, but not really.

I can't tell you much about what I had for dinner, because

when we all went into the dining room and I saw the way that the table was set, with about ten plates for each person and a dozen knives and forks, I almost keeled over. There were candles burning in silver holders and between the candles was a glass swan with flowers floating in water on its back. I had never eaten anywhere in my life where you got more than one fork. In fact, it had never occurred to me that you could *use* more than one fork. At the Avalon, we owned five forks, six spoons, five knives, total. Now on the left side of my plate there were three forks: a big one, a small one, and a fat one; and at the top of my plate there was *another* one, with a colored handle, and a little knife of the same color. And to the right of the plate were three spoons—*three*—two knives, and, in a little plate, another little knife like you use to dab putty. I felt like I was back on the golf links with that bag of clubs.

Well, I did my darnedest to watch Billy and use whatever he used, but by the time I looked around and made sure just which spoon he was using and how he was holding it and how he cooled off the soup without blowing it or slurping it, they took it away. That's what kept happening to me. There was this woman in a black dress with a white apron about the size of my handkerchief, and I swear she had orders to keep her eyes on me and the minute she saw that I had finally gotten myself to the point of putting some food down me, she was to zip over and snatch it away.

Part of the trouble was that while I was trying to figure out the knives and forks and gravy boats and salad servers, they were all talking to me and asking me questions, and trying to do everything at the same time—answer them, figure out the cutlery, and get some food in—was about as easy as circling your head and patting your stomach at the same time. But by the time the dessert came, which was vanilla ice cream with chocolate sauce, I decided the hell with it, and I picked up my biggest spoon and dug in. Ronald Colman wouldn't have approved but the Tyzzers just kept on talking and laughing about how we creamed the Blewetts, and I don't think they even realized I was using the biggest spoon.

Chapter Nine

I came breezing in with the new canary and said, "Look what I've got!" I thought I'd better seize the old initiative because I expected to have a hard time getting my mother to let me stuff the room with a bunch of canaries, but surprise of surprises, I didn't. And I knew once I got my mother, I got my father, too.

Mom was in a good mood because the shipment from the Windy City Hosiery Company had arrived, and there it was in the corner waiting to be delivered. Also, her swole-up jaw had uns-wollen and the relief check for $5.50 had come. Besides, she was probably impressed by how much money canary breeders made.

But the thing that *really* made her feel good was that she had received a letter from my brother Sullivan, the one I told you about who was farmed out to my aunt and uncle in Keokuk for two dollars a week. My father was behind in those payments, too, and my Uncle Nathan had already sent two letters about catching up.

I hated it when Sullivan was gone, because he was so funny and full of mischief and not like me always trying to get E-pluses. He was four years younger than me, but we had fun together except when it came to things like having to choose up sides to play ball. The trouble was he'd hang around even though he could see nobody wanted him. I once got into a fight to get him into a game, and then he struck out three times. When you're eight years old, you ought to bat against eight-year-olds, but Sullivan called eight-year-olds infants.

The only good thing about his being away was his letters. He wrote them all by himself, as you can see:

Deer Mom Pop Aaron and Skippy

I wuz sik last weak but now Im bettur. I lyked having a feever cuz evreewun sweeted me. My cuzzins are bean meen to me but thayair not so hot ether. Tom eets mor things than me but I eet mor of wot I lyk. Last nite thayair wuz wine and Unkle Naythun gav me a sip. Its smooth in the beegining but the going down part is sower.

Last nite at the taybull Reebekka told a purrmanent lie. I reely no. The othur thing is Tom is more uzzervant than me but I see more.

Yesturday on the way home from skool some Keeokuk rain fell in my eye.

If ud lyke me to cum home thats awl rite becuz I nevur hate to leeve whair I am becuz Im awlways so assited at whair Im gonna bee.

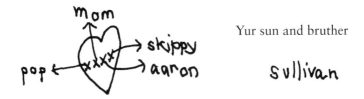

Yur sun and bruther

Sullivan

While I had been reading Sullivan's letter, my mother had been reading Mrs. Finch's booklet. "Well, now, it says you need a nest, special nesting materials, a breeding cage, and special kinds of food—here they are, with prices on them, and they're *quite* expensive." A lot of damp had fallen on her, I could tell.

"But we don't *need* all that guk," I said—note that I said *we*. "I've seen birds sitting in nests all over Forest Park and they didn't get them from Mrs. Finch." That's the thing about my mother, she can be reasoned with. She's not always yelling at me to call the *Post-Dispatch*.

We found an old tea strainer to use for the nest, and Mom got together little pieces of cotton and flannel from her scrap bag that you can bet were just as good as Mrs. Finch's carton of Sterilized Nesting Materials, fifty cents per. I said I would get the special food and cuttlebones with the two bits Aunt Minnie gave me every Friday for the movies.

"I don't know about that. You know how funny Aunt Minnie is. She may not like you to use the money for that."

"She won't know. I'll just go off like I'm going to the movies, stay away for a couple of hours, and she'll never know the difference."

"But that's cheating," my mother started to say, but then we both started laughing because that was *just* the way to spend Aunt Minnie's card money.

The only real problem was the breeding cage. I tried to make one out of some old window screen tacked around a grapefruit box, but I asked Billy Tyzzer and he said it was no good because the birds would cut themselves on the screen, especially the baby birds. Then it occurred to me to go talk to Ben. I didn't want to, I never *wanted* to talk to Ben, but if you caught him at the right time, when he wasn't feeling vicious, he'd do things for you. Actually I was about as crazy about Ben as I was about Patrolman Burns. If you had told me they were blood brothers, I'd have believed you.

Ben was the bellhop and he wore a greasy maroon uniform that hadn't been cleaned since the hotel was built. Neither had his teeth. He chewed a wooden match and was skinny and didn't like to shave. I never saw him carry any bags or fetch newspapers or do any of the things bellhops do in the movies. He did other things. Like lock people out. And he was a big shot in the lobby with the dance-hall customers who hung around at night. Mostly he threw them out. I would sure have liked to have seen Ben and Patrolman John L. Burns in a shoot-out. I'd have rooted for both of them.

I went down to the lobby and found Ben sitting in one of the mohair armchairs next to the dusty rubber plants in the window. I asked him if he had ever locked out anybody who had a big cage. He was proud of his lockouts and liked to be asked about them. He chewed on his match with the red tip bobbing up and down and thought while he scratched himself between the legs. Ben always scratched himself between the legs when he was thinking. "Now jus' who cuday've put the Ya-ale ohn who mott've hayed a big ol' cage?" Ben came from the Ozarks and he spoke this language that was harder to understand than French. He began to tick off all the people he had locked out over the past couple of years and it made me so depressed I wanted to shoot myself. Boy, was I sorry I asked him.

Suddenly he stopped chewing and scratching. "Wal, now acourse! Ginelli the Great Mahgician. Huh! He warn't even magical enough t'open mah ol' lock." I followed him down to the basement storage room: He kept telling me about the bunch of white mice Ginelli kept in this big cage, and the doves he had in another, and then about other people he locked out who had parrots and hamsters and canaries and God knows what. While he was unlocking the door, the biggest cat you ever saw came out of nowhere and began rubbing against his leg and purring.

"Wal, ef it ain't mah l'il ol' pussycat, Christian. Ha' ya, sweetheart?" I've seen tigers at the zoo smaller than his little old pussycat. "Thass whar them Ginelli mice went, rahte down into ol' Christian's tummy. Thar ain't much he cain't handle 'cept once thar was a parrot sho gave ol' Christian a hawd tahme." I wanted to stomp old Christian into the pavement right there and then. But he probably would have eaten off my foot right to the knee.

Ben waded through a mile of old junk. There must have been a thousand umbrellas. Ben said that even when people knew they were going to be locked out and had a chance to smuggle some of their stuff out, they always left their umbrellas in the closet. "Sorta for their conscious," he said. He found the cage behind a trunk. It was dirty but just the thing for Skippy's family. "Wachu gonna do, keep yo' money in there?" That made him laugh so hard he had to take the match out of his mouth. But he didn't ask me to pay him anything, just gave me the cage. Probably knew I'd put something nice and tasty for Christian in it.

When he had laughed himself out, he went over to a big trunk and took out a bottle which he put in a brown paper bag. "Give this to 310, willya?" I took the bag, what else could I do, but the last thing in the world I wanted to do was go near 310.

That was the beginning of what turned out to be the most putrid Friday night of the year. To start with, on my way down the hall Old Lady Heinson hooked me and wanted to get in this big discussion about *The Deerslayer*. Well, the next to last thing in the world I wanted to do right then was give a book report. I had read about fifty pages of *The Deerslayer* when I decided that if they ever had a world's championship for *boring* writers James Fenimore Cooper would win the Davis Cup. But I just lied and said I was in the middle of it and couldn't wait to get to the room to finish it.

What I really couldn't wait to do was clean up the old cage and put Skippy and Mrs. Skippy together, but when I got to our room I could hear Aunt Minnie droning away through the door. She always came early to get her fifty cents' worth. Maybe she was lonely. So I left the cage in the hall and knocked on the door of 310. I was praying no one was there yet so I could just leave the darn bag outside the door, but they were there all right. The tall one with the gray wavy hair that my father said was the best criminal lawyer in St. Louis opened the door. It was early still, so he was all right and just took the bag and thanked me. If it had been the next night, it would have been a different story. I sure wouldn't be knocking on their door on a Saturday night and handing them a bottle of whiskey. Not those three. Oh, yes, that's what was in the bag, a bottle of Ben's bootleg. That was another thing Ben did. He sold whiskey. Mr. Roosevelt had only given us beer, not whiskey yet, but Lester said booze was on its way and Ben wasn't going to be in *that* business much longer.

The Minnie dinner was a disaster because my mother forgot and served carrots, which Minnie hated. And then, instead of *passing* the chicken like usual, Minnie *served* everybody, for crying out loud, and I got the last thing on the plate, which was a drumstick. Now if there's any part of a chicken I don't like besides the you-know-what it's the drumstick. Then, in the middle of the meal, my mother began coughing and went down the hall to the toilet and didn't come back till the meal was almost over. Aunt Minnie said she looked pale, which she did.

After dinner we went to Minnie's room to play rummy, as usual, but I really wasn't in the mood for it. Finally, she won her games and said, "Well, looks like I've had a lucky run tonight," and handed me my quarter for the movies. I thanked her and got up to go, intending to look for cigar bands and save the two bits, but she said, "I think I'll walk you to the movies. I need a little air." Can you believe it? She never went anywhere at night, now suddenly she had to walk me to the movies. Boy, when a Friday night goes sour!

Once St. Louis got that hot, I always went to the Kingshighway Theatre. All that the Uptown Theatre did for the heat was to move outside into an open place in back of the theater, and put folding chairs on the gravel and show the movie that way. The trouble about that was St. Louis nights were as hot as the days and it was just as hot sitting outside in back of the theater watching the movie as it was sitting inside. Besides, a movie wasn't a movie for me if it wasn't in a dark secret place like the movie house. The lights went down and it was all black and quiet and you could be anywhere. Down on the bottom of the sea with Captain Nemo or anywhere. But sitting outside, with the sky and traffic sounds and all, it was not the same thing. That's why I preferred the Kingshighway. Also, it was ice-cooled. There were these big fans at the back with big hunks of ice in front of them, and the fans blew over the ice and if you knew where to sit you really got cooled.

So Minnie walked me to the Kingshighway, and who should be standing in the ticket line but Ella McShane and her mother and her aunt. The Kingshighway was giving away dish number 18 in its thirty-six-piece set and I liked that better than Bank Night, because I had never won a nickel on a Bank Night but on a Dish Night you always went home with a cup or soup bowl or something. We bought our tickets and went in, and of course we all sat together. It was the first time I had sat next to a girl in a movie. I mean a girl I knew. It felt funny, like I didn't know where to put my arm, whether being a girl she got the whole armrest or we shared it or what. She looked pretty good. She had on a white dress and her hair was fixed up and she had on a little bit of red lipstick. I think I told you she was fourteen.

It was a rotten movie with Joan Crawford, who always gave me a pain in the neck. So did Norma Shearer. Lots of mush and pretty faky. But Ella seemed to like it and she cried a little at the end when they finally took the bandages off Joan Crawford's eyes and she could see. My favorite actress was Marie Dressler. I always sat through Marie Dressler twice.

On the way back to the hotel, the aunt went into Walgreen's and bought a carton of ice cream. Ella told me that the aunt came to see them twice a month and took them to the movies and bought ice cream. They invited me to their room to share it and I wanted to refuse but I couldn't. I was very susceptible to ice cream.

Their room was the same as ours but they only had one exposure. The ice cream was Neapolitan, which I'm not crazy about, but Ella and I talked and she showed me her graduation book from Clark. She went to Blewett now. She didn't have her glasses on in the graduation book so I didn't recognize her. She had opened the top drawer of the dresser and taken out a package of cinnamon gum, and was just offering me a stick when it happened. The first thing I knew, her arm went stiff-out and she let out a little scream and fell to the floor. She was making a kind of grunting noise, and I was petrified. Her whole body was very stiff and I could see the rolled-up whites of her eyes, and her legs were jerking like someone was poking something hot at her feet. I was really scared to death.

Her mother ran over to the sink and got something and ran back to Ella. It was a stick like the doctor at school used to look down our throats. Mrs. McShane poked the stick in Ella's mouth. "Quick, Martha, quick!" she said to the aunt. "Raise her head, she's swallowing her tongue!" The aunt bent down and picked up Ella's head, and Ella's mother kept working the stick in her mouth till she pulled her tongue out. Ella's body was jerking all over now, and she was making little crying noises and she broke wind several times. I wanted to leave, but Ella was laying in front of the door. Oh, God, how I wanted to leave! I didn't know what to do. Walk over to the window and not look, maybe, but I couldn't seem to move.

Then, just as suddenly as it had started, it ended. All at once. Her eyes came back to place and she relaxed and her body smoothed out. Her mother took a wet cloth and wiped her face, and then they helped her to her feet. I picked up her glasses and handed them to her.

"Are you all right, dear?" her mother asked.

"Oh, sure," she said, trying to smile. She was very white and she had freckles I hadn't noticed before.

"I better be getting back," I said, and I thanked the aunt for the ice cream. I felt terrible. Really terrible.

"I'm sorry," Mrs. McShane said to me. "Ella hasn't had one of those for a long time."

"Was it awful?" Ella asked me. She was holding her fingers together very tight.

I didn't know what to say.

"Now, Ella, let Aaron be on his way."

"I just want to know if I did anything really bad," Ella said, her voice louder.

"Well," I said, wanting to die, "you were sick and now you're all right." I opened the door and stepped into the hall. She followed me.

"Here," she said, "you didn't take your gum." She offered me the stick of cinnamon gum which she still had in her hand. I took it and put it in my pocket and went on down the hall to our room. She was still standing there watching me when I went through the door.

So much for Friday.

Chapter Ten

Saturday wasn't much better.

The first thing I did was to scrub Ginelli the Great's cage and put it in the window in the sun to dry. Then I got Mrs. Finch's booklet and started to read. "When the male is placed in the breeding cage with the female, they may evince no interest in each other at first. However, eventually a conquest of the female by the male will occur, if the breeding process is to be successful."

I opened Skippy's cage door and he hopped out onto my finger as he always does. I carried him over and put him in the breeding cage. Then I opened the door of the little cage and placed it at the opening of the breeding cage, so that Billy's bird would fly in. I had named her Sooky. She was a little bigger than Skippy and all gold, whereas Skippy had half-moons of gray on his wings.

Into the cage she went, and I snapped the door shut and waited for the fireworks. My heart was beating a mile a minute. Imagine, all I had to do was to shut Skippy up with this pretty lady bird and I'd be rich! I had the tea strainer attached to the bars, the little pieces of Mom's cloth were piled in a corner, there was fresh water and seed, and out of all that I was going to make a fortune.

The two birds paid absolutely no attention to each other. Skippy was over at the feed cup cracking seed while Sooky hopped around on the bottom, sorting out good seeds from opened ones. I stood there for about two hours watching their every move. They never even *looked* at each other. I turned on the radio and got some soft music, but all that did was to make Skippy sing a little. While he was singing, Sooky just went on cracking seeds. It was so boring watching them eat and wipe their beaks and squeeze plops out of their behinds that I finally had to give up.

"He doesn't like her, that's what's wrong," I told my mother.

"Maybe he's been a bachelor too long," she said.

She was probably right. Poor old Skip. How'd I like it if somebody stuck me in a cage with some girl and expected me to have a flock of babies in a tea strainer ten minutes later?

I put on my Feltie and got out my racket and my two new tennis balls, but when I got to the door I remembered it was Saturday and juniors couldn't play Saturday or Sunday before one o'clock. I really hated weekends. I would never let any kid at Admiral Dewey hear me say it, but the fact was I hated any day I didn't have school. My father and mother had already had a big squabble, and if I had been in school I wouldn't have been there to hear it. They had a lot of squabbles. That's why you're never going to catch me married. If there was anything I hated, I mean really *hated*, it was squabbles. I brought some homework to Walter Eamons once when he was sick, and when I got to his kitchen door there was his mother and father having this giant squabble all over the kitchen, one of them following the other around the kitchen, both of them squabbling at each other. So I just leaned the homework against the screen door and left. I'd bet you even Dr. Tyzzer squabbled with Mrs. Tyzzer. I would just bet you.

Well, to get back to my mother and father, at the end of their squabble, which was something about money which their squabbles were about 99 percent of the time, my father had slammed out of the door, which was what he always did. My mother sat down at the table and put her face in her hands and cried. My mother cried quite a lot. Not very loud—I mean she wouldn't go "Boo-hoo-hoo!" all over the place, but she was a crier, all right. It always made me itchy as heck when she cried.

When she had finished her cry, she tied the Windy City Hosiery boxes together, and then she put on this straw hat she wears and I helped her carry the boxes down to the streetcar. She always went by herself because it was double carfare to East St. Louis, and that would have meant four extra fares if me or Pop had helped her.

The way she got into the Windy City Hosiery business was this. That time we were living in Chicago, before we came back here to the Avalon, my mother's sister Virginia was going with a guy who worked for the Windy City Hosiery Company. So after we got back to St. Louis and nobody could find a job and we couldn't pay the rent or eat, my mother wrote and asked Virginia to ask her boyfriend if Windy City had a salesperson in St. Louis. They sent her some samples to go door-to-door, and the deal was when she sent in the orders they'd mail her the stuff to take around to the customers. That way she got paid on the spot, kept her commission, and sent Windy City the rest.

They were silk things like panties and nightgowns and slips. They were cheaper than in the stores, but my mother had a hard time selling any until one day she rung a doorbell and there was this beefy blond woman who looked at all the samples and said, "Dearie, you have lovely things here and they are not expensive for silk things, but ordinary people don't have that kind of money right now. But maybe I can interest my sister." So she went to the phone and called her sister. "Betty, there's this darling little woman here with some precious silk things that are so cheap you wouldn't believe it. . . . You got any references, dearie? My sister wants to know." My mother told her she had worked at the Bell Telephone Company and the Woodward-Tiernan Printing Company, and the woman told her sister. "Dearie," the woman said after she hung up, "you're in luck. My sister said she'd take a chance on you." That's how my mother began to sell to these ladies in East St. Louis. They were rich ladies who had money and they used a lot of silk things. It seemed funny to me that they all lived in East St. Louis.

Crossing the street from the car stop, there was Patrolman John L. Burns waiting for me. He grabbed me by the ear and handed me a Robert Burns cigar band.

"I've been saving it for you," he said.

"That's stupendous," I said. That was his idea of a cigar band, a Robert Burns. But I had to put it in my pocket.

"Say, I don't see your old man riding around in his flivver any more. What'd he do, sell it?"

"No, he's got it."

"Where's he keep it? Out back in the lot?"

"Gosh, I don't know. I guess so."

"Don't he ever take you for a ride in it?"

"Oh, no, sir. I just go to school." That answer didn't make much sense, I admit, but I wasn't about to blab anything about the Ford. The finance company had been after it for a long time and my father kept moving it around so they wouldn't find it. There were these two finance-company guys my father called Repleviners who were always snooping around. They'd come by the parking lot two, three times a week. You couldn't miss them. They were both about six feet wide and wore black suits and gray hats, only one was tall and the other was short. You'd see them walking together you'd swear the short one had been sawed off the top of the tall one, that's how alike they looked. Of course, if they got their hands on the Ford my father's chances of ever getting the Elgin line would have been zero. Actually, he had the Ford hidden in the alley in back of the Piggly-Wiggly. It was a perfect place.

I was going through the lobby, massaging my ear, when Danny Desot stopped me and challenged me to flip baseball cards. Of all the stupid things there were to do on a stupid Saturday, flipping baseball cards was about the stupidest. It wasn't like shooting marbles or playing tennis where you did something. It was just standing there for a couple of hours and dropping those stupid cards on the floor. One side of the card had the picture of a baseball player and the other side had his life story—you know, batting average and if he batted right-handed and where he was born. You either matched pictures or you didn't match pictures, and that's how you got the other guy's card. Stupid. But that was my choice. Go flip those stupid baseball cards with Danny or go back to the room. Some choice.

"Where's your mother?" I asked.

"How should I know?"

I decided to take a chance on Mrs. Desot being off somewhere, because my father was probably back in the room and he was always pretty crabby when my mother was out selling hosiery. After all, *he* was the salesman, but he didn't have anything to sell. We went up to Danny's room, and after flipping those stupid cards for a while I got the bright idea of maybe going to the ball game. We could hitch a ride to Sportsman's Park and then get in with the Knothole Gang, which is what the Cardinals called the kids they let in free to sit in a section way out in left field. I had been to one ball game with a kid named Ralph Shultz when I went to Kennard School. I had carfare then. You couldn't see much from out there but it didn't matter. You got the *feel* of the whole place. And then that terrific thing happened to me in the seventh inning. I had raced up to the toilet, and on my way back I was going along the railing next to the field when there was Ducky Joe Medwick, the left fielder, standing on the foul line, unwrapping a piece of chewing gum. He had his glove under his arm and he was unwrapping this piece of chewing gum before going out to his position. I was standing there watching him as he pushed the gum in his mouth and chewed down on it. He saw me at the railing looking at him. "Here, Red," he said. Ducky Joe Medwick said to *me*, "wanna piece of gum?" Then he tossed me this piece of Doublemint Wrigley's gum he took from his pocket and I caught it, and he winked at me and trotted out onto the field. Of course, I never chewed the gum, which I have kept in my pirate box to this day.

"Naw, it's too hot," Danny said. He never wanted to do anything. So we kept on flipping cards and then the door opened and there was Mrs. Desot.

"Oh, there you are, my sweet baby, love of my life, fruit of my tree!" She came sailing at him with her arms open and this soupy look on her face. I wanted to jump out of the window.

She wrapped her arms around him and started to push her stomach against him. "You want to go back and live in Mummy's tummy for a while? Wouldn't that be nice? Mummy could carry you everywhere in there and you could swim around and be cozy. Wouldn't that be nice? Mmm, wouldn't it?" She kept saying "Wouldn't it?" and pushing old Danny into her belly and all the time kissing around on his cheeks and hair, and I can tell you if *I* had been Danny she would have gotten an elbow right into that belly where I once swam around. But Danny just had this sort of bored look on his face, like he always did when she started on him, and he let her do anything she wanted.

"Does Aaron know how sweet you were drinking all your milk out of my breasts? Does he know? Hmmm? Does he?" Now she had Danny's face mushed into one of her huge floppy breasts, still holding him up against her belly and pushing her breast at him like she was really feeding him. "Does Aaron know? Hmmm, does he?" Boy, did Aaron know. I had sat through this performance a hundred times more than Marie Dressler. It's hard to believe but she really had the breast part of her dress poked into Danny's mouth, all the time talking a mile a minute about milk, her wonderful milk and does Aaron know how sweet Danny was and telling him to drink his dinner like a good little baby boy. Then suddenly she started yelling, "Now you're being born, you're being born, my baby, my baby, my baby!" After a couple of hundred "my baby"s she finally let him go. The telephone in the other room had started to ring. She smoothed down the front of her dress and hurried out to answer it. There was a wet place on her dress where Danny had been drinking her wonderful milk.

I went on down to the room and I was plenty mad. What got me was why Mrs. Desot always wanted me around to watch Danny getting born again. I wasn't there the first time, was I?

My father wasn't in the room. I checked on Skippy and Sooky. Nothing doing. Still eating, opposite ends of the cage. Through the open transoms I could hear Mr. Criminal Lawyer and his pals heating up. It was quite a racket, like an argument. All the noises from there sounded like arguments. Except sometimes the blond lady would sing. Even when she had drunk so much I couldn't make out the words, I still liked to hear her voice coming through the transom. She sang in a high, chirpy voice, like a drunken bird.

I went down the hall and rapped on Lester's door, but no one was there. I had never been in Lester's room, or he in mine. If he had been there, he would've just come out in the hall and talked to me there. I never saw anybody go in or out of his room except him, but he said he lived with his "old lady." He always left me notes under our door when he wanted to see me. Anyway, he wasn't there. Or his old lady.

I don't know where the day went. I walked the gutters all the way to Skinker Boulevard and back without finding anything good. All the cigar smokers must've been out of town.

I went out to the tennis courts but I couldn't find anybody to play with, so I took one of my old balls and knocked it against the practice wall. I horsed around the courts and then the gutters till the sun went down. Found a Corona Corona and a Regalia Especial and a Bouquet. I gouged a little melted tar out of a street top and made a cud of it. But it was too hot to be Gus Mancuso. It was around six o'clock and cooling off a little by the time I got back to the hotel. By August it wouldn't cool off at all, sun up or sun down.

For the second time that day, Patrolman John L. Burns trapped me. This time I was on the lookout for him, as I usually am, but he was inside the Walgreen's, looking out the window, and he just stepped out and he had me by the ear before I knew he was there.

"Listen, you little bohunk, I thought you told me your old man kept his jalopy in the parking lot!" His jaw was out and he was mad. "What do you call that!" He was pointing across the street. Boy, was he mad! "He parks it in the Woodbine loading zone, that's where he parks it, and you better hustle up and tell him if it ain't outa there in two minutes he gets a ticket. Got that?" He was pulling my ear right out of the socket. "That isn't my father's car," I said, looking across the street. There was a Ford in the loading zone, but it sure wasn't my father's.

"Whaddya mean not your old man's car? You callin' me a liar? Okay, I was givin' you a break but there's no sense givin' a bohunk a break—they'll lie to you every time." He reached in his pocket and took out his ticket book. "You're a little smart aleck, ainchu? Well, I'm gonna write out this ticket, and you take it on up to your old man and tell him how you tried to tell a lie to Patrolman John L. Burns."

"Wait a minute, just a minute, Patrolman Burns, that isn't my father's Ford. I swear it! I can prove it. You can go over in back of Piggly-Wiggly, the alley there, and see for yourself."

"That the truth?" Boy, he had eyes like Bela Lugosi.

"Yes, sir. I swear it!"

He let go of my ear and put the book back in his pocket. "It'd better be. Go on, get outa here."

I reached up to my ear to test for blood, and as I did I sort of turned and looked back like maybe I could kill him with my viper look. That's how come I saw them. The Repleviners. Standing there on the street corner, talking to Patrolman John L. Burns, who was pointing in the direction of Cabanne and Union. And you know what was at Cabanne and Union? That's right, Piggly-Wiggly. My heart dropped to my ankles. I was stupid, stupid, STU-PID, to get tricked like that. Patrolman John L. Burns was a dirty rat, but I was STUPID. A really dirty rat to pull a mean trick like that on a twelve-year-old boy. I started to feel tears. Then I got mad. "Oh, no, you don't. Oh, no, you don't!" I was yelling it out loud as I raced down the block to the hotel. Lester was sitting out front reading a magazine.

"Lester! Look! The Repleviners! That dirty rat John L. Burns is telling 'em where the Ford is."

Lester took one look at Patrolman Burns, who he hated worse than me, and jumped up. "Come on!" he said, and I pitched my tennis stuff on the chair and we started to run.

"In back of the Piggly-Wiggly," I yelled, "but I haven't got the key!"

"Come on! Step on it!"

"And it hasn't any gas!"

One thing about us, we knew the neighborhood—every back-alley short cut there was. And what I do best is run, so I kept up with Lester pretty good. Right across Union and through Piggly-Wiggly and into the alley and there was our Ford. Lester yanked open the door, released the brake, and pushed me behind the wheel.

"You know how to steer?"

"Sure."

"Then steer."

He slammed the door, ran around to the back of the Ford, and began to push. What I meant about knowing how to steer was that I had sat behind the wheel many times and driven all over the map and worked the pedals but not with the engine on.

The alley was kind of uphill and Lester had to work like all getout. A couple of times we stalled, but I could hear him grunting and puffing as he got the old Ford going again. I rocked myself back and forward in my seat as hard as I could to help out. I could steer all right, but the seat was too far back for my feet to reach the pedals and I had a little trouble seeing over the top of the wheel.

It took us about three years to reach the end of the alley and I just knew the Repleviners would get to us before we really got going. Lester was grunting and heaving for all he was worth, but we were barely moving. "Come on, Lester! That's the way, Les!" I was yelling at him like I was the shortstop and he was pitching. "Now you're going! Atsaway! Give it the old muscle! That's it! That's the way, Lester! Atsaway!" I didn't know if Repleviners carried guns. Anybody in cahoots with Patrolman John L. Burns probably did. I didn't want Lester to get shot in the back. "Come on, Lester! Attaboy! Now you're moving! Now we're really rolling!"

The old Ford bumped out of the alley and I turned right onto Windermere, which was downhill. The Ford picked up speed right away and soon Lester began to run, still pushing, running the old Ford down Windermere, and I gripped the wheel tight as we really got going. I stretched up my neck as far as I could and sat on the tippy edge of the seat so I could see. By the time we got to the bottom of Windermere where it goes into Visitation Park, the Ford had run away from Lester and I could see him in the mirror getting smaller and yelling, "Keep going! Don't stop! Keep going!" He could have saved his breath, since my foot was about a yard short of the brake pedal.

I was really whizzing now and it was maybe the greatest feeling I ever had. I was also scared to death. It was getting darker and harder to see. At the end of Windermere, I turned left onto Arlington so as not to run over the curb into Visitation Park, and there were two cars turning onto Windermere, which if they hadn't I would have smashed them to pieces. Or they me. But they turned, thank God, and I went zooming down Arlington, which is even more downhill than Windermere. A car coming out of a driveway almost got me but I banged on the old horn and the driver slammed on his brakes, and I could see his face with his jaw dropped open as he watched this silent Ford whiz by with yours truly at the wheel.

The speedometer said thirty-five but I wasn't far enough to be safe from the Repleviners, and besides I didn't know how to stop even if I wanted. I decided that since I couldn't reach the brake anyway, I might as well get up on my knees so's I could really see. That was much better. I could steer now and see everything and I just kept banging on the horn and passing all the slowpokes in my way. I was really running that old Ford now and I was no longer scared. I passed this lady in a big Hudson as neat as you please, and when I turned right onto Enright I even put out my hand. What I wanted to do was to get down to Clara, which was a quiet street without much traffic, and try to stop there, but I almost cracked up at St. Luke's Hospital, which is on Enright before you get to Clara. There were a million cars pulling in and out of the hospital, and there I was zooming along with my horn blowing and them scurrying this way and that and me twisting and turning to try to get by.

But then clang! this ambulance came steaming out of the driveway right in my path and I thought I was a goner for sure, but I wrenched the wheel way over to the other side and we just missed each other, and then I wrenched back onto my side just in the nick of time to miss crashing into a truck that was coming at me. I was really scared again, more than before, so I scrunched way down to try to reach my foot onto the brake pedal but that made me not see anything and lose control of the wheel, so I popped right back up with my heart pounding and just missed ramming a coal truck parked at the curb. No more of that.

I careened around the corner onto Clara and the Ford raised itself way up on the left side, and I thought for sure I was going over as I got pitched way to the right, but then we bounced back down and swayed back and forth until I got control of the wheel again. Clara was uphill. But I was going so fast the old Ford rolled almost to the corner of Clemens before it stopped. My hands were glued to the wheel.

It was almost dark now and the streetlights were coming on, and I just sat there on my haunches with my hands glued to the wheel feeling like I'd just run a hundred-mile race. I let out this big sigh and put my forehead against the wheel and closed my eyes. Cars were going by with their lights on and I was sort of out from the curb but I didn't care. I wondered if maybe the cops had seen me and were after me, but I was too tired to care. Criminy, was I pooped. Sitting there, feeling pooped, was when the hand reached in and grabbed me.

"Gotcha!"

I jumped a mile.

It was Lester. He laughed at me and mussed my hair and gave me a punch on the arm that was one of the best compliments I ever got. I laughed, too, and he opened the door and I jumped to the ground and we had the kind of laugh together that only good buddies can have.

"Come on," he said, "we better move this."

"But I told you, Lester—no gas and I haven't. . . ."

He had taken his pearl-handled knife out of his pocket and now he crossed over to where a lawn sprinkler was whooshing and I followed him. "See if there's anybody on the porch." I walked over to the driveway and looked. There wasn't. Lester took his knife and zuck! zuck! cut a piece out of the hose. The sprinkler stopped working. Lester went back to the Ford and pushed it a few feet until it was alongside a Reo that was parked at the curb. Lester unscrewed the gasoline cap on the Reo and told me to do the same on the Ford. Then he put one end of the garden hose in the Reo's gas tank and the other end in his mouth. He gave a big suck on the hose, then quickly pulled it out of his mouth and dunked it into the Ford's gas tank. He spit some gasoline out of his mouth onto the street. He spit two or three times. He kept watching the street to be sure no one was coming.

After a couple of minutes, Lester pulled out the garden hose and flung it into the high weeds of a vacant lot. I put the caps back on the gas tanks as Lester opened the hood of the Ford and took out his penknife again. "When I tell you to," he said, "press down on the starter." He fooled around with his pearl-handled knife for a while. We were near a light, so he could see, but not good. I kept watching across the street in case the porch sitters came out and discovered their sprinkler wasn't whooshing.

Finally Lester said, "Okay," and I jammed down on the starter. The motor began to catch, flut, flut, flut, but didn't quite make it. "Give it more spark," Lester said. I pushed down the spark handle two notches. Then I pressed the starter again. Flut, flut, and then it started. Lester ran over and put up the spark and pulled down the gas lever about halfway. He closed the hood and got behind the wheel as I scooted over.

We drove a few blocks to the Eagle Ice Company on Euclid. There was a big truck in front loading up with huge chunks of ice that were sliding down a metal chute. Lester pulled up beside the truck and yelled at one of the men on the platform. "Hey, Mr. Marks, can I park this in the back for a while?"

"Who's that—Lester?"

"Yeah. Okay?"

"Sure, kid. Put it in the shed if you want."

"Thanks, Mr. Marks. Can you use me tomorrow?"

"Yeah, maybe around noon."

Lester drove the Ford around back and parked it in an old shed that was full of worn-out tires and things like that. We walked back onto the sidewalk.

"You know where you are?" he asked me.

"Sure."

"I'm late." He started to move off like he always does.

"Hey, Lester."

"Yeah?"

"Thanks. You know . . . my father really needs it."

He pushed his hand at me and left. He was embarrassed, I think. I shouldn't have thanked him.

Chapter Eleven

The first thing I did when I got back to the hotel was check on Skippy and Sooky. Zero. Both cracking away at opposite ends of the cage. It was the greatest eating match of the century. My father was glued to Fibber McGee and Molly on the radio, so I knew it was no use telling him about the Ford till it was over. Every week he'd sit there waiting for the big moment when Molly would want something and Fibber would say, "Oh, I have that in my closet," and Molly would say, "Oh, no, Fibber, not that!" but he'd go ahead and open the closet anyway and for about two hours there were these sound effects of junk falling out of Fibber McGee's closet, and my father would laugh and laugh and laugh as long as that junk kept clanging out of Fibber's closet. Every week the same thing. About as funny, if you ask me, as Skippy and Sooky eating at opposite ends of the cage.

My mother served us plates of macaroni and we ate while my father switched around to *Mr. Keen, Tracer of Lost Persons,* then Ed Wynn the "Fire Chief," Major Bowes and his amateur hour, and Fanny Brice with that throw-up Baby Snooks which she did. My father's big favorites of the week, besides *Amos 'n' Andy,* were Baron Munchausen, who was always saying "Vas you dere, Sharlie?" in a goopy German accent; Parkyakarkus, who spoke broken

Greek; Mr. Kitzel, who was Yiddish with Jack Benny; Mrs. Nussbaum, who was Yiddish with Fred Allen; and Molly Goldberg, who was Yiddish on her own. People with accents really broke up my father. Maybe his having an accent himself had something to do with it. It beat me. Anyway, I knew better than to interrupt his programs. But this particular night I had one thing to be thankful for—Rudy Vallee was resting his beautiful pipes.

When Gabriel Heatter finished the news and said goodnight, my father finally turned off the radio. I told him about Patrolman John L. Burns and the Repleviners and the Ford. He went through the ceiling.

"How many times have I told you to keep your mouth shut about that car? I don't care what he said! Any time he talks to you, tell him to deal with your father. You let *me* handle him. He knows he can't get away with that kind of stuff with *me!* You know what they may do at your Eagle Ice Company? They just may sell that car, that's what. How do I know anything about the Eagle Ice Company? Just because Lester Silverstone says hello to somebody, how do I know what they'll do to the car? How many times, how *many* times have I told you to keep your mouth shut about things that aren't your business? You take care of your cigar bands and let me take care of the car."

"Oh, Eric," my mother said, "he saved the Ford, didn't he?"

That *really* got him mad, and they started a big squabble over me. And then over everything. On and on and on. We put the screen between the beds and I covered Skippy and Sooky and we all undressed, my mother going into the closet, and all through it my mother and father squabbled. They kept on squabbling right into bed, but finally they told each other to shut up and turned off the lights.

It was a very hot night and neither exposure was working. The *Post-Dispatch* said it was the hottest for that date in the entire history of the weather bureau. I sure believed them. The music from the Good Times Taxi Dance was double loud, because on

Saturday night they had five pieces. There was a lot of laughing and yelling mixed with the music, and on top of that there were the transom voices of the drunks from across the hall. I just laid there looking at the lights on the ceiling from the parking lot and feeling miserable. About everything. Usually when I feel miserable, I can force myself to think forward to good things like a play I'm going to be in or a ball game coming up against Clark or Kennard or a super cigar band I just found, like that. I laid there poking around in my head for some good things to think about, but I couldn't find any.

I had really got my hopes up of making a killing in the canary business. I had gone through Mrs. Finch and added up how long it took till the eggs were laid, plus how long to hatch, plus how long till the baby birds were grown, and it just measured out right for my graduation. The class had voted on blue coats, white shirts, blue ties, and white pants. Plus I'd have to get shoes. I had looked in the windows on Delmar and made a list: Mound City Men's & Boy's Wear had a white shirt for 98 cents, a blue tie for 30 cents, and white pants for $1.75. At Horwitz's Haberdashery there was a boy's blue coat in the window with white buttons for $4.19. And Wheelock's had a big sign in the window, "All Shoes $2.98, None Higher." I added that up and it came to $10.20. Then there was the $1.00 for the graduation dance, which made it $11.20. Four birds at three dollars came to $12.00, so I could have made it with 80 cents left over. Could have, mind you, *could have.*

I began thinking every which way about how I was going to get my hands on $11.20. Wouldn't it be nice, I thought, if we were back at Lawn Avenue and I had the Nehi stand? You know when you get rich quick, the way I did with the Nehi stand, you just sort of take it for granted, like it's going to continue forever and always be that way, but that's how you get fooled. Next time I get rich, I want to get rich slow so I can appreciate it.

What happened with the Nehi stand was this. It was when we were living on Lawn Avenue, as I said, which is in South St.

Louis not far from the Anheuser-Busch beerworks. My mother had lost her job with the Woodward-Tiernan Printing Company, not because she wasn't good at it, only because Woodward-Tiernan didn't have any orders and they had to fire almost everybody. We had a little money saved, so we were eating but we weren't paying rent. That's how come we moved so much, and how come I went to eleven different grammar schools.

The thing that made us move so much was the concessions. My father had it in for landlords, but they were having a bad time like everyone else. Couldn't rent their places. You would walk down a street and it seemed like every flat or apartment had a "For Rent" sign on it. So what the landlords did, to get their places rented, was they offered what were called concessions. My father explained it to me. He would go to a landlord and say, "We like your place on Parker and we'll take it for two years if you give us a good concession." So the landlord would give a couple of months' concession in order to get his place rented because he was starving, too. Which meant that if my father paid the first month's rent, he'd get these concessions, which were two or three months' rent free. So we went from place to place, giving the landlord a month's rent, living free on concessions for a few months, then moving out into a new place with new concessions. Of course, the landlords never went after us for the leases my father signed, because even if they could find us, and they sued us, what did we have for them to get?

Well, the place we stayed the longest was Lawn Avenue, because the landlord gave us a five-month concession. It was summer and it was very hot, of course, and one day I asked my mother if she'd make me a pot of lemonade to sell. I was ten then. Lawn was just a block away from Kingshighway, which was nothing but empty lots way down south there, not anywhere near as built up as it was in the center, around Delmar. No hot-dog stands or ice-cream shops or used-car places, just miles and miles of empty lots. But I had noticed that there was a lot of traffic along Kingshighway which fed into Route 67, which was the main highway to the south, to Poplar Bluff and places like Arkansas. I figured people driving along there in that heat must have been doggone thirsty.

I was right. I printed a sign, "Fresh Lemonade 5¢," and plunked my pot at the curb in front of a vacant lot, and in about twenty minutes I was sold out. Now I had enough to buy a lot of lemons and sugar, and we made gallons of lemonade that went just about as fast as the first little batch. Well, one thing just led to another, that's all. By now, I had Jason Tindell and Ernie Rich helping out, and we were selling that old lemonade at five cents a drink just as fast as we could pour it. The cars would stop along the curb and we'd bring them their lemonade and they'd pay us through the window. That's when the Nehi man stopped. He saw this mob of cars. He was starving for business as much as the next guy, so he told me if I could put up a stand with a roof he could furnish me with a Nehi icebox and ice and all the flavors of Nehi soda.

Naturally to build a stand I needed wood and nails and all that stuff, but there wasn't any building going on in the neighborhood (where I could borrow all that stuff) because if you're a builder and you can't rent or sell what you've got, why build more? But I mounted my good old Century bike, which was really Silver and I was the Lone Ranger, and rode all over until I found a place where someone was building a garage. That night, me and Jason and Ernie snuck over there and got all the materials for the stand, which we then built and painted (Ernie's father was a paint salesman) in two days. The Nehi man brought the icebox and six cases of Nehi soda, which came in long thin bottles with this picture of a lady's leg with a garter on every bottle. The Nehi man also brought a big tin sign to put on top of the stand that had "Nehi" all around it, and in a white place in the middle it said in black letters, "AARON'S ICE COLD POP." I still think about that sign to this day. How it looked that first day we put it up. I had no idea he would bring a sign like that and it was like I was on Broadway or something.

Well, there's no use stringing this out, so I'll jump ahead. In no time at all, I had four Nehi iceboxes, hot dogs, and popcorn from a machine I bought for two dollars from a movie house on Chippewa that had gone broke. I also had eight kids on the block working for me and we were open nights. How we came to be open nights was pretty funny. That part of St. Louis still had gas lamps, and every night around six a fat little Italian man named Enrico would go by with his lamplighter pole over his shoulder, lighting the lamps on Kingshighway. He would always stop and have a soda, and one day I said, "Enrico, I wish you were lighting a lamp here, because people can't see us once it gets dark." Enrico knew all the kids who were working for me, because he had been lighting lamps up and down their streets from before they were born, so he said, with this big wonderful mustache smile he had, "Why not?" The next day, he came by in the afternoon pushing a handcart on which he had the top parts of two old lampposts. We hung them on the front corners of the stand, and every night after that when Enrico went by, he lighted our two lamps. Of course, from then on he got all his sodas free.

One other thing I did, I practiced a lot drawing the Nehi leg until I was really good at it. Ernie got a can of orange paint off his father, and one day we roped off half the street in front of the stand and I painted a huge Nehi leg on the street with an arrow. Boy, did we do business, I gave my mother some money, and saved some money in my pirate box and paid all the bills, and the Nehi man said I was the best customer he had.

Then one day Mr. A. W. Brown showed up and it all ended. He explained very nicely that he had been watching the business we did and had bought the lot to put up a root-beer stand and miniature golf course. As I said, he was very nice about it, and offered me a job either in the root-beer stand or the golf course, but no matter how nice he was, it was like Little Caesar coming in and telling me to get out of his territory. All the kids who had been working for me were standing in a circle around us and they were all looking at me, expecting me to *do* something, I guess, because none of their parents had any allowance money for them.

A. W. Brown's workmen started in the very next day, and it only took them about ten minutes to tear down our stand and cart it away. Enrico came for the lamplights, and in about a week the root-beer stand was open, with A. W. Brown's name on it, and the miniature golf a week after that. People didn't have money to eat, but they had money for miniature golf—it was sure hard to figure it out. I had my choice of drawing root beer at five dollars a week or pushing the heavy roller over the linseed "greens" of the miniature golf at seven dollars a week, so I took that. What finally happened between me and A. W. Brown was awful, really awful. But I just wanted to tell you about making all that money and what happened to it.

When school started that fall, I took all the money out of my pirate box and I put it in the Students' Savings Bank, where I already had $4.23 I had saved from before. The St. Louis schools had this savings system where they gave you a savings book with your name on it, and every Friday you could give your teacher anything from a penny on up and she marked it in your book. They paid you interest, but the big thing was that nobody could get at that money but you. The school promised you that. For me that was very important, because all summer my father had been taking my money, always asking to "borrow" a dollar for gasoline or carfare, but naturally he never paid any of it back. Once I put it in the bank, I didn't have it to "lend" to him any more.

I was a very saving type and I guess I'd still have had that money to buy my graduation things if it hadn't been for what happened to the Students' Savings Bank. Our teacher came in one morning and read us a bulletin from the principal, Mr. Herbert P. Stellwagen. It was his sad duty to tell us, he said, that the St. Louis Bank & Trust Co., which is where the Students' Savings Bank kept its money, had run out of money and gone out of business, and that all of the students' money was lost.

Mr. Hoover, who was President then, was always on the radio telling everyone that the bankers and the businessmen were going to save the country, and how we should trust them, so that night I wrote him a letter, President Herbert Hoover, The White House, and I told him about the way the bankers had cleaned out us kids and asked him to help us get our money back. I told him how I had worked so darn hard all summer for that money and how my father and mother didn't have jobs and would he please get that money back from the bankers for me. He never even answered my letter. That's when I started to hate Herbert Hoover. I never called him President after that.

So I laid there thinking about the good days raking in the money at the Nehi stand and wondering how I was ever going to make money like that again. Last summer when things were so bad, only not so bad as this summer, I thought I might be able to start all over again, selling lemonade in front of the Avalon, but nobody seemed to have a nickel for lemonade any more. Besides, there were three grown men along the sidewalk there, nicely dressed men with neckties, selling apples. One had a sign that said, "Last Resort," and another said, "Father of Four." It was no place for a kid.

The band down below had started up again and Mr. Criminal Lawyer was carrying on like he was making a speech to the jury. Every once in a while my mother would cough. It was a funny time to have a cold. It wasn't really a cold cough. More like something inside was tickling her. I began to feel very drowsy and I stopped thinking.

Suddenly I was awake. This terrible noise. This wild racket! I popped up in bed, trying to wake up. A shrieking, whirring commotion that seemed to be coming from . . . The cage! Skippy! I jumped out of bed just as my father turned on the light and came rushing across the room. Bits of feathers were flying out of the cage from under the cover. My father was reaching out to yank the cover off but I grabbed his pajama coat and pulled him back.

"Don't touch it!" I yelled. "Don't touch it! He's conquesting her! He's conquesting her!"

My father stopped, thought for a moment, then, wagging his head, went back to bed and turned off the light. I got back in my bed and laid there in the dark listening to the noisy battle and wondering if either bird would come out of it alive. Then, just as suddenly as it had started, the racket stopped and the room turned quiet. The band had finished playing. It was so quiet you could've heard a feather drop. There wasn't a sound from the cage. Not a peep. The twelve dollars jumped back in my head and it took me a long time to get back to sleep.

Chapter Twelve

My father's friend Mr. Able, in 340, was locked out while he was having his weekly dinner with his daughter and son-in-law. My father said of *course,* once a person gets the five days' notice if he's in his right mind he should never do anything on a regular basis. If they know you're out eating every Thursday, then what do you think? They're dummies? Nobody should let his stomach get the better of him, my father said. How come, my mother asked, if his daughter could take him to dinner in a restaurant she couldn't help him out with the hotel bill? Mr. Able is too proud for that, my father said.

Chapter Thirteen

"The male will shower attention on the female as she starts building the nest," Mrs. Finch's booklet read. "He will feed her and caress her. The female will take bits of the sterilized nesting materials and weave them into the bottom of your Mrs. Finch's Nest Cup." You'd think Skippy and Sooky had read the book. I was standing there watching old Sooky in the tea strainer sitting on my twelve dollars when there was a knock on the door, which was open to let in air, and there was Ella McShane.

"Hi," she said, "Maggie told me about your canaries. Can I see them?"

I told you how it was in the Avalon, that nobody went knocking around on anybody else's door, and the positively *last* person I expected to knock on mine was Ella McShane. You'd think, after what happened that night in her room, she would run and hide when she saw me. But there she was, standing next to me, peering in on Sooky.

"Isn't that *adorable*?" Ella said. "Maggie said you're going to sell them. How many are there?"

Maggie was one of my favorite people in the whole world but I wished she hadn't gone all over the third floor blabbing about my canaries. It's a wonder she didn't hand out cigars. But I did love Maggie. She was about a hundred years old and very skinny and only had three teeth, but I loved to look at her because she had this face that had seen everything and she knew a lot. She was not supposed to clean rooms that owed rent, but she did anyway. And gave us fresh sheets. I'd hear her shuffling down the hall in her busted carpet slippers, pushing her old squeaky carpet sweeper, and I'd feel better just hearing her coming. "Don't know why I bother," she'd say. "The carpet's so thin and the brush so worn they can't meet nohow." But I'd sure tell her not to go blabbing about my canaries.

"We had a canary once when we lived in Decatur," Ella said. "But I never liked him. Canaries are so *nervous*, don't you think? I mean they never sit still. They're always *doing* something, and if you get too near they get all nerved up and start to flap around and bits of their feathers fly off and, I don't know, give me a cat every time. They sit in your lap so peaceful and sleepy. I wish I had a cat. More than anything, I wish I had a cat."

"Well, there are a lot of toms that run around out back. What color do you want?"

"My mother won't let me. But sometimes I sit in the window and I can almost *feel* I have a cat in my lap, and I stroke it and rub it behind the ears and I can feel him purring into my lap. I really can."

This didn't seem the right time to tell her that if there's anything I loathed and despised, skunks, varmints, and bats included, it was cats. I sometimes practiced my fast balls on cats. I still have a scar on my right cheek where a darling little cat let me have it when I was three years old. I guess that's why I was so long getting interested in girls. This cat thing they've got. I never asked her, but I seriously doubt that Christina Sebastian was the kind of girl who liked cats.

"Would you like to have a hot dog?" Ella asked. "My mother left me two but I can only eat one." I hadn't had a hot dog for so long I'd forgotten what they tasted like, but the problem was that after a plate of ice cream and now a hot dog, I'd have to repay her with something and you can't put mustard on a marble or a cigar band.

"Thanks, but I have some homework," I said.

"Oh, come on," she said, yanking me by the hand, "you can *always* do homework."

She took the two hot dogs and put them in her sink and ran the bowl full of hot water. Then she took a jar of mustard and two pieces of white bread out of her bureau drawer and smeared the white bread with mustard. She left the hot dogs in the sink for about five minutes and then wrapped them up in the pieces of mustard bread. It was the best thing I ever ate.

"I wish we had some soda pop," she said. You see, that's what I meant about getting involved with hot dogs and ice cream. If I'd had a couple of nickels, I would have run down to the lobby and gotten the sodas. She probably thought I had nickels but I was too cheap to use them.

I guess I better put you straight about me and girls. To tell you the truth, this was the first time I was ever alone with one. Like the other night at the Kingshighway was the first time I sat in a movie with a girl. I guess what started me on girls at all was Lester. I don't mean that he was tossing girls at me, but I do sort of admire him, and since he was so almighty interested in them I figured they must have something to them. Also, some of the guys at school were walking around with girls' books under their arms, and they were always talking about girls, and just about that time I got transferred into Miss Mathey's class and there was Christina Sebastian sitting next to me. Right across the aisle. She was blond and just my height and she liked to talk to me. I could tell. At first, I had trouble saying anything at all, but once I found my tongue with her, you couldn't shut me up. I guess if I really came into some money, I'd take Christina Sebastian to a movie. But I don't know. Guys are always taking girls to movies, but I don't understand why. You buy their ticket; then you both just sit there in the dark and don't talk or pay attention to anything except what's happening on the screen. Then the lights go on and you leave. I mean I can see taking a girl to a dance, if you know how to dance, because you've got to have somebody to dance with. Or if you want to go get a soda and you'd like somebody to talk to, then okay, it costs you the nickel for the soda but she sits there listening and laughing at your jokes and all that. But why a movie? Sometimes if it's crowded, you can't even sit together. No, on second thought, even if I had money, I wouldn't take Christina Sebastian to a movie.

"I'd offer you some cinnamon gum," Ella said, "but you'd probably get nervous about me having a fit again." She laughed, and since I didn't know what to say, I laughed, too. She asked me if I would like to see her photos and she got out this enormous album that was full of pictures, but not the blurry things with heads cut off like you usually see. You never saw such pictures.

"My father took them," she said. "He was a photographer. He was killed taking pictures in Pennsylvania."

"They're beautiful," I said, not knowing what to say about her father.

"That's my father." She pointed to a picture of a tall man wearing boots and holding a camera. "They shot him with a machine gun for taking pictures."

"Who shot him?"

"The coal company. My father was there taking pictures of the miners in Duquesne. It was the Pittsburgh Coal Company and my father was taking these pictures for a magazine. The company had machine guns right there in the mines to keep everything peaceful in case the miners got out of line, and they warned my father to stop taking pictures or they'd use the guns on him."

"Is that what they did?" I was so horrified my voice squeaked.

"They shot my father, and when some of the miners went to help him, they shot them, too. Then they threw all the bodies in a coal cart, and a mule pulled it back to town. When my mother went to get him, my father's body was still in the cart. Nobody in the town would help her or touch that body, they were that scared of the Pittsburgh Coal Company. My mother had to phone her two brothers in Cincinnati to come help her." She ran the tips of her fingers back and forth over her father's picture. "I'm always expecting him to come home someday. Do you ever imagine unreal things like that?"

"Once in a while."

She sighed and turned the page. "I didn't have any . . . trouble . . . until after that. That's when it started. I never had anything like that when he was alive. But it's all right when I have my medicine. It's just when we get short. . . . But otherwise I'm fine."

She closed the book and held it on her knees. "But, oh, how I'd like to have a cat. I'd like a brown-and-white one with long fur and green eyes and I'd call her Stephanie. She'd wear a fresh ribbon around her throat every day and she'd sleep on the pillow next to me. Stephanie. Don't you think that's a pretty name for a brown-and-white cat?" Ella's glasses were too loose and she kept poking them back on her nose.

Her mother opened the door and came in, and I suddenly remembered I was supposed to meet Lester in the Vampire Room.

"Don't go on my account," Mrs. McShane said.

"I have to meet my friend Lester," I said.

"Goodbye, Aaron," Ella said, and she held out her hand. "Do come again." I shook hands. You'd think I was going off to the moon or someplace. I didn't know whether her mother was supposed to know that I'd wolfed down one of her daughter's hot dogs, so I decided not to thank Ella for that.

Going down the hall, on my way to the Vampire Room, I felt funny. Sad, I guess. I shouldn't have eaten that hot dog. Maybe it was Mrs. McShane's dinner. I wished I had something I could give to Ella. I didn't know what. Something. But what can you give a girl who wants a cat? Maybe she'd like to read *The Deerslayer.* I could lend her that. But still that's not *giving* her something.

I decided to take a look in my pirate box, but to tell you the truth, I knew everything in there by heart and I couldn't think of anything that would interest a fourteen-year-old girl who was hankering after a cat.

Lester was already in the Vampire Room when I got there, sitting down at the far end in the gloom playing the piano. Lester was full of surprises. I had no idea he could play the piano, but there he was sitting there in the dirt and cobwebs getting music out of that old three-legged piano. Then he began to sing:

"Grab your coat, and get your hat,
Leave your worry on the doorstep,
Just direct your feet
To the sunny side of the street.
Can't you hear that pitter-pat?
And that happy tune is your step,
Life can be so sweet
On the sunny side of the street;
I used to walk in the shade
With those blues on parade
But I'm not afraid,
This Rover crossed over.
If I never have a cent
I'll be rich as Rockefeller,
Gold dust at my feet
On the sunny side of the street."

It was as good as I'd heard anybody sing it on the radio. I gave Lester a big hand, and he stood up and put his arm across his stomach and took a serious bow. He really had a nice voice. I guess Lester could do anything.

"Listen, A, I think I'm on to a good thing for us. Selling tickets by telephone to the annual picnic of the Gas and Electric Workers' Union."

It didn't sound like much of a good thing to me. "Who would buy tickets to that?"

"All the stores. To stay in good with them. It's sort of, they've *got* to. I have this appointment tomorrow with the guy who runs it, but we've got to make you look older or he won't take you. You better shave that fuzz off your lip. Either you have a mustache or you don't, but that twelve-year-old fuzz is a dead giveaway. Here's my razor. Give it back to me tonight." He handed me a razor.

"Well, I better ask my mom." I did have some fuzz on my upper lip, all right, but I hadn't even *thought* about shaving. I mean, shaving was sort of, I don't know, like smoking cigarettes.

"Ask? Ask your *ma*? It's *your* fuzz, ain't it? Jesus, *ask!*" Lester was pretty impatient at times. "Do you ask her when you want to cut your toenails? You get permission to pick your nose? What's there to ask? Take the goddam razor and shave it off!"

"Okay, Lester, okay." I put the razor in my pocket. I still thought I'd better mention it to my mother, but Lester didn't need to know about it.

"Listen, I'm racing in a Hoovercart Rodeo tonight. You want to come?"

I almost said I'd ask my mother but I stopped in time. "Sure." I didn't know what a Hoovercart Rodeo was but anything Lester did was usually exciting. Besides, it was *One Man's Family* and Kate Smith on the radio, and I'd have done *anything* to miss that.

"You can be my starter. Meet me downstairs at five-thirty. Okay?"

When I got up to the room, my father was talking to Mr. Desot. My father had been very nervous about our room ever since Mr. Able was locked out. Mr. Desot was explaining to my father that he had no say in what was happening any more, that the bank that had the mortgage on the hotel had taken over because he had gotten so far behind in his mortgage payments. I had heard a lot about mortgages but I still didn't know what they were exactly, except they were the way the banks got hold of everything.

"You're up to $172," Mr. Desot said. "If you give me something by next Tuesday, I think I can get you by for a while. The man from the bank comes every Tuesday afternoon. He looks over the accounts and red-checks the rooms he wants locked out."

"But you could tell him I'm getting the Elgin line any day now and I'll take care of the whole thing. I also have my application in for a WPA job, when they get going."

"Yes, I can tell him," Mr. Desot said. "But he doesn't pay any attention to me unless I turn in money on an account. That's why I need a payment from you. Otherwise I can't do anything. The bank wants everybody out who isn't paying. The only steady money they get is the rent from the taxi dance. Now they've forced me to rent rooms to the taxi-dance people. You know I've tried to keep that riffraff in the basement. Well, now the girls come up and I have to give them a room. So far I've kept it all on the second floor. You understand I have nothing to do with it. I still run the hotel but they run the books."

After Mr. Desot left, my father went on a big rampage against my grandfather. My grandfather was one of my father's favorite rampages. "Thanks to your father," he yelled at my mother, "I can't go to the Chibners. They'd lend me the money just like that, but your father, the big shot, had to go ruin it for everybody. I hope he's satisfied! I hope he's sitting there in Chicago tonight, with his big cigar in his mouth, and he's satisfied!"

"What have I got to do with my father?" my mother asked. "I had nothing to do with what he did. Don't yell at me about my father. *I'm* not the one who went to Phil Chibner, am I?"

You know by now that I didn't agree with my father too much, but as far as I was concerned whatever he had to say against my grandfather wasn't enough. He was a short man, my grandfather, with a wide bristly mustache, a flat nose, and a voice that sounded like wagon wheels on cobblestones. He never talked. He yelled. He roared. He cursed everybody. He told lies as easy as you recite the alphabet. The only time I ever saw him look pleasant was when he was looking in the mirror.

My grandfather was in the restaurant business. He'd open up a place, put my grandmother in the kitchen, my aunts Virginia and Miriam would wait tables, and he'd sit behind the cash register. My grandmother was a marvelous cook and people would right away flock into the restaurant, but my grandfather didn't really know how to run a restaurant or what to charge or how to buy things, and all he did was sit at the cash register smoking up the cigars and being a big shot until he had to go out of business. Then he'd move everyone to a different city and start all over.

A couple of years back, he came to St. Louis and went to see Bert and Phil Chibner, who were our rich cousins. They were in the real-estate business and they owned office buildings and such where people were still able to pay rent. My father had been trying to get a loan from them to open a watch shop, and my mother had written about it to my grandmother. I guess that's why my grandfather came to St. Louis. He went to the Chibners and talked them into lending him enough money to open a combination delicatessen and restaurant on DeBaliviere Avenue.

Right away the restaurant had a lot of customers because you could smell my grandmother's good cooking all over the block, but it also had my grandfather in back of the cash register smoking up the big cigars and making a mess of things. My mother had a big argument with him one day. She had gone over the prices on the menu and asked him how he decided how much each dish would cost.

"I know what people will pay," he said, puffing away on a Dutch Masters.

"Well, let's take this one dish," my mother said. "Boiled beef, potatoes, vegetables, and coffee, forty-three cents. I have broken it down: the beef costs thirty-three cents, the potatoes two cents, the four vegetables nine cents, and the coffee three cents, making forty-seven cents in all, plus the gas and electric, rent, bread, butter, clean napkins and tablecloth—"

"You figured it out, did you?" my grandfather roared. "So how much should it be?"

"At least seventy-five cents."

"You see!" he yelled and looked around as if he was making a speech to ten thousand people in Sportsman's Park. "Miss Big Brain has figured it out! Seventy-five cents, *seventy-five* cents for a plate of boiled beef! At seventy-five cents no one would *touch* the boiled beef. At forty-three cents it's the biggest seller on the menu! Don't tell me how to run a restaurant! Go back to your typewriter, Miss Tillie the Toiler, and your unemployed husband and keep your nose out of things you don't know anything about! Huh! Seventy-five cents for boiled beef! What am I? The Waldorf-Historia?"

Even though my grandfather had beat him to the Chibners, my father kept on talking to them about the loan for the watch shop he wanted to open, and they said they thought they could manage it in a few months. That made my father very happy and he began to look around for a shop and to get watches all lined up, like Ingersolls that people could afford.

One afternoon after school, while I was playing on top of the potato bags in back of the restaurant, my grandfather came in with two men. I guess they didn't know I was in the back and besides I was only nine then.

"Is this the whole layout?" one of the men asked.

"Yes," my grandfather said.

"You want it just smoked or charred?" the other man asked.

"Charred," my grandfather said.

"Then it'll be a hundred."

"A hundred!" My grandfather got that rage look he always got. "What do you take me for? Mr. Dimitri said you would treat me right."

"How right can we treat you? We're giving you a five-hundred-dollar job."

Then they started to argue, all three of them yelling at the same time. Finally they agreed on fifty dollars, and my grandfather took some bills out of his pocket and paid them.

The next day, I came to the restaurant in the afternoon after school and it wasn't there. Neither was the dry cleaner, the Del Monte Grocery, the bakery, the Chinese laundry, the Hudson Funeral Home, the cigar store, and the Great Lakes Fish Market. The windows in Garavelli's, all the way down on the corner, had been blown out and there was spaghetti draped over the broken glass. There were policemen all along the street and a heavy rope had been strung along the curb to keep people off the sidewalks.

I stood there with my mouth open looking at where my grandfather's restaurant had been. The buildings on each end of the block were standing, but all the ones in the middle, on both sides of my grandfather's restaurant, were gone. It was like my upper teeth when I had lost the ones in the front. Imagine what those guys would have done for a hundred dollars! There probably wouldn't have been a building left standing in St. Louis.

I got as close as I could. I tried to figure out exactly where my grandfather's restaurant had been and where the cleaner's had been and where the Great Lakes Fish Market had been, but it was all one solid mass of busted bricks and plaster and glass. It seemed that my grandfather couldn't make a go of a restaurant either way. They went busted when he tried to run them, and when he tried to burn them down for the insurance he made a bust of that, too. Not only didn't the insurance company pay him a dime, but the police put out a notice that he was wanted for arrest. And on top of that, because of some sort of paper they signed for my grandfather, Bert and Phil Chibner had to pay out a lot of money. That's when they swore off, that they would never help any relative again. And they stuck to it. My grandfather never wrote them a word to apologize or anything. That was my grandfather for you.

But he went to Chicago and in three months he had another restaurant going. That's one thing he could do. Start restaurants.

When my father finally got through ranting and raving about my grandfather, he and my mother went off to the free clinic at the Barnes Hospital. My mother's cough had been bothering her more and more.

After they left, I checked on how things were with Mr. and Mrs. Skippy. He was busy running back and forth feeding her while she kept the eggs warm. I took out Lester's razor and went over to the sink to look in the mirror. Yes, no doubt about it, there was a lot of fuzz there. You know, you look at yourself all the time but you don't see things. Like when I described myself I told you about my auburn hair and freckles and all that, but I didn't mention this fuzzy lip because I didn't think about having all that fuzz until Lester told me.

I poked my face right up against the mirror and took one last look at my mustache. There was a lot there, all right. I examined the razor, then I soaped up my lip with the cake of Palmolive on the sink. The razor felt awkward in my hand. I placed it on top of the fuzz and scraped down with it. It hurt. It felt like getting your hair pulled out. I soaped my lip some more, then I took a good healthy swipe. My heart was beating a mile a minute. For some reason, I was all excited. I felt wicked. Like I was robbing a bank.

When I had it half off, I washed off my lip and looked at it. All I could think of was what my mother would say. But if I hadn't done it how could I have showed up at five-thirty to go with Lester? I soaped up the other half of my fuzz and lopped it off. I didn't look at myself again, but I still felt pretty excited.

I gave Lester back his razor when I met him at five-thirty but he didn't say a word about my shave. I almost asked him how he liked it but you don't ask Lester things like that. Besides, he was all wrapped up thinking about this Hoovercart business. It was in the Carondelet Ball Park, which was a kind of broken-down place that was almost full when we got there. It was one of those evenings where you paid two bits and got to see a million things. Cowboys on bucking horses, acrobats, a Jean Harlow contest to give a prize to whoever looked the most like Jean Harlow, a guy who dived off a platform a mile high into a saucer of water, a goldfish-swallowing contest, clowns, door prizes, but the big attractions on the billboard outside the ball park were Babe Didrikson and the Hoovercart Rodeo.

Me and Lester stood in a place where we could see what was going on until it was our turn, which was last on the program. Most of the events were pretty bad, like the girl who won the Jean Harlow contest was a dead ringer for Harpo Marx. But I was thrilled about getting to see Babe Didrikson. I had seen her in the newsreels running circles around everybody in the Olympics in Los Angeles, and now there was a prize of fifty dollars to anybody who could beat her at anything. When it was her time to come out, and the announcer was standing out there giving her this flowery introduction, she came over and stood right next to me and Lester in her track suit while she waited for the announcer to finish. I was so excited I couldn't breathe. She wasn't all that big, but she had terrific muscles in her legs and across her shoulders. She also had more fuzz on her upper lip than me before I shaved.

She went running out and a lot of men came out in track suits who had signed up to try to beat her for the fifty dollars. No one came near. There were six events—50-yard dash, hurdles, javelin throw, discus, high jump, and shot put, and the Babe polished off one group of those men after another. Then she trotted all around the park with her arm held high and everybody gave her a big ovation. Me, too.

As soon as she cleared out, they brought out the Hoovercarts, which actually were the back ends of old Model T Fords with big numbers painted on them. Then they brought out the mules and they hitched two mules to each Hoovercart. All the Hoovercart drivers lined up and a guy in a baseball cap went down the line and gave out numbers and whips. Lester got number 7, which happened to be my favorite. On the way to the ball park, Lester had told me what I was supposed to do, although he really didn't know too much about it since this was his first time in a Hoovercart race. The race was to be run over a course that circled the entire ball park. Ropes had been strung all the way around the park, so the Hoovercarts had to stay between the ropes on one side and the grandstands and outfield fences on the other. And they had to go over a lot of crazy obstacles all the way.

"Ladies and gentlemen," the announcer was saying, "we now come to our feature event of the evening. For a winner's purse of fifty silver dollars and opulent prizes for place and show, we present Fred R. Zekian's Hoovercart Rodeo! [Cheers, applause, hoo-ha!] Fourteen fearless gladiators riding roughshod across the hell-course of a hundred obstacles put in the way of these death-defying daredevils! [More cheers, applause, hoo-ha!] Will the gladiators please line up for the start?"

Lester had his number 7 pinned on his back now, and he got into the number 7 cart. Those fourteen flivver-ends with mules hooked onto them were sure a comic sight. My job was to lead Lester's mules up to the starting line, keep them steady, and then, when the gun went off, I was to give them a big whack to get them going. I had never been around a mule, horse, or anything else before but I told Lester I'd do the best I could. The mules were much bigger than I thought they would be and they were nervous and pulled around on each other. Lester showed me how to hold the one mule, said not to worry about the other, then he got in the cart and took hold of the reins. I had to hang on with both hands to keep that old mule from taking off. Lester kept yelling at me what to do and I hung on for all I was worth but the sweat was rolling off me. Finally, the man in the baseball cap got up on top of something and yelled, "On your mark!" Then he raised a pistol and boom! I let go. Lester gave his mules a big crack with his whip and I wound up and walloped the one mule on the ass as he went by. It felt like I broke my hand.

I stood in the center of the ball park with all the other handlers and whatnot and watched the race. The first thing the Hoovercarts hit was a whole bunch of old rubber tires that had been laid all across the track, and they jounced this way and that as the mules went whizzing over the tires and the Hoovercart wheels bounced around on them. I had no idea mules could whizz like that. I thought they were always sitting down and heehawing and being stubborn. Shows how much I knew.

Lester's mules went over those tires like they were pancakes, and old number 7 went sailing through the next obstacle, which was a stretch of gooey mud and water, like it wasn't there. Lester skidded a little and sprayed mud all over everything, but the mules whizzed right on. I was jumping up and down and yelling and screaming and so was everyone else. Some of the drivers were flailing away with their whips, but Lester's mules were really whizzing and he wasn't whipping them at all. They went over the chute-the-chutes, which was a stretch like a washboard, then grease alley, which was tin that had heavy grease on it, and the Hoovercarts skidded and banged into each other and a couple of mule teams slipped and fell and had to be pulled off the track. But on went old number 7.

There were ten Hoovercarts all bunched together when they went through the stretch where a bunch of men stood on each side of the track with fire hoses squirting water at full blast. One cart fell there, and then in the lasso obstacle, where cowboys tried to lasso the drivers and mules as they went by, two more carts went out. One of the lassos landed around Lester but he wiggled out of it and threw it off before the cowboy could pull him out of the cart.

Seven carts now and I was screaming myself hoarse. The next obstacle was fence posts but Lester's old mules just snaked right around them pretty as you please, and by the time they got through the next obstacle, which was a whole lot of searchlights, tin cans on the track, horns, screams, and God knows what kind of noise that turned on suddenly, those mules had Lester a little out in front of everyone else. But I thought the next thing would be the end. It was a wooden platform that slanted up so that the mules and Hoovercarts came off it sailing into the air. Some of the drivers slowed their carts but Lester whizzed right onto it, and he came off that jump like Santa and his reindeers. The mules landed on their feet all right, but the cart came down on its left wheel and ran way over to one side for a little bit and then skidded over onto its side. I kissed the fifty silver dollars goodbye but Lester jumped from the cart just as it was falling, ran along with it as the mules kept on dragging it, flipped it back up, and jumped aboard, and he was still in the race, even though most of the carts that were left had passed him.

There was only one obstacle left and then a long open stretch to the finish line. The last obstacle was fire—the whole track was lighted kerosene and I thought all those mules would surely go wild at that, but they just went careening into all that flame and smoke, and when they came out of it and headed for the home-stretch Lester was fifth. That's when Lester used his whip for the first time. He laid it whap! whap! once across each mule-end, and you should have seen them pick up and go! They just flew by number 9, and then number 3, and there was good old Lester right on the heels of the two leaders, number 13 and number 10, but as Lester started to pass number 13, the driver of 13 began to run his mules over into Lester's cart, trying to push him up against the grandstand to make him crash. But Lester yanked his mules so they leaned back in against the number 13 Hoovercart. That's when number 13 started to use his whip on Lester. The driver was a big guy in a leather jacket and a leather cap and he just suddenly raised his whip and reached over and whacked Lester across the back of his T-shirt and kept whacking at him, trying to get at Lester's face. Criminy, it was *Ben Hur!* That's when the number 3 cart passed them and you could see they were in cahoots and the number 13 cart wasn't trying to win, just to knock Lester out so's 10 and 3 could pick up the prizes.

"What's that bastard thirteen trying to do?" I heard a handler say.

"Them's Zekian's brothers. Mr. Zekian ain't hadda payoff a race yet and number seven's finding out why."

I went into action. There was a round hefty rock about the size of a golf ball right there at my feet, and I scooped it up and just as number 13 came by with leather jacket really giving it to Lester I let fly with my upshoot, which is my best pitch, and I got the outside mule right on the fanny. He let out a bellow and rised straight up in the air, and since the other mule was still going the whole cart did a somersault and flipped over in a tangle of mules and wheels. Lester's mules went charging free right down the middle of the track. They went whizzing by number 3 and they had their noses even with the wheels of number 10 as it hit the finish line. The big roaring noise of the crowd fell off and I heard someone in back of me yell, "That's the little son-of-a-bitch!" and when I looked, there was the guy in the baseball cap pointing at me, and two huge handlers started at me. The way I sprinted across that ball park and out through the grandstand exit I could have left Babe Didrikson in my dust. I lost myself in the crowd that was on the sidewalk outside the exit, and waited for Lester.

He came out a few minutes later. First I made sure those two killers weren't following him, then I caught up. His T-shirt was all covered with mud, and torn. There was a bright red stripe alongside his eye and down his cheek where the whip had got him. He didn't say anything for a while, just walked.

"What did you do to number thirteen?" he asked.

"I got his mule in the behind with my upshoot."

"That's some pitch. Number thirteen broke his arm."

"Oh, no!"

"I was hoping it was his neck."

Lester had won second prize, which was two free dinners at Duggan's Eatery on Carondelet Boulevard. We sat down at the counter and Lester gave the waitress the piece of paper that said we had two free dinners coming to us. She studied the piece of paper and chewed her gum. We were the only customers.

"I don't know nothing about it," she said.

"Where's Duggan?" Lester asked.

"He's over at the Hoovercart Rodeo."

"On the free tickets he got for these two dinners," Lester said.

"I don't know nothing about it. Come back when Duggan is here." She walked away. Lester sat there for a minute. Then he picked up the glass of water she had put in front of him when we first came in, and he sloshed some water on his hands and face. He used his napkin to dry himself off.

"Hey!" the waitress said, coming back to our end of the counter. "What in hell you doing?"

Lester flipped her the dirty napkin, which she caught, and then as he got off his stool, he took two apples and two doughnuts from some big plates that were on the counter.

"Hey, put that back!" The waitress, a blonde who was black at the scalp, ran around the counter. "Put that back or I'll call the cops." She reached out to grab the apples but Lester caught her nose between his thumb and forefinger. She began to squeal. Lester led her back around the counter by the nose, her squealing all the time; then he left her there and we walked out. She was whining and rubbing her nose when we left.

There was a bench in a bus stop at Carondelet and Holly Hills Boulevard, and we sat down there and ate the apples and doughnuts and Lester smoked a cigarette.

"Try a puff," he said, and he handed me the cigarette.

I had never puffed a cigarette before and I was plenty scared. I was not one of those kids who was dying to smoke cigarettes, and it was an awful big thing to do on top of having shaved. But I put my lips on the cigarette and sucked in a little smoke and puffed it out. I didn't cough or anything but the smoke tasted awful. I was glad I still had a little piece of doughnut left so I could kill the taste. Lester said he had to go, and I headed back to the hotel. I could still taste that rotten cigarette.

I walked across Hamilton to Clemens. As I was going along Clemens, I saw my father sitting on a stoop on the other side of the street. I got behind a tree so's he wouldn't see me. He was just sitting there on the steps of a house, and next to him were several boxes of glass candles. He had his handkerchief tucked around his neck inside his collar and he was staring at the ground. An automobile went by and its headlights lit up his face. He looked very sad and tired. After a while, he got up and picked up the boxes of glass candles and climbed up the stairs and rang the bell. The door opened and a man stood there, and my father began to talk to him.

I went on down Clemens and across Enright back to the hotel.

Chapter Fourteen

A lot of things were happening at sort of the same time, good and bad.

Good. We had our first graduation meeting and Miss Mathey announced the pairings of the speakers. The way they had graduation at Admiral Dewey, you would have thought we were getting out of Harvard. But I told you what kind of a school it was. Everybody was to wear these robes, boys black, girls white, and we all tried them on for size. Then there was to be a ceremony where everybody got a chance to show off in front of their parents and relatives. A boy was paired with a girl and they would get up, these pairs, one after the other, and recite little speeches that we had to memorize. The boy and girl of each pair had to say their lines back and forth, so you had to practice together. When Miss Mathey announced that I had been paired with Christina Sebastian, my face caught on fire. She turned and smiled at me and gave one little clap with her palms. I guess because I was the best public speaker in the class.

Bad. The Blewett Junior High School nurse brought Ella home from school one afternoon and told Mrs. McShane that Ella couldn't go to school any more. Ella had a slight attack, that's what Ella called it, a "slight attack," in the lunchroom, and that's how the school found out about her condition. Students in her condition, the nurse explained, were not allowed to attend public school. Ella came in and told me all about it. She didn't seem to mind too much because she didn't like the kids at Blewett anyway. She had had her attack because they had run out of money and Ella was only taking her medicine every other day. She was supposed to take it every morning.

Good. All four eggs hatched with a chip-chip-chip chip-chip-chip early one morning and even though the baby birds looked like four blobs of furry margarine, the pictures in Mrs. Finch's booklet showed how quickly they would sprout feathers and get out of the nest. The business of pretending to Aunt Minnie that I went to the movies on Fridays, and keeping the money for seed instead, worked fine. I also had this friend, Mr. Donaldson, who ran the fruits and vegetables at Piggly-Wiggly, who wrapped a lettuce leaf or two and a couple of split grapes in a newspaper and left them for me every day back where they kept the pop empties. Mr. Donaldson had to be careful about it because all the stores were very strict about giving out *anything*, because you can imagine what a ruckus there would've been with so many people grubbing for food. But Mr. Donaldson had a canary himself, so he did this for me. He also had red hair and freckles, and he used to say us types had to stick together. I went to the pet store and told Mr. Farley that the birds had been born and he gave me a bottle of vitamins, free, to put in the water. He said he had a lot of canary customers in the summer and he would be glad to have my birds.

Bad. They locked out 338, but no one on the floor knew who lived there. Maggie said that when she cleaned there, before 338 got in arrears, whoever lived there was always out. It was a man, because there was a holder with four pipes in it. In some ways it was more scary to see a lock on a door and not know who lived there.

Good. My father received a letter from the Elgin Watch Company that said he had been recommended by Mr. Sid Gutman and would he fill out the enclosed questionnaire? It was only one page long but my father spent two whole days on it, and he tortured over every question like it was the semester test in algebra. My mother did the actual writing since her penmanship was much better and my father misspelled a lot of words. Or is it mispelled? Chip off the old block, I guess.

Good and bad. Our last baseball game was against Kennard and the winner would wind up in second place. Almost the whole school showed up, Christina Sebastian included, and I really pitched my arm off. Moose Brennan, who was the catcher, showed me his hand which was red and really puffed up from my upshoot. We had it, 2-0, going into the last inning, but I walked the first batter, got two pop-ups, and then Bruce Livesly, the left fielder, came running in for a fly ball that went sailing over his head and landed right where he had been in the first place. That tied the score and I was the first batter up in our half of the inning. Everybody was yelling and screaming for me to smack it out of there. I swung at the first pitch and hit a little pop-up that sailed out beyond second base. The center fielder came charging in and the shortstop and second baseman went charging out, and they all arrived under the ball at exactly the same time. I was running with my head down, but when I heard that crunch I knew what had happened and I really turned on the old Pepper Martin. As I went into second, I took a look out there at all those bodies and I saw two of them get up and go for the ball and bang into each other again. Finally, the third body got up and picked up the ball and fired it to third base, where old Pepper was coming in like wild horses. The ball hit me right in the behind and it stung like holy hell but I just chugged right on around third base, and Mr. Belifont, the physical education teacher who was our manager, was there in the coaching box yelling at me to stop, but all I really heard was the crowd and Pepper Martin wasn't going to stop for anyone as he came steaming down the last white stripe on his way to pay dirt. Their catcher was a fat guy and he was spread out in front of the plate with his mask off and his glove up yelling for the ball. He stood there with his shin guards and belly protector and his backward cap, and

Pepper came flying at him, and when he reached his glove forward I knew the ball was on its way, so Pepper took off in a sailing headfirst dive, like a swim-dive when you're racing, right between the catcher's fat shin-guarded legs. Pepper had his hands stretched out as far as they would go and they whacked on top of the plate just as the fat boy boomed down on me with his glove, and we went down in a giant heap all over home plate. I was knocked a little cuckoo for a second or two, then I heard the umpire yelling "Safe!" and my teammates were shoving old fatso off of me and pushing me to my feet and brushing me off and banging me on the back while the other team was having this terrific argument with the umpire, who kept yelling, "A tie favors the runner!" Bruce Lively, who must have felt terrible about that fly ball getting over his head, got his shoulder under me and so did Moose Brennan, and they pushed me up in the air and paraded me around while all our kids cheered and all the Kennard kids booed, and then some of them started throwing wadded-up paper at me and then other things and I was a dead duck sitting up there getting pasted with all kinds of slop by those Kennard hotheads. But the Admiral Dewey kids came to my rescue by charging into the Kennard kids and pretty soon there was this mangle of kids fighting all over the stands and the playing field, and once I got myself down to the ground I was in there with the rest of them. But nobody really *socked* anybody when they were all milling around like that. Just a lot of pushing and headlocks until it died down. But it was quite a thing for a kid from the Avalon to wind up on their shoulders and to have two whole schools fighting over him.

But there was bad on top of the good that afternoon and the bad part was this. Billy Tyzzer was our equipment manager and afterward, when we were back at school and had taken off our uniforms and all, he asked if he could take a look at the baby birds which, of course, I had told him about. We were just walking out of the schoolyard. I couldn't think of anything for a while, so we just walked along, me getting more panicky every step. I was looking at that ratty lobby as Billy would see it and that dark dingy hall and then coming into 309, with its hot plate and our laundry hanging in the window and the cinders out back and my father sitting there in his undershirt, and the shame of it was awful.

"Listen, listen, Billy, I'm sorry," I blurted out, "I'd sure like you to see them but my brother has smallpox."

"Smallpox!"

"Yeah. It's awful. I wouldn't want you to catch it."

"*Small*pox! But hasn't he been vaccinated?"

"Well, he caught it in Keokuk. They don't vaccinate in Keokuk."

"You sure you don't mean *chicken* pox? I've had chicken pox."

"Oh, no, chicken pox—what the devil, everybody has chicken pox. I mean this poor brother of mine has *small*pox and they've got quarantine signs on every door."

"I'll have to tell my father about it. I don't think I've ever heard of anyone with smallpox."

"Well, I wish you wouldn't. I mean tell your father. You see we're trying to keep it as secret as we can."

"And your brother's all right?"

"Yeah, he's not great, of course, but I keep giving him transfusions and they say he'll be all right."

"That's . . . that's very nice of you," Billy said. He gave me this funny look; then he looked down at the ground, then another funny look, and then he started away. "I'll be seeing you," he said. I knew the minute I had said that about the transfusions it was a mistake. But if my poor little brother had smallpox I wanted to help him every way I could and somehow giving him some of my blood was the best way I could think of. But it ruined me with Billy Tyzzer.

That's why I hated to make friends. If you went to their house, they expected to come to yours, and I hadn't lived in a house a friend could come to since Art Hill Place, which was third grade.

Not only that. No sooner did you make a friend than you had to move away, and then you had to try to forget him. To tell you the truth, I'd rather have no friends at all than to have to forget one. By the time I got back to the hotel, all the joy of the baseball game was gone and all I had was this heavy heart because of the way I had treated Billy Tyzzer.

Good. At first Mr. Verney, who was in charge of the Gas and Electric Workers' Union picnic, didn't want to take me, even though I kept my voice down pretty good, but Lester talked him into it. Mr. Verney was not all that old but he had no upper teeth. All gum. Must have been some kind of accident, Lester said later, but the fact is that when you speak to people with no teeth they really drown you in spit. This Mr. Verney talked a mile a minute, you never heard anybody talk so fast—not even Walter Winchell with his "Hello, Mr. and Mrs. America and all the ships at sea, let's go to press!" I couldn't pay too much attention to what Mr. Verney was saying, I was so busy dodging the spit, but I did make out that we'd get five cents on each dollar ticket sold, and twenty cents for every three-dollar ad in the picnic program. Mr. Verney gave us long lists of names and phone numbers to call, and we were to phone in at the end of each day with a list of the ones who bought tickets and ads. Mr. Verney's office was in a building on the corner of Delmar and Vandeventer, which was not too bad to walk to. He had three girls in the office clacking away at typewriters, and the phones were always ringing. He gave us, all typewritten up, what we were to say to people when we got them on the phone, and there was some other stuff to read in case they asked us questions. He shook hands with us and walked us to the railing outside his desk. "Godspeed and good luck," he said as he clapped Lester on the shoulder. Then he turned to me. "Don't worry about your voice," he said. "If they think you're a woman, so much the better."

Really bad. My mother had twice been to the Barnes Hospital free clinic, sitting around there all day long on those long wood benches in the hall waiting for her name to be called. They had taken X-rays and blood tests and told her they had found a small spot on her left lung. My parents are the types who would have kept all this from me except one night I heard them in bed on the other side of the screen talking about it. They thought I was asleep but I was being Charles Lindbergh in *The Spirit of St. Louis* fighting to keep awake as I crossed the Atlantic. There was a terrific thunderstorm with lightning snapping all around and I was nosing my little plane down to the wave tops to keep from being struck. Colonel Lindbergh was a big hero of mine, especially because of that time he flew back to St. Louis for all the school kids. This was just after he had come back from Paris and was paraded all over New York City. What he did was to get in *The Spirit of St. Louis* and fly it back to St. Louis. I was about six years old then and in the first or second grade. All the children in St. Louis were let out of school and put in streetcars that took them down to the Mississippi levee. We were all given badges in the shape of streetcars with our names, schools, and grades on them, and they were pinned onto our clothing in case we got lost.

All the St. Louis children were lined up along the levee according to school and we waited and waited, and finally there was a big roaring cheer and a little silver airplane came flying along the river, right past our eyes, and it was Colonel Charles A. Lindbergh in *The Spirit of St. Louis*. He flew back and forth in front of us, so close we could see him waving, and we waved back at him. Finally, he went all the way upriver, so far I thought he was flying away, but then way out there, a speck, we could see him turn and start back, and he did something that made him my hero for life.

He was headed toward us now, getting lower and lower until he was only a little bit above the surface of the water. Between us and him there was a bridge, the Eads Free Bridge, and he was heading straight for that bridge, and when he got almost on it, so close all of us St. Louis kids let out a giant shriek, he ducked the plane down and flew right under the bridge, so close to the water the wheels of *The Spirit of St. Louis* got wet, and as he zoomed by us, the wheels dripping, he waggled his wings and waved goodbye.

So every once in a while I fly the Atlantic in *The Spirit of St. Louis*, and that's how come I was awake to hear my mother and father talking about her condition. "Are you still spitting blood?" was the thing I heard my father ask that got my attention, and I listened to everything after that. The fever and the cough and the spitted blood and the spot discovered by the X-ray, the doctors had told them, were all signs that my mother had consumption, a word I knew because I had heard many times how she had had consumption when I was twelve months old. I had gone to stay with my grandmother while my mother had been sent to the Fee-Fee Sanatorium, which was outside of St. Louis in a district called Creve Coeur. She had stayed there for eight months, and had never had any trouble since then. But now she was in trouble again, and the doctors were deciding what to do. She was supposed to go back to the Barnes Hospital free clinic once again, for more tests and to be examined on a certain day by a big chest specialist who only gave one free afternoon a month to the clinic.

"Do you think they'll make me go back to the sanatorium?" my mother asked. "What about A? How will he manage? And poor Sullivan, will he *ever* get back home?" My mother began to weep. "Oh, Eric," she said. "Don't let them put me out there. For the boys' sake."

"What are you talking about?" My father sounded angry.

"Shh, you'll wake A."

"If it's consumption you've got, then you'll have to do what they tell you. Do you want the boys to catch it? You know how dangerous it is. Aaron may have it already. Don't worry about him. I'll take care of him. Just worry about yourself. It's you who's got to get well."

"Well, let's don't tell him. If I have to go away, I don't want him to worry. We'll just say I've gone for a visit somewhere." She coughed two or three times and continued to weep. Suddenly she said, "God, isn't it enough!" Her weeping turned to real crying. My father didn't say anything. I wondered whether he was touching her, patting her shoulder or smoothing her forehead, but in the dark with the screen there, I couldn't tell. Knowing my father, probably not.

Chapter Fifteen

Mr. Evans, in 328, was stopped at the desk when he left the elevator carrying his piano-tuning bag. He hadn't had any work in a long time, so he was far behind in rent. I used to sit and talk to him in the lobby, and he told me stories about the times when he used to be a pianist and play concerts in England and France. He was so gentle and quiet it was hard to picture him tossing his hair around and pounding his hands on the keyboard. But I believed him. His hands shook now, but I could see that once upon a time he might really have played the piano.

"You know the rule," Mr. Neville, the room clerk, said. "Rooms in arrears can't carry out nothing without special permission from Mr. Desot." Nobody ever fooled Mr. Neville. He had the eyes of a chicken hawk and the nose of a bloodhound. "But it's just my piano-tuning equipment."

"Don't matter if it's your false teeth—if you had 'em in a box, I'd have to confiscate 'em."

"But how can I earn any money to pay my back rent if I can't use my equipment?"

"You shoulda thought of that when you got behind in rent," Mr. Neville said, and he took Mr. Evans's bag and put it in back of the desk. He said Mr. Evans would have to discuss the matter with Mr. Desot.

When Mr. Evans went back to his room, he found that while he had been down in the lobby arguing with Mr. Neville, Ben had locked him out. It sure wasn't fair, but that time when I worked for A. W. Brown and got fired, I learned about fair. Just always expect the worst, I found out, and you're never far wrong.

Chapter Sixteen

Every day when I came home from school, I spent two hours on the telephone selling ads and tickets for the Gas and Electric Workers' Union picnic. Lester had discovered that the room next to his, which was empty, had a phone in it that didn't go through the hotel switchboard. There was no furniture in the room, just this phone on the floor left there by somebody who had put in a private line, and I guess the telephone company had forgot to disconnect it.

The first afternoon we started calling numbers, Lester lasted about one hour before he quit. Of course, a lot of people hung up on you or called you a bunch of names for bothering them, and this riled Lester. I didn't care. I just pushed my voice low and talked fast and sometimes they hung up and sometimes they didn't. "Madame, why should I buy tickets to a gas workers' picnic?" I got asked. The answer was right there on Mr. Verney's information sheet. "Because the electric and gas workers are going to remember their friends when you need service and they make out their cost sheets."

"You mean they'll charge me less?"

"Let's just say," I read off Mr. Verney's paper, "that a ticket, or especially an ad, buys you a lot of good will."

I sold two tickets and an ad ("Compliments of Busy Bee Grocery") that first afternoon, and every day as I got better at it, I sold more and more. I phoned in my orders and Mr. Verney complimented me and said I should have a pretty penny when we settled up on the day after deadline for payments. Since I would have enough from the canaries for my graduation, I planned to give my gas workers' money to my mother. Well, maybe a dollar or two for myself, but most of it to my mother. Ever since I had overheard her talk with my father, I had been very worried about her. She really looked terrible, especially the black under her eyes.

The day finally arrived when the big-shot chest specialist was going to see her at the free clinic. I told her, after I'd heard that nighttime conversation, that I knew about her condition, so that she wouldn't try to play that silly game with me and pretend she was off visiting the Queen of England, or somebody. Why is it parents think they help their kids by pretending things are better than they are? If there's no dinner there's no dinner, and there's no way my mother can pretend that I have a big fat hamburger and mashed potatoes in front of me. So I guess I know how crummy life is, don't I, so why suddenly shouldn't I know the truth about my mother being sick and having to go to a sanatorium? Is that different than having no food in my plate? No, it's all part of the same thing, and I think kids only get nervous and act up when they don't know what's happening. That's spooky. It's like as if you were in the crazy house at the Forest Park Highlands, with all those tilted rooms and mirrors and whirlarounds and whatnot, and the lights suddenly shorted out. Of course, if you've got the kind of parents who just sit around and hold their heads and tell you all the time how awful things are and there's no hope and maybe we should all jump into the Mississippi, that's worse than the pretenders. Oh, look—all my complaining, don't think I don't know that it's murder to have kids.

Anyway, this afternoon I'm about to tell you about, my mother and father were at the Barnes Hospital free clinic seeing the big-shot chest doctor and I was waiting for them in front of the hotel sitting in one of the sidewalk chairs reading *Nicholas Nickleby.* From where I was sitting, I could see and hear Patrolman John L. Burns giving hell to some motorist he had ordered over to the curb. He was asking questions like, "Do you think I'm standing out there for my health?" and, "If you're so blind you can't see my hand, why don't you get yourself a tin cup?" When Patrolman Burns had these little talks with motorists, which he had all day long, he put his face right up against theirs and barked at them in a voice that scared the lions all the way over at the Forest Park zoo. So naturally any person trying to read *Nicholas Nickleby* could not possibly have kept his mind on it while Patrolman Burns's voice was rattling the neighborhood. That's how come I was looking at the intersection when it happened.

A big truck with Swift & Co. on the side was crossing Kingshighway when another truck, Buster Brown Shoes, started to cross Delmar at the same time because Patrolman Burns was not there to keep them apart, and they both had to slam on their brakes and they bumped. Not a serious bump, just enough so the gate across the back of the Swift & Co. truck popped open and right in front of my eyes an enormous steer came tumbling out of the truck onto Kingshighway. Then there was another and another and another, five in all, these giant steers, which I thought were bulls because they had the biggest, sharpest horns I could imagine.

The two truck drivers had rushed around to the front of their trucks and were so busy yelling and screaming at each other about who was to blame they didn't see these monster steers until a big black one with white patches suddenly let out a terrific trumpet noise and headed for them. I never thought guys with potbellies could move so fast. That black steer came right at them with his big horns and they practically flew off the street and into the Buster Brown truck. The black steer looked in the window of the truck at them, and then he backed up and charged the truck door, hanging one of his horns right into it. It made a tremendous clang and the

Swift & Co. man, who was sitting on that side, jumped into the lap of the Buster Brown man and they both cringed in the corner.

The other four steers, who had been milling around in a nervous circle, got going now, fast, moving in a pack away from the truck and down Kingshighway. The black-and-white steer galloped after them and caught up. They went smack down the center of Kingshighway as drivers on both sides ran up on the curbs to get out of their way. They were passing right in front of me now and I was just getting to the curb to get a better view when for the first time I saw Patrolman Burns. He was running as fast as he could after the steer pack, yelling in that voice of his for the motorists to pull their cars across the street to block off the steers, but the motorists of course were doing just the opposite. Patrolman Burns was red with fury, his face yelling and full of rage, and as he came abreast of where I was, he pulled his gun out of its holster. The steers had worked up a good head of steam by now and were down to just about where the B'rith Sholem Synagogue is at the corner of Kingshighway and Kensington. Something was going on at the synagogue, because the sidewalk in front of the synagogue was packed full of people talking to each other. I always knew when it was a Jewish holiday from the crowds on the sidewalk. Nobody ever seemed to be *inside* the B'rith Sholem, and I often wondered if anything ever really took place in there.

Anyhow, there was this sidewalk full of B'rith Sholem people, and there was this galloping pack of horns, and there was Patrolman Burns puffing along with his pistol in his hand trying to take aim at the behinds of those wild beasts. By now I was running along slightly to the rear of Patrolman Burns. Just as the steers got to Kensington, Patrolman Burns began to fire. The noise of the gun panicked the steers even more and they went somewhat apart, but Patrolman Burns kept firing away, his arm bobbing up and down as he ran. The people on the sidewalk had just barely got their first glimpse of the running steers when the shooting started. They screamed and bumped into each other and tripped and dived this way and that. I saw one man standing at the curb, holding on to the roof of an auto, blood running down his face, and then there was another stretched out on the sidewalk with his arms spread out, and as I watched, a woman grabbed at her stomach, the way bad Indians do in the movies when the cowboys get them, and she doubled over and held her stomach as two men rushed over to help her.

"Stop! Stop! You're killing them! You're killing them!" I yelled at Patrolman Burns and he kept shoving bullets in his gun and firing, but all he was hitting were Jewish people and not the steers.

Finally, the steers veered into Cates Avenue and up and across some of the lawns and then into somebody's back yard where the fences stopped them. I will say for Patrolman Burns that he had good wind, because he was into that yard right on the hoofs of those steers and he went charging right up to them. They were only a few yards away now and he had a better shot at them. One of them was spurting blood from where the bullets had hit his leg. They were all packed together, up against a corner of the fences, when Patrolman Burns started to fire. He shot them one after the other point-blank in the eyes, and they fell and got up and staggered around and bled all over that back yard. Patrolman Burns kept reloading and firing until all the steers were down for good, and the back yard, which had been green, was bright red.

I had been standing in the driveway watching all this, not able to make a sound or move, but I moved plenty fast when a Swift & Co. van, marked "EMERGENCY" in red below the Swift & Co., came whizzing into the driveway at top speed and screeched to a halt. The van doors burst open and out spilled butchers, ten of them, wearing long white coats and white rubber boots and tight-fitting white skullcaps. They jumped from the van with long knives and butcher saws and they sailed into those five steers. The man in charge of them kept yelling at them to hurry. They paired off two butchers to each steer, and they rolled them on their backs and started to slit them open. A police car pulled into the driveway and four policemen got out. Patrolman Burns, who still had his gun in his hand, saluted one of the policemen so I guess he was a big shot.

The butchers really went to work on those steers. They stripped off their skins and then began to carve them up. First they sliced open the front of them and they emptied all their insides into two big wheelbarrows that they brought out of the van. They had a scoop as big as a snow shovel and they filled it full of intestines and all that gook and shoveled it into the wheelbarrows. When the wheelbarrows got full, they carted them back to the van and up a ramp they had put down at the back, emptied them inside the van, and then wheeled them back to the steers for another load.

They hacked off the hoofs with the sharpest ax I ever saw and then they went to work with the saws. They were much bigger than the saws I'd seen in butcher shops. Nothing was wasted. Every bit of skin, the tails, the heads with their horns, the lungs, the hearts, even the balls were loaded into that van.

The air was full of sirens now, so I guessed the city ambulances had finally come for the people on the B'rith Sholem sidewalk. When it came to speed, the ambulances could have learned a lot from Swift & Co.

When every single little bit of those five steers had been loaded into the van, the big-shot policeman signed some piece of paper for the big-shot butcher. Then all the policemen, including Patrolman John L. Burns, who had put away his gun, got into the police car, backed out of the driveway, and pulled away.

The butchers, now red and white, took up their ramp and climbed back into their Emergency Swift & Co. van as the lady of the house pulled up in the family car. She had been shopping and she had two brown paper bags full of groceries. She looked at the red-smeared butchers and then at her bloody yard, and the two bags of groceries fell from her arms.

"What have you done!" she cried up at them.

The big-shot butcher reached down into the van and picked up a huge hunk of steer meat, running blood at both ends.

"Here you are, lady," he said, and he pitched the meat hunk onto the ground in front of her. She looked down at the meat, which had splattered blood all over her spilled groceries, as the van pulled away.

I ran down the driveway and watched them go off. They headed north away from where the people were being loaded into ambulances in front of the B'rith Sholem.

Chapter Seventeen

I went charging back to 309 to tell my parents what had happened and how Patrolman John L. Burns would probably get electrocuted for having shot all those people. My mother was sitting on the side of her bed, all dressed, a shopping bag at her feet, waiting for me. My father was standing at the window staring out at the parking lot. I knew right away there was a lot of bad news in the room.

My mother said that the big-shot chest doctor had ordered her to Fee-Fee immediately, but that he was very optimistic because the consumption was not very far along and that she would probably be all right in a couple of months.

"But I'm worried about you, A."

"About *me*? Gosh, what's there to worry about me?"

"How will you and your father manage? Who will cook for you?"

"Now, Anne," my father said, coming away from the window, "I told you not to worry about us. That's why you're in this condition, worrying about everything. Now you've got to stop worrying."

"I'm not worrying. But he's a boy, Eric, and you know what kind of hotel this is."

"Don't you think I can cook hamburgers and make baloney sandwiches?" I asked.

"What if you get the Elgin line and have to travel?" my mother asked my father.

"Then I'll have to travel. But I'll arrange things for Aaron. He's a big boy. He takes care of himself very well. And anyway I haven't got the Elgin line, so there you are again, worrying about something that hasn't even happened yet. Now, come on, we're supposed to be there by six o'clock and you know how far it is." He picked up her shopping bag and went over and stood by the door. She looked at me, with her eyes all sad, biting the inside corner of her lip. She stood up and came over and kissed me on top of the head. "I won't be here for your graduation," she said.

"That's all right. It's not such a tremendous thing, a graduation." She was trying hard not to cry. I could tell.

"You can come on Sundays to visit," she said. "Not the first two weeks, but after that."

"He's not allowed in," my father said. "Fee-Fee's very strict."

She wasn't listening to him. "Who will wash out your things?" She started to cry. "And cut your hair?"

"Mom, don't worry, I'll be all *right*, it's okay."

My father opened the door. "Anne," he said.

"I'll write you, Mom, all about everything. Especially if I get lucky one of these Fridays and beat Aunt Minnie at rummy." It was the only joke I could think of, but she kept on crying. I was feeling a little funny myself. In my throat.

"It's terrible to miss your graduation," she said.

I suddenly thought of something. "Would you like me to bring you one of my birds when he's old enough? Choose one, why don't you? He would be very cheery for you."

"Oh, A, how sweet, but they don't allow anything like that. It's a very serious place."

"Anne," my father said.

She took my face in the palms of her hands and looked at me and I looked at her, and then she walked out with my father. When the door shut, I thought, Well, she'll never come back. She's going to die in this Fee-Fee place and I'll never see her again. I swear to God, that's what I thought. There they go protecting me again is what I thought. The big-shot specialist probably said she had two months to *live* and they turned it around to protect me. That's the way they were. I could tell from the way she looked at me, I could see it in her eyes, right through the tears, that she knew she was going to die and she didn't want me to know.

I went over to her bed and sat down in the dent that was left from where she had sat. I tried to think about how things were when times had been better, but I couldn't remember anything. I tried to think of something me and my mother had done together that had been fun, but I couldn't think of a thing. The best I could do was think about her brown diamond, which I knew meant a lot to her, and hope that my father was right that his pawnbroker friend Lou Solomon would hang on to it for her. It was pretty, all right, this big brown diamond with all the little white diamonds around it, but I could never understand how people could put all their money on their fingers instead of into a Pierce-Arrow or something reasonable like that.

I guess we had lived pretty good at first, but I wouldn't know since I'm pretty blank about everything when I was two and three and four. The earliest I remember was my father's fur office in the Holland Building. My father liked to carry on about how it was the Night and Day Bank that did him in—criminy, don't get him started on the Night and Day Bank! But I remember hearing all the time about how he was always losing money on buying furs at the wrong time. It was my mother's job at the Bell Telephone Company that kept him going. Of course when the Night and Day Bank caved in along with all the other banks, and only paid two cents on the dollar, that was the end of my father's fur business, but the thing that really kept us going before and after the Night and Day Bank was my mother's job.

She was secretary to a vice-president and we lived very nicely on Art Hill Place. She had had to lie about being married to get the job, since the Bell Telephone Company was very strict about not allowing married women to work for them. I guess she would have still been working there and we wouldn't have had all this trouble if it hadn't been for me. My chin suddenly hurt thinking about it. It had happened after school and I had gone over to the schoolyard to see if I could get into a pick-up baseball game that was just getting started. I was in the fifth grade at DeMun then. I was the new kid in the neighborhood so I got chosen last, and then they asked me if I could catch. New kids never want to admit that they can't do something, or don't want to, so I said sure I could catch, even though I had never caught before.

This was hard ball, but nobody had a mask and I had to catch without one. I was doing pretty good, considering it was my first time, but along about the fourth inning a foul ball ticked off the bat and caught me smack on the chin, splitting it open and knocking me cuckoo. One of the kids ran inside the school and found the nurse, who was still there. They brought me into her office, and after she phoned the doctor she looked in the file and found that my mother worked at the Bell Telephone Company. It just so happened that when the nurse phoned, my mother was away from her desk and her boss picked up the phone himself, and the nurse said to tell my mother it was an emergency, that her son had been seriously injured in a baseball accident and would she come to the school immediately.

That's how I lost my mother her job, and I still felt bad when I thought about it. And when I thought about it, my chin hurt. I got up from the bed. I didn't want to sit there moping about my mother even though I felt scared that she was going to die. And I really didn't think me and my father *could* get along without her.

Eating or anything else. And that was certainly the end of the fifty-cent Friday-night dinners with Minnie.

The room started to fill up with the black stink from the fire Martin started in the ashpit every afternoon around that time. He lit up the rubbish in the ashpit and it would send up this black stinking smoke for about an hour. It was like the smell we used to get when we lived over Sorkin's delicatessen and they killed chickens in the back. The rabbi came early in the morning to make the chickens kosher by slitting their throats with his knife and hanging them up by their feet on a clothesline so they'd run their blood out of their necks onto the ground. There were two big, sweating, shirtless Negroes who handed the shrieking chickens to the rabbi. After the blood had drained out of the chickens, the rabbi left and the Negro men began to pluck the feathers. The white feathers stuck to their sweating black skins in the St. Louis sun until they looked like some kind of scary birds.

When they had finished plucking all those chickens, then came the smell. They had this fire burning in a big oilcan, a high blaze fire, and they'd hold the plucked chickens over the flame to burn off all the pinfeathers that remained on the skin. The stink of those chickens being singed in the fire would rise up in the heat and seep into our rooms, and closing the windows nor anything could keep it out. I tried everything, even a wet towel snugged across my nose and mouth, but the stink came right through the towel. It burned my nose and curdled my stomach and made me want to give up breathing.

The stink from the Avalon ashpit was almost that bad, except it wasn't so near, so if there was any kind of breeze blowing against it, not so much of it got into the room. But mostly there was never a breeze.

I went over to the sink and washed my face and combed my hair. Christina Sebastian had invited me to her house to practice our graduation parts, and I was glad I had a reason to go somewhere and get out of that stinking room. Especially to see Christina. I had already been to her apartment to rehearse one afternoon after school. She lived in a big place on Westminster that was as pretty as she was. And so was her mother, who looked more like her sister than her mother. That first time I was there, Mrs. Sebastian called me Red and made us milkshakes in a machine like they have in drugstores. She even gave me a choice of chocolate, vanilla, or strawberry!

Another thing happened that first afternoon at Christina's. After me and Christina had rehearsed our parts—I was talking about this and that for a while, and I was having a good time and feeling wonderful being with her when her father came home and Mrs. Sebastian invited me to stay for dinner. Now, one thing about me is that when I am stupid once I am not stupid twice. All I had to do was sit down at that dinner table—*Mon Dieu!* (as D'Artagnan would say), what stupendous smells were coming out of the kitchen!—and it would be just like it was with Billy Tyzzer. Only worse. I couldn't go stuff myself with Mrs. Sebastian's roast beef and not invite her daughter to my house or somewhere in return. So, swallowing my spit, I had said I'd sure like to but my mother was expecting me.

"Well, why don't you phone her?" Mrs. Sebastian had said. "Perhaps she wouldn't mind." Everybody was always shoving a phone at me and telling me to call my mother.

"The problem is," I had said, "she's having this dinner party and I know I have to be there."

"Oh, I see. Well, another time, I hope."

Some dinner party, us and Minnie Rosenthal slurping up a plate of soup meat while Major Bowes was gonging out some poor dope who was trying to play "Ramona" on the musical saw.

Now I was going over to Christina's for the second time, and I sure hoped they wouldn't embarrass me by inviting me to dinner again. I changed the drinking water in the birds' cage and put a saucer of water on the bottom in case they wanted to take a bath.

Then I plunked my old Feltie on my head and left, first checking to be sure I had a handkerchief.

Christina knew more of her part than I did. We rehearsed a little, but mostly what we did was listen to some records by Bing Crosby singing with the Boswell Sisters, and by my favorite singer, Ivie Anderson, singing, "It Don't Mean a Thing If It Ain't Got That Swing." While we were sitting there listening, I'd sneak a look at Christina, who was listening with her eyes closed, and I guess I never saw anything as pretty as she was. I couldn't keep my mind on Ivie Anderson.

Mrs. Sebastian came in to say it was time for Christina's dancing class. "Did you ask Aaron?" she asked.

"I was just going to," Christina said. She seemed a little embarrassed. "You know about the graduation dance, don't you? Well, you know the silly thing that the girls ask the boys, and I thought if you wanted to think about it, I mean I don't know what your plans are, but perhaps we could go together."

Of course I had never been to a dance with a girl before—in fact, I couldn't even dance—but this was school and not like being asked to a person's house for dinner, so it was all right to go. But I had this sinking feeling about not being able to dance, and especially here she was going to *dancing* class, for cripes' sake! "Oh, sure, I'd like to." Was that *me* talking? Well, last time I had turned down the dinner invite and I just *couldn't* turn down another invite, especially this one, or they'd think I was a snob. That almost made me burst out laughing. I mean me being a snob. Actually, I had *been* to two dances, but I hadn't danced. Both times I had spent the whole evening sort of losing myself in the stag line and watching everybody. One time was when Walter Eamons took me along to his Sunday School youth group, and the other was when Priscilla Noonan had this birthday dance in her back yard and practically invited the whole school.

But I had vowed not to go to any more dances, because even though no one seemed to pay any attention to me, I was sure they could tell I didn't know how to dance. Also, both times I was the only boy there who wasn't wearing a jacket. Now here I was busting my vow. So maybe I'm wrong—stupid once, stupid twice. But Christina Sebastian had *asked me!* Do you know how that made me feel? On hundred-foot stilts, that's how! I'd burst any vow any time for Christina.

"It's raining cats and dogs out," Mrs. Sebastian was saying. "Why don't we give you a lift home?" That sure chased that goopy look off my face. A lift *home!* As we went out the door, I desperately tried to think of something. I began to babble things like oh, it's just a short distance, and don't bother, and, for gosh sakes, I like the rain, but Mrs. Sebastian just hurried us into their car and off we went.

"Where do you live?" she asked me.

Nice direct question. Well, she wasn't about to get a nice direct answer. "Oh, over on Kingshighway."

"Where on Kingshighway?"

"Oh, I'm sure it's out of your way. Why not drop me, uh, oh, around Delmar would be fine."

"Now, Red, we're going to take you right home. That's the direction we're going anyway."

We were getting close to Delmar and Kingshighway and I was getting close to a heart attack. Christina and her mother were in the front seat and I was sitting on the edge of the back seat chewing off my thumbnail. "Well, if you insist," I said as we drove right past the entrance of the Avalon Hotel, "it's down there at the corner of Fountain Avenue. That white house on the corner with the porch." I had always admired that house when I went by there looking for cigar bands.

We pulled up in front of it, and I thanked Mrs. Sebastian and ran up the stone steps to the front door. Wouldn't you know they just sat there at the curb watching me? So what could I do but punch the bell. That made some big dog inside mad as hell. Criminy, if they didn't get going they were about to see the stupendous sight of the master of the house getting his behind bit off by his own dog. The door opened as, thank God, Mrs. Sebastian pulled away. A big man with fat jowls stood there holding a huge Doberman by the collar. The Doberman had his lip back and he was doing everything he could to break jowly's arm.

"Whaddya want?"

"Sir, I am selling tickets to the Gas and Electric Workers' Union picnic." Luckily I had my sales book in my pocket and I held it up for jowly and the Doberman to see. "And I wondered if I could interest you—"

"Ring this bell again, and he eats you for dinner." The door whammed shut.

I ran back to the hotel, not getting too wet, and hoped my father would be there but he wasn't. The rain seemed to make the room hotter. I tried to think of somewhere I could go, but where could I go? So I just sat in the window watching the rain making a black sea out of the cinders and thinking about everything. "At least that's the end of Patrolman John L. Burns!" I said that out loud. I often talk out loud when I'm alone. Thinking about Patrol-man Burns like that—well, that's the way with me, always pawing around in the clinkers to find a lump of coal.

I *had* to get out of there. I went down the hall and knocked on Ella's door. First time I ever went to see her.

She was glad to see me. Her photo book was on the table, so I guess she had been thinking about her father. She looked even paler and skinnier than the last time I had seen her. But she had a nice way about her. She would have made a good sister, except for her being sick like she was.

"Ella, is it hard to learn how to dance?"

"Oh, no, it's easy."

"Then why do kids go to dancing school if it's so easy?"

"Oh, that's for manners and white gloves and bowing at the waist—you ever see dancing-school kids dance? They look like they had wind-up cranks in their backs. Dancing school! You might as well go to breathing school. Dancing's just as natural as breathing. Say! Don't you know how to dance?"

Her eyes suddenly brightened up and some color came into her cheeks. That's how it is with girls, I've noticed. They can really brighten up over girl things. Like playing house. When I was little and some girl came around eating an ice cream or candy bar that she wouldn't share for beans, all I had to do was just *mention* playing house and she practically jammed the Eskimo Pie down my throat. You be the daddy, I'll be the mommy, and you're just coming home from a busy day at the office and I'm in the kitchen cooking dinner and you come in . . . cripes, it was enough to make you throw up the darn Eskimo Pie.

So Ella immediately zoomed over to the radio and tuned around till she found some music. Then she showed me how to move my feet not lifting them off the ground, and held my hands as we looked down at our feet and moved around, me trying not to mangle her feet. It wasn't so easy, because my Keds kept sticking to the carpet. But then she made me take them off and I really began to get the hang of it sliding around in my socks. "That's it, Aaron, you're getting it. That's the fox trot." I really didn't know what I was doing but if I was getting it, whatever the fox trot was, that was fine with me. I was beginning to get pretty warm. I didn't know dancing got you so heated up. The music kept on playing, one song after another, and we kept on fox-trotting around Ella's room and I was beginning to feel like Bojangles Robinson himself. "Don't look at your feet," Ella said, "look at me." We danced some more. "You're biting your tongue," she said. I put my tongue back in my mouth. "You're getting it," she said.

Then suddenly she let go of my right hand and moved close to me and put her arm around me. "Now let's see how you do cheek-to-cheek," she said.

I nearly collapsed because, to tell you the truth, outside of my mother I had never been that close to a girl before. I mean I could feel her body up against mine. I mean even her *breasts*, for crying out loud, and she put her cheek against mine even though she was a half head taller and then she reached down and took my right arm and pulled it around her. I forgot all about my feet.

"You're very well coordinated," she said, and I nearly jumped out of my skin when I felt her lips moving right next to my ear.

"I don't want to tire you," I said. Frankly, I suddenly had this guilty feeling that Christina was looking at us and here I was wound around with Ella doing something I was supposed to do with Christina. Just the thought of dancing like this with Christina almost made me keel over.

"Why did you say that?"

"Why did I say what?" I'd honestly forgotten what I had said.

"About me getting tired. You're afraid I'll get . . . sick, aren't you?"

"Oh, no, really, I just meant. . . ." I tried to pull my head back, but our cheekbones were wired together.

"Don't worry. Not when I have my medicine. My mother can even go out and leave me alone. I love to dance. Oh, I'd forgotten how much I love to dance! Are you sure you never danced before? You know what we should do? When the band in the dance hall plays at night, we should dance to it."

"You mean go down *there!*" She winced a little because I had raised my voice, and with this cheek-to-cheek business you've got to watch the volume.

"No, silly, I mean dance here. And you won't have to pay me ten cents a dance." She laughed and we danced on and on. Our cheeks were glued together from the heat. The door opened and her mother came in and I tried to jump away, but Ella hung right on to me. "Look, I've just taught Aaron to dance," she said proudly as we fox-trotted right in front of her mother's eyes. "Would you believe he never danced before?"

I mean, cripes, there I was stuck smack up against her daughter with my arm around her and Mrs. McShane could plainly see that Ella's breasts were mushed up against me, and here was Ella asking her mother to give me the Medal of Honor for dancing, for Pete's sake! But all Mrs. McShane did was watch us and sort of clap her hands in time to the music, and at one point she came over and fixed the way I was holding my hand on Ella's back.

The music finally stopped and somebody started to sell Post Toasties. We pulled our sticky cheeks apart and I thought my skin would come off. "Well," I said picking up my Keds and heading toward the door, "I'm sure grateful to you, Ella. I was always sort of afraid of dancing."

"Don't forget. We're going to dance to the band tonight, aren't we?"

"Now, Ella," her mother said, "I don't want you to overdo it. I think you'd better rest tonight."

"Oh, I'm so *sick* of resting," Ella said in a quiet voice. She sat down with a plunk on the floor and leaned her back against the bed. "It was the first fun I've had." Her paleness had come back. "Sometimes a little fun is better than rest," she said.

"I know," her mother said nicely.

"Sometimes you want to fly a kite or play with a kitty or dance with a boy. Sometimes you can't stand books any more. Or yourself any more. Do you like to fly kites, Aaron? I used to make my own animal kites, and I'd have purple elephants and pink kangaroos dancing in the blue sky."

"I better go," I said. I was getting nervous about her. Very nervous. Her mother was over at the sink paying no attention to her. I began to think about my mother out there at Fee-Fee and I suddenly felt a big squeeze of sadness inside me. I left and went on down the corridor in my stocking feet.

My father still wasn't back. I was starving hungry. I looked all through the drawers and on the closet shelf where my mother kept food but there wasn't anything. Not a crumb. It was okay, though, because first thing in the morning I was to go see Mr. Verney and get all my money. The Gas and Electric Workers' Union picnic was Sunday and tomorrow was the day to settle up.

I went over and turned on the radio. It was Fred Allen. I didn't much want to listen to him, but then again maybe he'd tell a few jokes that would get my mind off my stomach.

Chapter Eighteen

On my way to Mr. Verney's office the following morning, I couldn't believe my eyes when I saw Patrolman John L. Burns out there directing traffic big as life. And on his chest he had a red, white, and blue ribbon that hadn't been there before. And there was Mr. Lucas, the barber from the Woodbine, walking through the traffic out to the middle of the street to shake Patrolman Burns's hand. They stood there talking, Mr. Lucas in his white barber's coat with a scissors in the pocket, while the traffic whizzed around them, and Patrolman Burns was laughing and had his chest out like he'd just won the World Series single-handed.

On my way down Delmar, I saw Johnny Cafferetta standing in the doorway of the Dew Drop Inn and I asked him about Patrolman Burns's red, white, and blue ribbon. Mr. Cafferetta just shook his head sadly and motioned me into the restaurant. He took a copy of the *Post-Dispatch* out from under the counter and handed it to me. Circled on the front page was this:

TRAFFIC OFFICER DECORATED FOR HEROISM

Patrolman John L. Burns, a veteran traffic officer sixteen years on the force, won a special police heroism citation yesterday for diverting a pack of rampaging steers from charging into a group of worshipers outside the B'rith Sholem Synagogue.

The steers had panicked on escape from a slaughterhouse truck and were on the verge of charging into the synagogue members when Patrolman Burns fearlessly and without regard for his own safety pursued the steers and opened fire on them with his service revolver.

Unfortunately several of the bullets ricocheted into the crowd, wounding several people, including Harold C. McManus, who was a passerby and not affiliated with B'rith Sholem. However, Patrolman Burns's resolute action, according to the police citation, effectually detoured the charging steers from what would have been a mass catastrophe.

Two of the wounded are in critical condition but all are expected to recover.

I gave the paper back to Johnny Cafferetta and he put it back under the counter. "One of those people died this morning," he said. "A Mrs. Lewis. I knew her. She used to eat here once in a while." I suddenly saw that lady getting shot in the stomach and folding over as she held herself. "A very nice woman. And *he* gets a medal." He picked up his counter rag and threw it down and said something in Greek as he walked on back to the kitchen.

I kept seeing that woman getting shot in the stomach as I went on down Delmar to Mr. Verney's office, and I started to look for cigar bands to try to get my mind off it. I didn't have any luck either finding anything good or getting rid of that woman being shot. Finally, I got to Mr. Verney's office and as I climbed up the two flights I got out my list and counted up the tickets and ads so's to be sure he wouldn't cheat me. The way I figured it I had sold sixty-two tickets and eighteen ads, which should add up to $6.70 if everybody paid up. Even if it only came to five dollars, say, it was still the hugest amount of money I had made since the Nehi stand. I could get my mother some nice things to eat, and we could buy gasoline so's the Ford could get us out to Fee-Fee to see her.

The door to Mr. Verney's office was open and I walked right in. There was no one there but an old Negro man with white hair sweeping up. The telephones and the typewriters and office junk were all gone and the place looked cleaned out.

"You lookin' for that Verney?" the Negro man asked. I nodded. "So's the landlord, and a lot of other people."

"But . . . where is he?"

"Go ast that young lady in there." He gestured toward the small office at the rear that was Mr. Verney's. I went back and opened the door, and there was one of the typists sitting at the desk with her head down on her arms crying. She looked up at me and said, "He's run out on us, the bastard," and went back to crying.

"But what about the picnic?"

She looked up again, her nose all red and runny. "There *is* no picnic!" All of a sudden she was screaming. "The gas and electric workers don't even have a union! No one ever heard of Mr. Verney! And he owes me three weeks' wages! I even spent my own money for carfares! He said he would pay us everything today but the bastard has cleared out and hasn't even paid the rent! He just printed up these fake tickets and took all those people's money and beat it! How much does he owe you?"

"Six dollars and seventy cents."

"He owed me sixty-eight dollars! *Sixty-eight* dollars! And my landlord will be waiting for me when I get back! Oh, God, I'm going to be out on the street tonight!" She threw her head down and began bawling again. I left her. The old Negro man had finished sweeping up and had disappeared. There was no one there. I went over and opened a few desk drawers. I took out my order book and threw it in one of the drawers. Then I ran out of there and down the stairs, two at a time, and out onto the sidewalk. I swear I could hear the typist crying all the way out there.

Chapter Nineteen

But it turned out to be not such a bad day after all, since that very afternoon my father received the Elgin watch line. Eighty-five watches in velvet-lined trays in a big leather case. Most of them had no insides, just the cases with their straps or chains, but they were a beautiful sight. I never saw my father so flushed and excited. I sure didn't blame him, after a wait like that. He even received a card in a leather case that said he was the official representative for Iowa, Kansas, and Oklahoma, signed by the Elgin president. He carried it around all over the hotel and the neighborhood and showed it to everyone, just the way he always carried around my report card the day after I got it and showed it to everybody, even strangers practically.

I guess my father overbragged about my report card because he didn't have much else to brag about. I could understand about my report card, but in a lot of ways he went too far. Like he'd brag about my twelve-year-old molar that had got pulled. He carried it around in his pocket and he'd take it out and show people the cavity and tell how he had rescued it from my mouth just in the nick of time. Then he'd make me open my mouth and show the empty spot where it had been. I hated opening my mouth for him, but the one time I refused he threw a terrible tantrum. But, I ask you, what father brags about yanking a molar that got pulled because he didn't have the extra fifty cents to get it filled? Ye gods and little fishes!

There was one other brag my father had on me that was even worse than the molar brag. I guess I must've had to listen to it ten thousand times. It was about how when I was crib-size, about twelve months old, and my mother was in the sanatorium that first time, I cried a lot during the night. "Well," my father would brag, "you want to know what a smart baby he was? The first couple of nights when he pulled his crying act, I got up and picked him up and he stopped crying. But then I realized that all he wanted was attention. So the next night when he cried, I went and got a glass of cold water and I went over to the crib with it and I said, 'You see this, it's a glass of cold water; now you stop crying or you'll be sorry.' But he went on crying, so I threw that glass of cold water right in his face and he stopped crying just like that! And from that night on, whenever he started to cry, all I had to do was grab a glass and show it to him and he'd stop crying. Now, that's a smart baby for you!"

Anyway, to get back to that day my father got the Elgin watch line, he sat me down and said we had to have a talk. It was just about the only talk we ever had, not counting the hilarious time he sat me down to explain the facts of life. I better tell you about that. Of course, I knew as many facts of life as he did, from hearing the guys at school yap about them all the time, but I played it dumb just to see how it'd turn out.

"You know, Aaron," he had said, "there are some things like Santa Claus that you believe when you're little but then when you get older you've got to find out the truth. Well, that's how it is with the stork. It's just something for when you're little, but now that you're eleven I have to tell you in a grown-up way about babies." What had brought on this talk was that the night before, my father's friend Carl Klein and his wife, Gertrude, had been talking about some woman in the paper who had quadruplets, and

I had asked if they had been brought by four storks or one stork with a super-giant beak.

I had been feeling mean because my father had just told Carl Klein to call the *Post-Dispatch* about a big argument they had had over whether eating fish was brain food. My father had said it was. So I put on this little-boy face and piped my voice up and gave it to him about the stork. Actually, I was feeling mean about my father in general. I mean there I was eleven years old at the time, and he had never done one single solitary father thing with me in my whole life. I had played ball that very afternoon with Bernie Rasmusson, whose father ran Tip-Top Cleaners, and he showed me how his father had taught him to throw the knuckle ball. If my father had ever put on a glove and told me to show him my smoke ball, I would have keeled over.

So now he was about to have his first father talk with me, hallelujah! (I had overheard my mother giving him hell the night after the Kleins: "Now, Eric, you've *got* to speak to the boy. No, I'm not going to do it for you. Yes, it *is* for you, because it's not a mother's place to tell a son about babies. That's what fathers do and God knows you do little enough for A. It was just *too* embarrassing with the Kleins. You've got to do it first thing tomorrow, and don't put it off like everything else.")

"You mean the storks don't bring babies!" I exclaimed.

"Well, ah, yes, you see, uh, well. . . ." He was fishing around for some way out but I wasn't helping him at all. "You remember last Easter that pet store that had the chicken in the window sitting on those eggs? Well, that's just how it is with mothers."

"You mean I came out of my mother like a chicken?"

"Yes, just the way it is in Sandoz's picture of your brother Sullivan."

"But how did I get inside her?" I thought I had him there.

"You just grew, that's all."

"But what do fathers do?"

"Well, they put their arms around their wives and kiss them."

I waited. But that was supposed to be the whole father works. "You mean every time a woman gets kissed she has a baby?"

"No, just some of the time."

"Then how do you know when you make a baby?"

"You don't. That's why you have to be very careful who you kiss."

So now we were having our second talk. Can you imagine that you're twelve years old and this was only the second time you'd had a talk with your father? Well, what he told me was that they hadn't given him the territory he wanted but that beggars couldn't be choosers. That he had arranged with Johnny Cafferetta for me to eat supper every night at the Dew Drop Inn, and that Arnie, over at the delicatessen, would fix up a sandwich every day for me to take to school. "Of course, you're not going to get roast beef and ham," he said, "but he promised it would be something healthy like liverwurst." I asked him how he had arranged this, and he said he had given Johnny and Arnie two of the Elgin wrist-watches that had works out of his sample line. "Soon as I earn a little money, I'll buy watches to replace them." My father had also given an Elgin watch with works to Mr. Desot, who had given him a seventeen-dollar credit on the bill. "That way, as long as I'm paying a little something, they won't bother us."

He gave me fifty cents for spending money and said he would send me more just as soon as he started taking orders. He had figured out on a piece of paper how much gas and hotels and food would cost him, and it looked like he could just barely squeeze by on his drawing account.

"Now you be sure to go see your mother every Sunday," he said. "They won't allow you in to the visitors' room because you're a child, but you can talk to her from the lawn outside. She'll be very lonely so don't forget—every Sunday, two to four."

"When will you be leaving?"

"Now. Right now. I've got to be in Davenport, Iowa, first thing Monday morning."

"Then you can see Sullivan! Listen, I want to send him some marbles!"

"No, no, I won't. Keokuk isn't on my route. They've really got me spread out all over the map."

"How long will you be gone?"

"I just can't tell. A territory like that."

"But will it be days or weeks or years or what?" I couldn't picture places like Kansas and Oklahoma.

"Oh, not years!" He laughed. "I'd say several weeks. Quite a few weeks."

"Months, then."

"Well, I just can't tell. But I'll get back as soon as I can because I'll be worried about you."

"Is there any place I can write you? I mean what if I have to get in touch with you?"

"I guess there isn't. I'll just be moving from town to town and staying in the cheapest hotels I can find. What bad luck that your mother is sick just now. I should put this off, I guess, but you know how jobs are. . . ."

"Oh, listen, don't you worry about me. Long as I can eat at the Dew Drop and Arnie's, I'll get along fine. After all, I have my friends, Lester and everybody."

"It's just the worst time to be getting this job, wouldn't you know." He got out his suitcase and began to pack.

"Will they let you leave with that?" I asked.

"Yes, Mr. Desot said it was all right as long as I just took a few of my things and I let them inspect the suitcase on the way out. After all, I just paid him seventeen dollars!"

I walked my father to the Ford, which he had switched to the rear of the Kroger parking lot. I suddenly didn't want him to go. At least to wait a few days while I got *prepared*. Right at that moment, I felt a little scared.

He had unlocked the door and slid behind the wheel. He took out his handkerchief and wiped off his face and shined up his glasses. Carrying the suitcase had perspired him. I had offered to help but he wouldn't let me.

"I'd give you a lift back but I can't risk the Repleviners."

"Will you write me?"

"Oh, sure. All the time. You and your mother."

"Shall I still play rummy with Aunt Minnie?"

"I should hope so. It's your movie money, isn't it?"

"Well, it's been my bird money."

"Aren't they about ready for sale?"

"Just about."

"That's wonderful. You'll have some money in your pocket."

He started up the engine. I shut the car door. He reached over and put his left hand on top of mine, which were on the window opening. "You be a *Mensch*," he said. It was one of his favorite words, *Mensch*. I took my hands off the rattling door and stood back from the Ford. My father started it going. As he moved away, he stuck his hand out of the window and waved. I waved back. I guess he saw me in the rearview mirror. I stood there until the Ford bounced out of the parking lot and onto Page and disappeared. Then I started back to the hotel. He hadn't even *mentioned* my graduation. I put my hand in my pocket and made a fist around the fifty-cent piece. I just wished he hadn't gone so soon. It would have been all right if I had been prepared. There must have been a million things I hadn't thought to ask him. Like how to get to Fee-Fee. It just occurred to me I didn't know how to get to Fee-Fee. Things like that. And what to do about the mail. Not that we got very much. Or there was anything in it.

A lady came walking out of Kroger's with a bag of groceries followed by a kid about my age wearing a Feltie sort of like mine, and I don't know why but I suddenly got this terrible feeling about the birds. I can't explain it. I mean I can't figure out the connection but I had two terrible feelings. First, it really socked me about what a low-scum Verney was (now I knew how he must've lost those teeth of his), and then it hit me about the birds. My whole life now depended on those canaries, but with the super-lousy luck I was having ever since I flubbed the caddie money and now the picnic money, it just struck me there in the Kroger parking lot that some awful thing had happened to the birds and I was going to flub that, too. And that would be the end of my graduation clothes. Oh, no! What about the dance and Christina? Oh, no! I lit out of there and my old Keds grew spikes and I was Glenn Cunningham giving it the old kick on the last lap. Glenn really turned it on, passing the entire field, weaving in and out, going "Beep-beep, beep-beep" to let them know he was coming, his barrel chest way out at the Avalon tape, a new record for the outdoor mile as he took the stairs two at a time and over the white tiles to the finish.

The 310 door across the hall opened and there stood the wavy-haired criminal lawyer. "Why, hello, lad, I thought you were brother Ben." His deep voice was like a church bell. "Have you by chance seen him?"

"No, sir."

"Well, now, I wonder if you would go on an important mission for me? It is imperative to locate brother Ben and fetch us a package from him. Can you do that?"

"I'll try."

"There's a good boy."

What could I do? Just behind my door, my poor canaries were facing some terrible peril, I knew, but I had to desert them and go off and find icky Ben.

It didn't take me long. He was asleep on a cot in the storeroom. He got a paper bag and went to the trunk and put a bottle in it and gave it to me and went back to sleep without saying a word.

The lawyer took one look at the bag and greeted me like I was a judge. "Come in, come in, lad," he said as he took the bag from me. The blond woman was standing at a table putting ice in some glasses. The other man was sitting in a chair at the window.

"Isn't he cute?" the blonde said, coming over to give me a closer look. "What's your name?"

"Aaron."

"What?"

"Aaron."

"How do you spell it?"

"Big A, little a, r-o-n."

"What kind of a name's that?" She was disappointed.

"Moses's unruly brother, the upstart Aaron," the criminal lawyer boomed out. "You worship the golden calf, do you?"

"I don't care if he does," the blonde said, reaching over and mussing my hair. "He's cute, aren't you, Red?" Her hand smelled of cigarettes.

"When the hell," the man in the chair said, "are we going to open that bottle?"

The blonde took the bottle over to the table. The lawyer reached in his pocket and took out a nickel. "Here you are, my little man, for your trouble." I suddenly didn't want his nickel.

"Thank you, but I did it as a favor."

I ducked across the hall and into 309, leaving him with the nickel in his hand. The guy at the window was John Dillinger, and I would capture him as soon as I checked on the birds.

I tiptoed over to the cage. My heart was beating a mile a minute, mostly from that blonde mussing my hair and John Dillinger snarling from the window, but also because I was prepared to see six feathered bodies strewn around on the bottom of the cage.

It took a few seconds for my eyes to get adjusted to the dark. Then I saw them. Sleeping all in a line on the same perch, Skippy, then Sooky, then the four babies, all on one foot with their heads under their wings. I got tears in my eyes. They looked so contented and beautiful and family. Mrs. Finch had warned that the father might resent the baby birds and attack them, or the mother might neglect them, or the strong babies would peck up the weakest one, but not Skippy and his family. He had fed Sooky while she sat on the nest, and then they had taken turns feeding the babies when they were in the nest, and now they all got along just fine.

I felt very sad at the thought of breaking up Skippy's family. Billy Tyzzer had warned me about this feeling and advised me not to name the babies because you got worse attached to them when they had names. I put the cover over the cage, turned on the light, and looked around. My mother's and father's things were gone from the dresser top and there was no sign anybody lived there. It was an awful feeling. I sure hoped Lester was in. I didn't want to stay there for a minute. It was like everybody had gone off to a funeral.

I closed the door softly so they wouldn't hear me across the hall; then slowly I slid my hand to my shoulder holster, unleashed my trusty G-man .45 Colt automatic, and blasted away at the door of 310. Dillinger tried to get to his feet but the first bullets cut him down.

There was no answer at Lester's room, which meant I'd have to go back and write him a note and slip it under his door. He may have an old lady, like he said, but either she was never there or she never answered the door. When I passed the McShanes, I suddenly felt like I didn't want to go back to 309 even to write a note, so I knocked on their door. Mrs. McShane answered.

"Oh, come in, Aaron," she said. "I'm sure Ella would like to see you."

Ella was in bed. Her face was whiter than the sheet. "Hi, Aaron. Come on over." Her voice was white, too.

"What's wrong?"

"Ella had a rather nasty attack, I'm afraid," Mrs. McShane said. "Even with her medicine."

"I'm all right, though."

"The doctor said she just had to rest."

"Well, gosh, I shouldn't disturb you." I just couldn't stay there with Ella sick like that. I mean I didn't have it in me to stay there. Any other day I'd have been glad to sit there and play cards with her or whatever, but this was the wrong time. But I felt so doggone sorry for her. Just her white face poking out of the sheets like that. I really felt bad that I couldn't stay.

"I'm sure it's all right for you to stay a bit," Mrs. McShane said.

"I'd like to, I sure would, but Lester is waiting for me in the Vampire Room."

"Vampire Room?"

"Oh, that's what we call it. But I'll come see you tomorrow."

"Promise?"

I should have stayed, at least for a couple of minutes, but I just couldn't. I wrote the note to Lester and went down the hall and slipped it under his door. On my way back, as I passed Old Lady Heinson's door, she called to me. "That you, Aaron?" She had a great pair of ears, all right. Well, I did not want to gabble with her about James Fenimore Cooper or hear about the Johnstown flood for the two-millionth time. I pushed open the door to tell her I couldn't hang around, but the sight I saw made my breath suck in.

The room was all dark except for the candles. Old Lady Heinson had put a little table in the center of the room, between the stacks of newspapers, and covered it with a long white cloth on which she had these high white candles. In the middle of the candles she had a framed photo of her nephew in his navy uniform, with flowers all around the frame. Laid out on the table in front of the photo were things like a cross with Jesus, some beads, a Bible with silver on it, and other religious stuff. Old Lady Heinson was kneeling on a pillow in front of the table, with a white shawl over her head. Her back was to me.

"Come help me pray, Aaron."

I didn't know what to say, I had never prayed in my whole life. I didn't know how to pray. "What are you praying for?"

"My nephew Jonathan. We'll pray together and the Lord will hear us."

"What's wrong with your nephew Jonathan?"

"He's on the *Akron*."

"But he's been on the *Akron* for a whole year and you haven't prayed for him."

"Don't you know about the *Akron*?" She turned her head and looked at me with this fierce look on her face.

"No, Ma'am."

"Don't you read the paper?"

"Not for a while, I haven't."

"It's all over the radio."

"One of our tubes blew out." During *Amos 'n' Andy*. You should have heard my father banging on the radio and cursing.

"The *Akron* is down in the stormy sea and they are out there searching. The Lord must help them find Jonathan. He's all I have, as you know. We must pray with all our might so the Lord will hear us and save Jonathan. He's all I have."

"The *Akron* fell down! Why, that's not possible!" The whole world knew that the *Akron* was absolutely unfallable. I saw it once when it sailed around St. Louis for all one afternoon with this tremendous American flag hanging out of its belly. They let us out in the schoolyard to look at her as she floated by. The hugest silver thing you ever saw.

"Crashed in the New Jersey sea in a raging storm. Thunderbolts and lightning. Four of the crew have already been plucked from the sea. Let us pray that one of them is Jonathan."

"How many are there?"

"How many what?"

"How many men were up there?"

"Seventy-seven. Kneel, lad, and pray with all the might that's in you. Pray as you've never prayed before."

I got down on my knees beside her and copied her, clasping my hands and bowing my head. She smelled nice, kind of musty like once when we had to press some flowers in a book for botany and afterward I took them out and smelled them. The candles made a lot of heat on my face. I looked at her nephew in his navy suit and he had this face that all guys get when they put on a sailor suit. I tried to think of something to pray, but it's really hard to pray for someone you never met, especially when you never prayed before. I only knew one prayer and it wouldn't have helped Jonathan.

It was this prayer I had heard Jamie Nichols say that time when we were living on Concordia Lane and he invited me for a sleepover. It was the only time I'd ever been invited for a sleepover, so I didn't know about kids praying when they went to sleep. At first I thought old Jamie was looking for something under the bed, until I realized he had his palms together under his chin and his eyes closed. Then he started in on this prayer: "Now I lay me down to sleep, and pray the Lord my soul to keep. If I should die before I wake, I pray the Lord my soul to take." Well, that was just about the morbidest thing I ever heard. In the first place, how many nine-year-old kids go to bed and wake up dead? Nobody I ever heard of. But here was Jamie worried about being the first nine-year-old in history to kick off in his sleep. When I found out that kids all over America got down on their knees every night ascared about their souls if they died in their sleep, it really put me off praying.

The closest I ever got to religion was last year when Marty Abramson, who since moved back to his parents in Cincinnati, asked me if I wanted to visit his youth group at Temple Israel. Marty was boarding with his St. Louis married sister, like Sullivan was boarding with my Keokuk aunt and uncle. His sister belonged to this temple that was at the corner of Kingshighway and Washington, just a block from the Avalon. It was a very ritzy temple that always had limousines parked in front on Friday nights. So I was interested in seeing what went on inside, and I said sure, I'd go with him to this youth group that met every Sunday afternoon.

They met in what they called a vestry room at the back of the Temple. It was a giant room, as big as a basketball court, where they put on dances and pageants and had speakers with colored slides. Those rich kids were nice, I guess, but I would have had no interest in ever going again if the vestry room hadn't been, as I said, the size of a basketball court. It so happened that Marty was as keen about basketball as I was, so I suggested he ask the man in charge of the group how about playing basketball there. The only time me and Marty got to play was when we had climbed over the fence of the schoolyard a couple of times, and only got caught once, but this could be a place where we could play regular and have a team.

What was decided was that the group could use the vestry room for basketball if me and Marty put up backboards and hoops. Of course, that was quite a problem. Marty solved half of it by getting his sister to buy a pair of hoops, and I solved the other half of the problem by removing a section of the fence that surrounded the Yellow Taxi Cab Company. It was a section way down at the end, and me and Marty did it at night and carried the boards over to Temple Israel. We borrowed the janitor's tools and sawed the boards the right size, nailed them together, screwed on the hoops, and attached the backboards to the walls. The Temple Israel group bought a basketball, and for one solid week, every day after school, a bunch of us showed up and practiced. I think it was the most fun week I ever had. We elected Marty captain and one of the limousine kids said he had talked to his father about putting up the money for uniforms. The T.I. Fireflies is what we were going to call ourselves.

Then the whole thing blew up. It was Sunday afternoon, after the youth meeting was over, and we were just starting a game when these men came parading in. The one man who wore pinch-nose glasses had a wonderful face like you see on foreign money. He turned out to be the rabbi, Leon Harrison. The other two men turned out to be detectives. The three of them marched right through our game over to the wall and began looking up at the backboard. I had been dribbling the ball when they first came in and I just kept on dribbling and trying not to look at them.

"The one that's dribbling," one of the detectives said real loud.

They came over and stood around me, so I finally stopped dribbling. "These gentlemen are looking for a section of fence that disappeared from the Yellow Cab Company garage," Rabbi Harrison said, in a kind of Leslie Howard voice that went with his face. "They seem to feel that you might know something about it."

"Me? The Yellow Cab Company?"

"Where'd you get them boards?" one of the detectives asked. *He* sounded like Victor McLaglen.

"Why, they were just a bunch of old boards from in back of the hotel."

"What hotel?"

"The Avalon. There was just this pile of old boards."

The detectives got a ladder and took down the backboards. I zapped both of them with my Buck Rogers disintegrator gun. There was something stamped on the boards that matched what was stamped on the boards in the Yellow Cab Company fence.

"Well, somebody must have thrown them there in the back of the Avalon," I said. "How was I to know?"

The Yellow Cab Company came and got the lumber and the youth group canceled my membership, and that was as close as I ever got to getting religious.

"Oh, Lord, save him, save him, save him!" Old Lady Heinson suddenly shouted, scaring me to death. "Are you praying, Aaron?"

"Yes, Ma'am."

"Oh, dear Lord, save him, save one of your devoted sons!" She went back to praying and so did I. I thought about my mother and I prayed that the spot on her lung would go away, and I thought about my brother and prayed they would treat him nicely and that I'd get to see him soon. I prayed for Ella and for my father out there on the road with his Elgin watches.

I would have liked to have gone on praying all night. I had really worked myself up into the mood for it. Who knows, maybe I'd take it up. It seemed to me it was a pretty good thing for people who lived alone.

Chapter Twenty

I had thought that the worst time would be at night getting in bed alone, with the Good Times band playing and the noises from the lobby and the hall, especially when the criminal lawyer and his pals were there, coming into the room and nobody to say good night to. But actually the worst time was the morning. Waking up in the empty room with nobody there to say good morning to. I was sure glad I had the birds to talk to. It was also too bad that the radio was burned out, because a radio voice sort of keeps you company. And I could have found out about the *Akron*. It wasn't until later in the day that I finally heard the news that all seventy-seven of the men were lost except four, and Old Lady Heinson's nephew wasn't one of them.

That afternoon I had an experience at the Barnes Hospital that I should mention. When my mother went to Fee-Fee, the doctor there arranged for me to go to the free clinic to have a chest X-ray, since it would have been possible for me to have caught my mother's consumption. I had been told to go to the main desk of the clinic at four o'clock that day and that they would have made arrangements for my chest X-ray.

The corridors of the clinic were packed with people sitting on wooden benches waiting for their names to be called. They were sick and bent over and coughing, and it was really a terrible sight.

They looked like they had been there on those wooden benches for a couple of weeks. The corridors were so full of these waiting, suffering patients you had to push into them to get through. The smell was something fierce. I felt sorry for them, like I wasn't one of them, but just passing through in my gilded carriage on my way to the castle.

The main desk for the free clinic was in a large room at the end of one of the corridors, and I had to push my way down the entire corridor to get there. I realized when I got started that I had gone into the hospital by the wrong door. People kept deliberately getting up and clogging my way, afraid, I guess, that I was trying to push ahead in the line. It took me a long time to get down the corridor because if you're a twelve-year-old kid you can't go barging into some old man with brown splotched skin who's been sitting there on his bony behind since daybreak waiting for some free doctor to look at him.

I finally got to the main desk. It was circular and full of people as busy as soda jerks. It was hard to get anybody's attention, especially at my height. I finally found an opening at the counter. There was a woman with her back toward me bent over the files.

"Can you help me, please?" I said.

The woman stood up and turned around. It was Christina Sebastian's mother. She had a red band on her arm that said, "Volunteer."

"Aaron!" she said after a little gasp. "What are *you* doing here?"

For a second there, my eyes crossed, but then, as I always do, I grabbed hold again. "Oh, me? Why, I'm looking for my uncle."

"Your uncle? Is he a patient?"

"No, oh, no." I let out what I hoped sounded like a little laugh. "He's a doctor. We're supposed to have lunch."

"Oh, what's his name? I'll check on him for you."

"Uh, Dr. Ungudunger. He's in gall bladders." I had once seen a Marx Brothers movie in which Groucho was a Dr. Ungudunger and for some cockeyed reason that was the name that popped out of me. "But don't bother to check. I'll just go to the gall-bladder department. I know where it is. I meet him there all the time." I started backing away from the counter as fast as I could, and I beat it out of there with Mrs. Sebastian watching me go with this kind of funny look on her face.

If I went to all that trouble to keep them from knowing I lived in the Avalon Hotel, I sure as shooting wasn't going to let them find out that I was a free-clinic charity case at the Barnes Hospital. The minute I got out of that room I took off. I snapped on my mask and jumped up on Silver and rode lickety-split through the canyon till I got to my hiding place at the tennis courts.

I went around back of court 9 where there were trees, and sat down with my back against the tennis fence. Cripes, what a shock that was when that bent-over lady turned around and it was Mrs. Sebastian. Fate was always walloping me like that. I began to think about other times that I had been walloped, which was a bad habit I had when I got to feeling really sorry for myself. I tried not to, because I knew I'd wind up thinking about A. W. Brown, and I did *not* want to think about A. W. Brown. But I did.

I told you that A. W. Brown had given me a job on his miniature golf course, pushing a roller over the "greens," which were really dyed linseed. It cost a dime to play, and players were given a putter and a ball that had "A. W. Brown's Miniature Golf" stamped into it. When a player got to the last hole and putted into the cup, there was a pipe connected to the hole that carried the ball back to the starting shack. There was one hole, the sixth, where the player stood on a little platform and had to hit the ball over a puddle to get to the green. Sometimes there would be these muscle types who would smack the ball clear over the fence. They were very cheesy balls and A. W. Brown would go out in back of the fence every evening and collect the balls that had been hit there.

One afternoon, a bunch of us were playing softball in a vacant lot about two blocks from where the miniature golf was.

Somebody knocked the ball out of the lot and into the street where it rolled into a sewer opening. We pried off the sewer cover and I climbed down into the dry sewer. I not only found our softball but to my surprise I found four A. W. Brown golf balls, which must have rolled all the way down the street and landed there after being knocked over the fence by the muscle men.

Later in the afternoon, me and Jason Tindell and Ernie Rich made our own miniature golf in Ernie's back yard. We nailed sticks together to make putters and we had a great time putting around our miniature golf course with the A. W. Brown golf balls, until this really creepy fat kid named Harold Buckley came around and tried to get into the game. He kept asking if he could play, and Jason kept saying, "Yes, we have no bananas," and it made Fatso Buckley madder and madder until finally he threatened us that unless we let him play he'd go snitch to A. W. Brown that we had four of his golf balls. Jason gave him a couple more bananas and off he went to snitch to A. W. Brown.

Two minutes later, A. W. Brown sent for me. It was my intention to tell him the truth about how I got the golf balls, but when he said to me, "Aaron, I hear you have four of my golf balls," I sort of panicked and said, "No, sir, they belong to Ernie Rich."

"That's a lie!" Fatso Buckley said. "They got your name stamped right on them, Mr. Brown."

"He's just mad because we wouldn't let him play with us," I explained.

"I want to see them," A. W. Brown said. "Go get them and bring them here. That way we can see who's lying."

I went back to Ernie's and told them what had happened. Ernie went down into his basement and got a long iron file for us to file the names off the golf balls. We filed the names clean off, and then we went to face A. W. Brown. I was really pretty scared, because if he didn't believe me about these being Ernie Rich's old golf balls, I would lose my job. And I was the only one in the family who was working.

I held out the golf balls for A. W. Brown to see that they weren't his. He took one of them and looked at it, and then he took an old coffee can off the shelf that had a yellow liquid in it. He got a piece of wire, twisted it around the golf ball, and dipped it into the yellow liquid. After a minute or so, he pulled it out and dried it off with a rag. In the very place where we had filed off the name, there it was again—"A. W. Brown's Miniature Golf." He held it up in front of my nose so'd I'd get a snootful of it.

"How many did you steal?" he asked.

"Listen, Mr. Brown, let me tell you what really—"

"You're a liar and a cheat, and if you ever set foot around here again I'll throw you to the cops."

"I didn't *take* them, honest, I *found* them. . . ."

"Get going. You're just lucky I don't send a cop around to see your parents. Get going."

The next day, I snuck around the back and looked through the fence to see who had gotten my job. I should have known it would be Fatso Buckley.

Yes, thinking back on it, that was the worst wallop fate ever gave me. Don't forget I was the one who had put A. W. Brown in business.

Chapter Twenty-One

The canaries were six weeks old on Monday of the week before graduation, but I had to wait until Wednesday to take them to the pet store. That was because Mr. Farley said I had to bring them in when Mr. Yamo made his rounds, and Mr. Yamo only came to Mr. Farley's pet store on Wednesday afternoons. Mr. Yamo was this Japanese man who was an expert on birds.

I put Sooky and her four babies, who were now as big as Sooky, into the little cage Billy Tyzzer had given me. Skippy kept jabbering all the time, probably scolding me for taking them away. I stopped by Billy's house on the way to the pet store and gave Sooky back to him, and he said the four babies certainly looked wonderful. So did Mr. Farley when I brought them into the store and put the little cage on the counter. He said Mr. Yamo ought to be coming in any minute.

I don't know why, but I was very nervous. I also felt bad about taking everybody away from Skippy. I stood there at the counter, with my arm around the cage, watching the door for Mr. Yamo and feeling nervous, like I had to go to the bathroom even though I had just gone to the bathroom when I left the hotel.

Mr. Yamo finally arrived, later than Mr. Farley had said. He was very small and smiled all the time. He took off his hat and hung it in the back of Mr. Farley's store; then he rubbed his hands together like it was freezing outside instead of about 1,000 degrees Fahrenheit. Mr. Farley showed him a parrot and some other birds he had at the back of the shop, and Mr. Yamo examined them and they blabbed and blabbed about them. Finally, Mr. Farley brought Mr. Yamo over to look at my birds. Mr. Farley put an empty cage on the counter beside mine. Mr. Yamo put his hand in my cage and plucked one of the birds from its perch. He really knew how to pluck birds off perches. He held the bird in his left hand, on its back, and he examined it carefully while it tried to peck his fingers. Mr. Yamo released the bird into the empty cage and took another and another until all four birds were in Mr. Farley's cage.

Mr. Yamo smiled at me with all his teeth and patted me on the head. "They very nice birds," he said. "Very healthy. All females."

"Are you sure?" Mr. Farley asked.

"Oh, yes. Very sure."

"Well, I'll be darned. A whole litter like that."

Mr. Farley took Mr. Yamo to the back of the store and got his hat for him, and I just stood there trying to understand what had happened. My brain seemed stuck. And all my blood seemed to have drained into my Keds. I wanted to say something to Mr. Yamo as he went past me toward the door but I couldn't think of anything to say. After he left, Mr. Farley stood at the door for a moment and then he came back to where I was.

"Now that's a tough break," he said.

"Aren't they worth *anything?*" I asked. "I can't take them back home. We only live in one room."

Mr. Farley rubbed his hand along the side of his face. "There's no market for females," he said, "since they don't sing. The most I could give you is fifty cents for the lot of them."

I nodded my head and Mr. Farley rang up the "No Sale" on his cash register and handed me a fifty-cent piece. "I'm really sorry it can't be more," he said. "First time I've known that to happen."

"That's all right," I said. He was a nice man and God knows it wasn't his fault, but I felt myself boiling up angry. That's the way with me when I've really lost out on something and I have a big disappointment. I don't sit down and cry; instead I get mad and my blood sloshes all around and that's what started to happen to me. Up sloshed my blood from my Keds and I could feel my face getting red and I was getting madder and madder. The way I felt, I wanted to break something. Jump on something and hear it split and crack and rip in two. Criminy, wasn't anything *ever* going to go right? I wanted to take that half dollar and fling it through the pet-shop window all the way to Oklahoma. Could fifty cents buy a jacket or a pair of shoes or pay for the graduation dance? If I had a gun, I would've stuck it in Mr. Farley's ribs and punched open his cash register and taken the twelve dollars. I really would've. Not just pretend, like when I'm Pretty Boy Floyd or Baby Face Nelson. I mean really. Twelve bucks, Mr. Farley, or I'll blow you to kingdom come. Ninety-eight cents for my white shirt and 30 cents for my blue tie and $1.75 for my white pants and $2.98 for my shoes and $1.00 for the dance and $4.19 for that blue coat with the white buttons from Horwitz's Haberdashery. You know how many times I have laid there in bed at night and looked at myself in that blue coat with the white buttons and seen myself dancing cheek-to-cheek with Christina Sebastian, holding her tight up against my blue coat? Don't you think I had enough? Don't you think they ought to have left me alone? It was graduation next Friday. What was I supposed to do? I hated them all. Billy Tyzzer and those damn birds and all those movies I had to give up. And what did I have to show for it? Nothing. *Nothing.* Zero. I tell you I hated them. All the times I cleaned that cage and worried about them and got them lettuce leaves from the Piggly-Wiggly and they turn out to be *girls!*

I was standing at the door, not going out in the street, clenching the half dollar in my right fist like I could mush it, not wanting to go out there and leave my birds with nothing to show for it.

Right next to the door was a little pen with wire sides, and one of the kittens in the pen had her paw through the wire trying to get at my sleeve. She was tan and white and about the size of my hand. I watched her quick paw playing with my sleeve for a while and I began to feel less angry.

I picked her up and looked at her and she looked back at me without blinking.

"How do you like my calico kittens?" Mr. Farley asked.

I took one more look at her and made up my mind. "Could I buy her for this?" I asked.

Mr. Farley looked at the fifty-cent piece for a moment, and then he looked at me and then he smiled. "Sure," he said. I gave him the money. He opened the door for me and I left with the kitten.

When I got to the hotel, I put the kitten inside my shirt because animals weren't allowed (except if you were Danny Desot), but she didn't let out a peep. I should say a meow. I went up the stairs so Arletta wouldn't spot her in the elevator, and just as I got to the third-floor corridor I saw Mrs. McShane going into the toilet. I took the kitten out of my shirt and put her up against me and she made tiny little purrs you could scarcely hear.

Ella's door was half open so I peeped in. She was asleep. I tiptoed over to her bed and gently put the kitten on the pillow beside her. The kitten looked at me and then she nestled over to Ella. Ella opened her eyes and saw the kitten and touched her with her fingers to make sure she was real. "Oh! Oh, Stephanie!" she said. "Stephanie!" She put her hand around the kitten and pulled her up against her. "Oh," she said. "Oh."

I was over by the door. Ella hadn't seen me. I took one last look at her with the calico kitten and I left. I can't say how I felt exactly, but I certainly wasn't mad any more.

Chapter Twenty-Two

Once he heard about my father having to take off, Lester had come by pretty nearly every day to look in on me. There was one afternoon he left a note for me not to eat at the Dew Drop Inn. He told me to be downstairs at five o'clock and I was. He pulled up in a Marmon coupé that had headlights like a locomotive and a motor longer than my bed.

"How do you like it?" he asked.

"It's colossal. Whose is it?"

"What do you mean, whose is it? It's mine. Get in."

Off we went. You had to talk loud to be heard above the engine and the brakes didn't work very good, but it was the most scrumptious car I ever saw.

"Aren't you afraid the Repleviners will get it, pulling up in front of the hotel like that?" I asked.

"Repleviners? This car is *mine*, I told you."

"Oh." I didn't know. I thought that all cars had Repleviners looking for them.

"Watch this," Lester said. There was a pretty blonde standing there, waiting for a streetcar, and Lester pulled up in front of her, pushed a button on the dashboard, and the rumble seat popped right up. The blonde, who was trying to pay no attention to Lester, burst out laughing.

"Hop in," Lester said. "I'll take you where you're going."

The blonde climbed up the rumble steps, giggling, and settled into the seat. "I'm going down to the Loew's State," she said as Lester zoomed away. "But I'm not in a hurry."

Lester took her to Loew's State and she climbed down from the rumble and thanked him, but she seemed disappointed. Lester drove on.

"With that rumble seat," Lester said, "I've got blondes like that coming out of my ears."

"Does the button close it?" I asked.

"Nah. It's just the popping open that counts."

"Where we going?"

"My sister's having a *bris* for her baby. You ever been to a *bris*?"

"I don't even know what a *bris* is."

"You circumcised?"

"Yes."

"That's a *bris*. It's just the way the Jews do it, that's all. The reason we're going is for the food. One thing about a *bris*, you really eat, and from the look of you, you could use a good stuffing. What's that Greek been feeding you?"

"Oh, whatever he sorta has left."

"That sounds really appetizing. And Arnie?"

"Baloney sandwiches on white."

"Is that what you want? You ask for baloney?"

"No, I really don't like it."

"Then tell him to give you something else. Your old man gave him a good watch, you should get a good sandwich."

"I'm afraid he'll get mad and give me nothing. He's a hothead like my grandfather. Besides, I trade off the baloney sandwiches with the dumb little kids. They don't know the difference."

Lester looked down at my feet and smiled. "How do the shoes fit?" he asked.

"Perfect," I said, and I wiggled my toes inside them. The way I got the shoes is this. The day after the canary disaster, I got hold of Lester and told him what had happened.

"Well, the problem's not getting hold of twelve dollars," he had said, "the problem is getting hold of those clothes for the graduation, that it?"

"Yes."

"All right, then, we've got to outfit you. The jacket's no problem. I got one that's way too small for me. It ought to just about fit you. Ditto a white shirt. The blue tie I'll borrow from my friend Newton Pfeffer, who's a clotheshorse. That leaves the white pants and the shoes. The first time it rains, we get the shoes."

"The first time it *rains?*"

"Leave it to me."

Two days later, it rained cats and dogs and Lester came banging on my door. "Let's go," he said. He was carrying a big black umbrella with an old wooden handle. "You got an umbrella? Bring it."

I told him about the $2.98 window at Wheelock's, but he said no, when it came to your feet you ought to get the best, so we traipsed down Delmar in the rain to the Florsheim store. There was nothing cheaper than eight dollars in the window. "Come on," Lester said, and he collapsed his umbrella, and so did I, and we went in.

"A good pair of black shoes in his size," Lester said to the salesman. I think I told you I had never been in a shoestore before, so when the salesman put the foot measurer on that little wooden ramp I didn't know that he wanted me to put my foot on it. The only shoes I had ever got were bought somewhere at a bargain sale and brought home to me. The salesman picked up my foot and put it on the measurer. Then he disappeared and came back with three boxes. I was awfully embarrassed about my busted Keds with the round rubber label on one of them hanging loose, but it didn't seem to bother Lester at all.

Those Florsheims were the most beautiful shoes I'd ever seen, but Lester didn't like any of them. The salesman brought out three more boxes. You never saw shoes like that. I'd try them on and walk around and they fit so good my feet felt reborn, but Lester kept saying no, they wouldn't do, and he asked for things like wing-tips and brogues and I really didn't know what he was talking about. I happened to see some of the price tags, and would you believe there was a pair of shoes there for fourteen dollars?

Finally, we must have had about a thousand shoes piled around us. "Well," Lester said, getting up, "there's just nothing we really like. But thank you, anyway." He picked up his umbrella and started out. I squirmed into my wet Keds and scooted after him. He wasn't going to strand me in there with all those enemy shoes. But when I got to the door I remembered my umbrella. The salesman was right behind me with it. He didn't look at all mad. I guess they were used to nuts like Lester. Besides, they weren't exactly overrun with customers.

Lester was waiting for me under the awning outside. "Put up your umbrella," he said. He had his hung over his arm. He held my umbrella over the two of us and we started back up Delmar. I knew him well enough to know that this wasn't the time to ask him anything. He was whistling this little tune he whistled between his teeth when he was busy thinking about other things.

When we got back to the hotel, we went straight to the Vampire Room. "Well, I'll be darned," Lester said, "it's raining in here, too. You feel the rain?"

"What rain?" No doubt about it, poor Lester had gone goofy.

"Why, I'm getting drenched!" he said, and he opened his umbrella. Two of the prettiest black shoes you ever laid eyes on fell out. The fourteen-dollar ones. They landed at my feet like two black diamonds and I let out a whoop that must have carried all the way back to the shoestore. I flung off my Keds and slipped my feet into the new shoes and I was Cinderella. I couldn't stop whooping.

I skipped around the room. Bill Robinson. Lester started banging out some music on the old piano. I started to dance like a madman. Popping my feet around. Fred Astaire. Tap-dancing like a demon—well, not really, you know what I mean, making a terrific clackety-clack and Lester pounding away and singing:

LESTER: I can't give you anything but love, baby!

ME: Baby!

LESTER: That's the only thing I've plenty of, baby.

ME: Baby!

LESTER: Dream awhile . . .

ME: Scheme awhile . . .

LESTER: We're sure to find,

ME: Happiness . . .

LESTER: And, I guess . . .

ME: All the things we've always pined for . . .

LESTER: Gee, I'd like to see you looking swell, baby . . .

ME: Baby!

LESTER: Diamond bracelets Woolworth doesn't sell, baby . . .

ME: Baby!

LESTER: And till that lucky day you know darn well, baby . . .

ME: Baby!

LESTER: I can't give you anything but . . .

ME: I can't give you anything but . . .

TOGETHER: I can't give you anything but love!

The tap-dancer collapsed with exhaustion and the piano player spun around on his stool and looked at him, a sweating, panting mess sitting in the middle of the floor, and from the way the tap-dancer looked at the piano player I guess he understood how much he thanked him for those shoes.

So that's how come I was wearing those beautiful black shoes in the Marmon that day on the way to the *bris*. As long as I'm at it, I suppose I ought to interrupt and tell you about the white pants, too, the ones I was wearing and the ones I was saving so'd they'd be clean for the graduation. Here is how I got them. Just as Lester had said we'd get the shoes the first day it rained, he said we'd get the white pants on the first Monday it *didn't* rain. It didn't rain that Monday, so Lester showed up and we walked over to Lindell Boulevard, that stretch between DeBaliviere and Skinker that runs along Forest Park. Actually, we didn't walk along Lindell, but along the alley that ran in back of the houses. The St. Louis sun was burning up the sky and all the back yards were full of Monday wash.

Every time we spotted a pair of white pants, we stopped and tried to size them up. Of course you couldn't be sure from as far away as the alley but they all looked like grown-up pants. But in one back yard there were four pairs flapping around, and you could tell they were different sizes. It was a family that obviously specialized in white pants.

"Now remember what I told you," Lester said. "From the time you ring the bell, I need two minutes. You've got to stall 'em."

I circled around the alley to the front of that house. It was two stories of red brick and white stone and there were two lions on each side of the steps in front of the door. I felt scared in my stomach, but I pulled out the copy of *Liberty* magazine that I had in my back pocket and I forced myself up those steps. I touched the bell ever so lightly but it went off with a clang that made me jump. The lions, I noticed, had very fierce expressions on their faces. I just hoped and prayed there wasn't another Doberman inside. Two minutes is a long time when a Doberman is drooling after you for dinner.

There was no sound of barking inside, but the door suddenly jerked open and there was a woman who looked fiercer than the Doberman. I mean it. Certain people really have dog faces. The woman had a little chow in her but she was mostly Doberman.

"Yes?" she barked.

"I have this marvelous . . ." My voice stuck to the roof of my mouth and I had to start over. "I have this marvelous offer from the publishers of *Liberty* magazine—"

"Oh, for Chrissakes!" she growled and slammed the door on me, but I had slid my foot forward and the door banged into it. I had turned my foot so the door hit the sole of my shoe and didn't hurt a bit, but I put on some act. I am not the number 1 actor in the Admiral Dewey Dramatic Society for nothing! The door popped back from my foot and I went lurching to the ground, being sure I landed on the doorsill, holding my foot and carrying on like every toe had been fractured. It was a very nice performance, if I say so myself, and it brought a lady down from the second floor on the run to see what had happened.

"My word," she said to the Doberman, "what happened?" She had an English accent and wore pearls.

"This kid selling magazines caught his foot in the door."

I kept on moaning and rubbing my foot.

"Oh, you poor child," the woman said. "Can you stand on it?"

I let her help me up but took my sweet time about it. I then walked around a little, carefully testing my foot. "Oh, I'm sure it will be all right," I said bravely. The two minutes were more than up.

The lady took me by the arm and guided me into the house. "Come in and let's have a look at it," she said. "Bring us some tea and cookies," she said to Fido.

What could I do? She took me into this fancy sunroom full of white furniture with yellow cushions and sat me down. I took off my shoe and we inspected my foot for swollenness. We agreed it was a little puffed around the anklebone.

Doberman came in with a huge tray full of teapots, cookies, chocolate-covered brownies, and fruit. The lady kept heaping up my plate and I kept emptying it. They were the best brownies my teeth had ever sunk into. Finally, when all the brownies and most of the cookies were gone, I pointed out that the swollenness had just about disappeared. I got up and tested my foot, and from the way I walked you could tell I'd recovered.

Lester was sitting on an ashpit at the end of the alley, worried about what terrible thing had happened to me. When he saw the chocolate smeared around my mouth and found out I'd been having a tea party while he was climbing fences and lifting pants off of clotheslines, he almost tossed the pants into the ashpit. But I took the two brownies out of my pocket that I had stashed away for him, and even though they were pretty mushed, he enjoyed them. Turned out he'd taken two pairs of pants to be sure one of them would fit me.

So now I was wearing one of the pants (the second-best fit; the best fit I was saving for the graduation) and my new black shoes to this *bris*. To be honest with you, the idea of going to a great feast because some kid was getting circumcised wasn't the most appetizing thing I could think of, but if there was as much food as Lester said there would be, I would probably forget about why I was eating it.

The *bris* feast was held in an empty lot behind a synagogue on Newstead Ave. It wasn't much of a synagogue. There was a delicatessen on the corner and then a door, and you climbed up to the second floor and that was the synagogue. The roof was sagging a little at one end and it hadn't been painted since Noah left the ark. What with B'rith Sholem and Temple Israel and whatnot, I was getting to be an expert on synagogues.

All the people invited to the *bris* passed through the synagogue and said hello to Lester's sister and her husband, who were standing there with the baby. Of course everybody also clucked over the baby. Then we filed out the back of the synagogue and down some rickety wooden steps into this vacant lot where the feed was going to take place. A huge tent had been set up there, with rows and rows of long tables and folding chairs. Before we went into the tent, Lester took me into the back of the delicatessen to show me where the food was being prepared. You never saw such a sight. All these fat women dressed in white, with white cloths around their hair, running back and forth, mixing, baking, slamming oven doors. God, what a sight! Mounds of chopped liver, herring, vegetables, potatoes, millions of brown chickens in rows, enormous baked fishes, other round and rolled things that looked delicious but I had never seen before, slabs of boiled beef as big as third base, and pastry of every kind, strudels, pies, cakes with chocolate swirls in them—just too darn much for my eyes and nose to handle.

There must have been a million people inside that tent packed together at the tables, which were all set with dishes and glasses and silverware and bouquets of flowers. The tent kept the sun from broiling the guests but it also kept the heat inside.

Lester sat at one side of the main table in the family section. I sat at a table to the other side. People were fanning themselves and yelling back and forth and waving at friends, and it was like a party. I didn't know what to expect. There were a lot of kids, little ones running around and bigger ones sitting together, but the table I was at were all grownups. The only one who said boo to me was a powdered lady in long white gloves with fatty arms that spilled over the tops of the gloves. She asked me if I was related to Myron or Thelma. I said Thelma.

Somebody banged on a water glass and everyone quieted down. The rabbi came in and went to the center of the main table, next to the family section. He was a small, skinny man, not so old, with a thin black beard and a black silk skullcap. He was carrying a little black leather bag like doctors carry. He opened the bag, and the first thing he took out was a long white scarf that he draped over his shoulders. Then he took out a Bible and opened it to a certain place and put it on the table. Next he reached in his bag and took out a round of leather, which he untied and unrolled. There were scissors and knives lined up in elastic bands inside it.

Now there was a big rustle and stir in the crowd, and then people started saying "Ah" and "Oh" as Lester's sister entered carrying the baby. She was a tall, pretty woman and she held up the baby for everyone to see and they laughed and applauded. Then her husband came in and stood next to her, and the *bris* got going. The rabbi read a lot from the Bible in Hebrew and the baby got handed back and forth a few times, finally winding up on a blanket on the table in front of the rabbi. Everybody hunched forward in their chairs and craned their necks up. The rabbi took a water glass and dumped a whole container of sugar in it. He took a string from his pocket that had a wad of cotton tied to its end. He dunked the cotton in the sugar water, leaving the string hanging over the edge of the glass, like a tea bag.

He took a little bottle of oil or something from his bag and put a few drops on his fingers, and then rubbed it on the baby's penis. He slid one of the scissors out of the leather holder and wiped it off with the napkin. The cutting end of the scissors had a funny shape to it. The rabbi pulled the cotton out of the sugar water and put it in the baby's mouth. The baby seemed to like it. Lester's sister sat down and the baby's father leaned over and held the baby's legs. The rabbi had been saying Hebrew prayers every time he had done any of these things, and now he raised his voice and you could tell he was saying a serious prayer.

Once that was out of the way, he picked up the baby's penis with his left hand and pinched the top skin between his thumb and forefinger, pulling it tight. Then, zuck!—that quick—he picked up the scissors with his right hand and snipped off the top piece of the skin.

The baby spit out the sugar cotton and howled bloody murder. The rabbi dipped it in the glass again and put it back in the baby's mouth. The rabbi uncapped a bottle and poured something on a cloth and wrapped it around the baby's bleeding penis. Then he wrapped the baby up in the blanket and handed him to his mother. The baby was yowling to beat the band. The rabbi kept dunking the cotton in its mouth and the baby kept spitting it out, but everyone was happy and applauding and you'd think the kid had just delivered the Gettysburg Address. The rabbi had a few wind-up prayers which he said while drinking down a couple of glasses of wine. In fact, everybody was drinking wine now, which was thick and had a blackish-red color. Even the kids. I took a sip—first time I ever tasted wine—and I almost urped. It tasted like Lysol smells.

The rabbi washed his hands in a basin of water that was brought to the table, and then he washed off the scissors and dried them on the napkin. The baby was carted off, still yowling, and as the rabbi sat down the food started streaming in. It came on huge platters carried high in the air and then plunked on the table, everyone to help himself. Plunk, plunk, plunk, our table was getting heaped with chopped liver, herring, smoked salmon, huge loaves of twisted bread, mounds of raw vegetables which were put in bowls and covered with sour cream, pancakes stuffed with cheese, and one platter with an entire fish on it, head and all. The bowls and platters were whizzing around the table, and my plate was already pretty full when the fish arrived. Fatty long gloves had been sort of helping me shovel things out of the serving bowls, and now she speared a big hunk of fish, which had carrots and onions clinging to it, and thrust it on my plate in the one empty spot between the chopped liver and the cheese pancake.

"Watch out for the bones," she said, and we picked up our forks and went at it. After all the Dew Drop Inn leftovers, you can imagine how these things looked to my starved eyes! I started with the golden brown pancakes stuffed with the creamy white cheese, and had just gone to work on the chopped liver when it happened. She started to cough in a loud, funny way; then one of those gloved hands grabbed my arm and she sort of yelled out, "I've swallowed a bone!" and then she started to choke and make this terrible throwing-up sound trying to get the bone out of her throat. People began to jump up and crowd around and she was still grabbing my arm so hard I thought it would break.

The rabbi jumped down from the head table with a piece of bread in his hand. "Here, quick, swallow some bread," he said. "It will force down the bone." The woman was sucking hard to breathe but she managed to chew a piece of the bread and swallow it, but all that did was to lodge in her throat with the bone and then she couldn't breathe at all. Lester was pushing the people back and saying to give her air but there wasn't any air to give her. People kept yelling to call an ambulance and somebody ran to the telephone, but the woman wasn't able to breathe at all and her face was a terrible color and her eyes were pushed out. They had pulled her off my arm and were holding her up and pounding her on the back but she couldn't breathe. She wasn't even making any throat sounds any more. Spit with pieces of food in it was running out of her mouth and down her chin. I pushed away from the table. Everyone was yelling and screaming at everyone else to do something. My head felt funny, and when I started to move my legs almost gave way. I held on to a table for support and suddenly right there in front of me were all the rabbi's things, the Bible and the shawl and the knives and scissors. And there on a napkin was the circle of flesh the rabbi had cut off the baby's penis. It looked like a rubber washer.

I somehow managed to get out of the tent and up through the synagogue and out into the street before I got sick. The way I was sick you'd have thought I had eaten everything in that kitchen instead of just a golden pancake with some cheese in it.

Chapter Twenty-Three

Ella and her mother left the Avalon to go live with the aunt I had met that time at the movies. They were not very much behind with their rent. The aunt paid what they owed and they were able to just pack up and go.

Ella came to 309 to tell me goodbye. She was all in white, even a white straw hat with a big brim that sat on the back of her head. Stephanie was on her shoulder, in the crook of her neck. Their eyes were somewhat alike.

"I wish I was going to your graduation," Ella said.

"Oh, listen, it'll just be a stupid graduation like everybody else's."

"Still, who's going to be there?"

"I dunno. Maybe Lester."

"But you've got to have some relatives or *some*body."

"Why? I'll take my diploma with me when I go to see my mother, and that amounts to the same thing."

"No, it doesn't. You know it doesn't. Oh, I think it's beastly that you're all alone here and now we're leaving you, too."

"Well, I'm sorry to see you go, Ella. I really am. But you'll be a lot better off with your aunt, won't you?"

"I guess so." Her face was very sad. Very delicate and sad.

"What will you *do?*"

"Why, I'll just get along until my mother comes home. You know me!"

"It's not all that easy, and you know it."

Stephanie yawned and made a little squeak. "We're boring Stephanie," I said.

"Oh, Aaron," she said suddenly, "knowing you was the only good thing that happened to me at the Avalon!" She put her face up to mine and touched my lips with her lips, and then she turned and ran on back down the hall, Stephanie holding on to her very tight. I watched her white hat go bobbing around the corner and disappear. My God, I thought, I'll never see her again. It was like one more person dying.

Chapter Twenty-Four

I woke up at six o'clock on the morning of my graduation, too excited to sleep. I had taken out my graduation clothes the night before and lined everything up, so that first thing in the morning when I opened my eyes, there would be my black shoes on the window sill, white pants over a chair, blue jacket over another chair, and my shirt and tie on the table. I had washed out my socks, underwear, and a handkerchief the night before and hung them on a hanger in the window to dry. That St. Louis heat, they were probably dry before I fell asleep.

The white pants fit me absolutely perfect, and you know about the shoes, but I had a couple of problems with the shirt and coat. It turned out that Lester's idea of too small for him didn't mean small enough for me. The shirt wasn't so bad, because I turned the cuffs of the sleeves up and buttoned them that way and that made the arms all right. Then I found that if I didn't button the collar and just knotted the tie very hard into my Adam's apple it pushed the collar in and it didn't stick out from my throat. I really hate to see guys with ties on and the front of the collar is about thirty yards away from the guy's neck.

There wasn't much I could do about the coat, though. It was pretty roomy and the sleeves came down to about the middle of my palms, but Lester showed me that if I didn't button it and just let it hang open you couldn't tell if it fit or not. I tried walking around the room that way and looking in the mirror and I guess he was right. Besides, we weren't actually wearing our coats for the graduation ceremony. As I told you, the school had these robes which we were supposed to wear, and from the looks of them they had probably been given to the school by old Admiral Dewey himself. We each had to bring fifty cents for having them cleaned afterward, so there went the fifty cents my father had given me.

I must've tried on my clothes about a dozen times waiting for it to be time to go to the graduation. I told you how I'm always looking past the bad things on to the good things ahead, and I was sure looking forward to (1) playing the violin in the orchestra (I had stayed at school and practiced every afternoon), (2) standing up there with Christina Sebastian and reciting our parts, (3) the party Billy Tyzzer was having for all the boys afterward, (4) the dance in the evening, from seven to nine, when I was going to have my first real date with Christina. Actually, my first date with anybody. Lester had given me the dollar for the dance. I hadn't wanted to take it but it made Lester mad. Really mad. So I had to take it to keep peace.

We all assembled a half hour early to have a group picture taken in our robes, girls in front, boys in back, and if you wanted one for thirty-five cents you signed up. I would have liked one to take to my mother but it didn't look like I'd have thirty-five cents for quite a while.

Those of us who were in the orchestra took off our robes and went out and tuned up. When the parents and everybody were all seated, Mr. Kelly, the music teacher, came in and bowed and got a big hand. He knocked his baton a couple of times to get our attention, especially the little kids, then he swept his arms up in the air and we all set off on *Pomp and Circumstance*. The little kids kept speeding up, so I guess it sounded a little like we had an echo. But then came the part where me and Wanda Fabian, who played the cello, had this section all to ourselves. I didn't feel a bit nervous and my fingers hit every note right on the nose and so did Wanda, so nothing sounded sour and when we finished and everybody cranked up together again, the little kids in the lead, there was a nice round of applause for me and Wanda.

When it was over, Mr. Kelly took a couple more bows and us graduators went back and put on our robes and all of us trooped in and sat down on the stage, boys in black left and girls in white right. Our principal, Mr. Herbert P. Stellwagen, made a little speech and then we went up in pairs and gave our recitations. Christina Sebastian looked so pretty in her white gown with her blond hair falling out from under her cap that I almost forgot my opening lines. But you could tell we had really rehearsed and I gave it a lot of elocution and gestures. Even though Christina was nervous at first, we ended up with a bang.

The diplomas were handed out by Mr. Jansen K. Little, who was Superintendent of all the St. Louis elementary schools, and as we had rehearsed, we took with the left and shook with the right. Every kid's group in the audience gave him a big hand when he got his scroll from Jansen K. Little, but I began to get worried, as the alphabet got closer and closer to me, about what would happen when he called my name. I knew Lester was there—you couldn't miss him in his white T-shirt—but how would it sound with just one person clapping for you? I began to get fidgety and it got very warm in that robe of mine. I began to wish that Jansen K. Little would never get to my name.

But he did, and I went over and took with my left and shook with my right, and the only real applause I got was Lester's. He applauded as loud as he could, but that made it worse because it stood out all the more. There might have been a couple of other little palm taps here and there but you could barely hear them. It made me feel pretty miserable, I can tell you. On the way back to my seat, I kept my head down so's I wouldn't have to look at any of the other kids. Nancy Inwood was already going up to get her diploma so maybe it wasn't as noticeable as I had imagined. But when I sat down with my hands curved on the smooth round of the diploma, I felt pretty awful, and the good feelings from the violin and the recitation had washed away. Why is it, I sat there thinking, that the good things that pop up almost always get clobbered by these miserable darn things that seem to choke out everything like stinkweeds? I just sat there with my hands clenched around my diploma, grinding my teeth together, getting madder and madder, and shutting out, best I could, the bursts of applause each kid was getting.

Finally, thank God, it was over, and Herbert P. Stellwagen took over again and blabbed about how we would all be going forth to McKinley and Soldan High Schools, carrying with us the treasures of knowledge we had been given at Admiral Dewey. "I now take pleasure," Herbert P. Stellwagen said, "in presenting the Admiral George Dewey Achievement Award to that member of the graduating class who possesses that combination of scholastic ability and extracurricular accomplishment, good character and wholesome personality, sports ability and pride in his work and school—in short, that combination which best exemplifies what we seek in our young people going forth toward a higher education." He then announced my name, but to tell you the truth I was still feeling very sorry for myself about my diploma applause and my mind was so far away from Herbert P. Stellwagen that when I heard the biggest applause of the day, with all the kids around me applauding, I just applauded, too. Finally, Billy Tyzzer reached over and gave me a big shove on the back and I sort of woke up and everybody laughed and applauded all the harder.

I was all flushed and confused but I managed to walk stiff-legged over to where Herbert P. Stellwagen was standing with a big smile on his face. First he handed me a rolled-up scroll, which I took with my right and shook with my left, then tried to shake with my right but I stuck the scroll in Herbert P. Stellwagen's hand and everybody laughed. We finally got our hands together, and then he handed me a velvet box with a medal in it and finally a gift box, tied with a ribbon, that said, "P.T.A. Gift to Admiral George Dewey Achievement Award Winner."

I thanked Mr. Stellwagen and started to go back to my seat but he took my arm and held me there and said, "Aaron, I just want you to know in front of all these witnesses how much pride I take in having students like you pass through the learning halls of Admiral Dewey. As teachers, we have learned as much from you as you have learned from us. Thank you from the bottom of our hearts."

Everybody burst out applauding and this funny feeling suddenly swelled up inside me. I stood there with Herbert P. Stellwagen holding my arm, trying to keep this funny rising feeling down inside me, and I could see Mr. and Mrs. Tyzzer smiling at me and applauding, and Mr. and Mrs. Sebastian carrying on like I was their son-in-law, and all my teachers applauding, especially Miss Mathey, who was right in the front row and clapping hardest of all.

Afterward, everyone out on the sidewalk patted me on the back and smiled at me and I felt simply wonderful. Lester drove me back to the Avalon in the Marmon. He said there wasn't a pair of shoes up there on that stage that could've held a candle to mine.

I went on up to the room because I wasn't due at Billy Tyzzer's for about an hour. I opened the velvet box and took out the medal. It was bronze. Engraved in a circle, it said, "Admiral George Dewey Achievement Award 1933," and then engraved straight across the middle was my name. I opened the scroll. It said just about the same thing, with my name printed in big letters. I never knew that seeing your name like that could make you feel so important. Like it was proof that there you were—somebody. I suddenly missed my parents very much. My father, too, because he'd be running around the lobby and all up and down Delmar with the scroll and the medal, showing everybody with that overpride of his, but this time I wouldn't have minded because I was the Admiral Dewey Achievement Award champion. I wondered if the *St. Louis Post-Dispatch* would run it.

It didn't seem right that there I was with that beautiful medal and scroll and nobody to show it to. Sure, I'd take them out to show my mother when I went to Fee-Fee, but that wasn't the same. That second, right then and there, all dressed up and everything fresh, I wanted somebody who I could tell about what had happened to me in front of all those people at the Admiral Dewey graduation. But Ella was gone, Old Lady Heinson's door had been shut, and Minnie didn't care about anything except her rings, playing rummy, and feeding her stomach.

I washed my face and combed my hair and looked at myself in the mirror. I had to admit that there was something about a necktie that made you look like you had money in your pocket. I pinned my Achievement Award medal onto my lapel but decided not to carry the scroll in my pocket because the guys at Billy Tyzzer's might have thought I was showing off. So I took some thumbtacks out of the oilcloth on the table and stuck the diploma onto the door so's every time I left the room it would be there for me to look at. It looked beautiful stuck up there like that with my name across it.

I had opened the door to leave when I suddenly remembered the P.T.A. present. Criminy, how could I forget a thing like that? The box was heavy. I took off the ribbon carefully and unwrapped the gold paper so's not to spoil it. Inside the cardboard box there was white tissue paper. And inside the tissue paper was a large book—*The Pathfinder*, by James Fenimore Cooper.

I had a good time at Billy Tyzzer's party except for the end, and that was awful. The party was in the back yard, and we played softball and had hot dogs and ice cream and a watermelon race. Each team had a watermelon and we had to race with it in a relay and then slice it open, divide it up, and the first team to eat its watermelon won. We were doing all right except for Perry Armbuster, who kept being very polite and taking the seeds out of his mouth and putting them on his plate instead of just spitting them out on the lawn like everyone else. But it was fun even though we didn't win.

All that part of the party was fine, but then at the end came two hard knocks. One was that Billy Tyzzer discussed the dance with me. First he asked me if I was sending Christina a corsage of one gardenia or two. He said the guys who were sending two were just showing off, and he hoped I was just sending one like he was. He then said that after the dance his father and two other fathers were going to take a group in their cars to Medart's on Clayton Road for hamburgers and shakes, and I was one of those invited to come, with Christina. Everyone was going to chip in a dollar and that way there wouldn't be all that divvying up at the end. He told me where to meet after the dance. That was the first knock.

The second was when I went to the toilet before I left. I was in the toilet when several of the guys came into Billy's room and they didn't know I was in the toilet.

"Hey, did you see that jacket Big A Little a is wearing?"

"That's not a jacket, that's his overcoat."

"Does he have a big brother?"

"Naw, he's just planning for the future. That's the way it is with Achievement Award winners."

"What I like is the shirt. The collar is puckered like it's on a drawstring."

"Maybe he thinks it's a costume party."

"He'd win first prize, all right."

They all had a good laugh. Of course I knew who belonged to the voices, especially Rudy Lavolette, who was jealous because he had wanted to go to the dance with Christina. I waited until I was sure they were gone before I came out. All the way home I kept telling myself I didn't care what they thought of my jacket and shirt, they were probably just jealous of my Achievement Award, but when I got back to the room and started to think about the dance I got more and more deflated. I didn't know about the gardenias; no one had told me. I didn't even know what a gardenia looked like, for crying out loud. On the way back to the hotel, I had gone into the Woodbine florist and he had shown me one through the icebox window that he said I could have for fifty cents. So that, plus going to Medart's, was a dollar-fifty and it could just as well have been five hundred. I stood in front of the mirror and looked at myself. Maybe they were right. Maybe that's how I looked. I took off Lester's jacket and threw it against the wall above the table and it landed on the table in a heap.

Even if I had a jacket that fit, how could I possibly get my hands on a dollar-fifty? There was the radio but I didn't know how to pawn things, and besides I just couldn't do that to my father, even if they let twelve-year-old boys pawn radios, which I doubted. Lester wasn't there. When he dropped me off, he had said that he was driving to Rolla and that he was going to stay overnight.

The more I thought about how things were, the more I knew I couldn't go to the dance. But I didn't know what to do about Christina.

"Christina Sebastian?"

"Yes."

"This is Dr. Diamond calling. I have bad news for you. Aaron is at death's door but he says for you not to worry, that he'll pull through and you're to go to the dance and have fun."

"Hello, Christina Sebastian? This is police headquarters. Aaron has been kidnapped and. . . ."

"Hello, Christina Sebastian? This is the White House calling. Mr. Roosevelt has sent for Aaron. . . ."

"Christina Sebastian, it is my duty to inform you that the *Nautilus* is forty-eight hours overdue and it is feared that Aaron and the complement of thirty-six men are trapped on the bottom of the sea. . . ."

What I wanted to do was hide there in the room and do nothing. But I just couldn't stand Christina up, could I? She had a right to go to the dance in her pretty new dress with a gardenia pinned on it, didn't she? And to go to Medart's afterward with a guy who looked like something, and have a hamburger and shake. She had the right, didn't she?

I really didn't know what to do. Usually when things really squeeze me I can think of something, some way to help myself, but no matter which way my mind squirmed around it seemed hopeless. Finally, knowing it was hopeless but trying anyway, I went down and asked Johnny Cafferetta. Just for a dollar. To loan it to me till my father got back. He said he would have if he could have but he couldn't. In fact, he said he didn't know if he could open his doors one day to the next. So all that did was give me a new worry whether Johnny would go out of business and I'd have nowhere to eat.

I'm ashamed to admit that it even flicked across my mind that I might sell Skippy and his cage to Mr. Farley. But it was only a flicker. I had my cigar bands and my bag of marbles, but who would buy those in the next hour? No, you see, it was hopeless. In the back of my mind was forming the only solution I could think of. I didn't want to think about it, but the more I couldn't think of anything else, the more this rotten solution nudged itself up to the front of my mind, and I finally realized, the time being what it was, that it was just about the only thing I could do.

I went down the hall to the room with the telephone I used when I was soliciting for the gas workers' picnic. I looked up Rudy Lavolette's phone number in the book that was under the phone.

"Hey, Rudy, listen, this is Aaron. This thing has come up, I know it's at the last minute, but I've developed this terrific stomachache and the doctor thinks it might be my appendix, and I wondered if you could take Christina Sebastian to the dance."

"Oh . . . sure. You bet."

"I'm sort of in bed now and I've got to keep ice on my stomach, so I wondered if you would call her and explain about everything and tell her I'll call her tomorrow."

"What if you're in the hospital?"

"Yeah, well, I'll call her from the hospital."

"Sure, Aaron, sure thing. Gosh, that's a tough break."

"I don't feel like dancing, I can tell you."

"Well, don't worry about anything. Oh, one thing—have you sent her a corsage?"

"Uh, not yet. Matter of fact, I was going to pick one up on my way."

"Gosh, I'd better hurry out and get one."

"But call her first."

"Oh, I will, I will. And I hope you'll be okay."

"Oh, sure, don't worry about me. I've got an appendix like iron."

I went back and took off my necktie and rolled up the sleeves of my shirt. I unpinned the Achievement Award medal from the jacket and put it on the crown of my Feltie. Then I went on out and walked the gutter all the way down to Grand Avenue, looking for cigar bands and thinking about things. It was just like Old Lady Heinson said when she heard her nephew was dead. The Lord giveth and the Lord taketh away. I guess when you came right down to it, the Bible made a lot of sense.

Chapter Twenty-Five

The way to get to the Fee-Fee Sanatorium, I found out, was to take the Delmar streetcar to the end of the line and the Creve Coeur trolley after that. There were no transfers and each ride cost a nickel. I sold Danny Desot my agate shooter, ten blueys, and his pick of fifty baseball cards for his weekly allowance of twenty cents to finance the trip. The reason it's called a trolley instead of a streetcar is because it's different. I had never been on a trolley before. The seats were sideways—not seats really, but two benches back to back and you faced the sides but there weren't any sides. That was the peachy part of it. You could step up into the trolley anywhere and you could hang on to a post while standing outside on the boarding step if it was crowded, but it wasn't that crowded. It was a really nice ride. Trees and country all the way through Creve Coeur and we even passed a lake where men in straw hats were fishing.

The conductor was a jolly man with a white mustache who kept red-striped peppermints in his vest pocket and told me stories about how it was out that way when he was a boy and the Indians and then the French lived there.

"You know what Creve Coeur means, son?"

"No, sir."

"Broken Heart." He handed me a peppermint and unwrapped one for himself. "Yes, Busted Heart in French. I guess this was pretty wild country back then and it caused a lot of heartbreak. There's a conductor on the other run, Linus Tremaine, got a cock 'n' bull story about an Indian princess and a French captain madly in love and he is killed by a jealous brave and she dies of a broken heart, so that's why it's Creve Coeur, but I'll tell you, m'boy, that Tremaine drinks a lot, and when the Irish drink, as you'll find out, they tend to tell stories that cause a tear. You're not Irish, are you?"

My mother was on the second floor of a white frame building that had a screened porch running all around it. There was bed after bed after bed all along this screen, and all you heard was coughing, the kind where something comes up at the end. My father had explained to me that the cure for my mother was lots of fresh air and sunshine and things like cream and eggs to eat.

I went to the information desk to find out where she was and to send my parcel of things up to her. When I finally located her by walking around the building and looking up at the people in the beds, she already had my parcel. She was so glad to see me, and me to see her. She looked much better. But it wasn't very private talking to her with everybody in their beds on the first floor and second floor listening. They didn't have anything else to do, so they just looked out at me and listened. I felt like I was on the stage. There were two other visitors standing on the lawn talking up to people in the beds, but I swear everyone was listening to me.

There were a lot of things I wanted to tell my mother but I'd have had more privacy on the *Major Bowes Amateur Hour*. While we were talking, I could see that some patients were walking along the aisles between the beds with tin cups in their hands. When they coughed and brought stuff up, they spit it into the tin cups. The people in the beds had tin cups, too, that they spit into, but all the time I was there my mother never coughed once.

We talked about my father and what he had written in the letters to us, and I told her all the details about my graduation. She looked at my scroll and my medal and her face was all happiness. I had wanted to wear my new black shoes and my white pants, but then I didn't think I should tell my mother how I had got them or lie to her about them.

I stayed on the lawn trying to think of things to talk about until the bell rang that meant visitors had to leave. I had almost forgotten to tell her that her last shipment from the Windy City Hosiery Company had arrived. This bothered her.

"Oh, dear," she said. "I'd forgotten. They have to be delivered."

"I'll deliver them," I said. "Where do they go?"

"No, I don't think you should . . . but. . . ."

"Why not? It's in East St. Louis, isn't it? Well, I know where East St. Louis is."

My mother was suddenly very disturbed, which mustn't've been very good for her. I was sorry I had told her about the Windy City package.

"Well, I guess I have to send you, A," she said. "It's best to arrive there around three o'clock."

"Okay. School's over now."

"You look in my order book under Betty Haskins. She's a real nice woman. Just tell her I'm sick. You just go there and go right home, hear? Oh, if only your father were here to do it."

I couldn't imagine why she was so upset. It wasn't a big box and God knows it wasn't heavy with all those silk things in it, and if I could get myself to Creve Coeur I could certainly get myself to East St. Louis.

"Well, I guess it will be all right but be careful changing streetcars. When you collect the money, twenty dollars goes to the company. You just take it to the post office and get a money order. The two-seventy-five commission—you keep the seventy-five cents and mail me a two-dollar bill inside one of your letters so no one can see the money through the envelope."

The next day, I left the Avalon around two o'clock with the Windy City package and changed streetcars at the Eads Bridge.

I had never been to East St. Louis before, but it was just across the Mississippi and a cinch to find. As the streetcar started across the bridge, we passed through a million shacks in a Hooverville that was packed in between where the bridge started and the edge of the water. They were the worst-looking dumps I ever saw, with hunks of rusted tin, cardboard, and old boards patched around to form sides and roofs. There were little kids and wives living in them and laundry lines with ragged clothes on them strung between the shacks. I had been through a couple of other St. Louis Hoovervilles but this was by far the worst.

The streetcar passed low over the shacks and little kids in dirty rags stared at us as we went by. I was looking at this one starved kid with a dirty face, holding a one-legged Raggedy Ann, when my eyes fell on Mr. Evans leaning against a shack. Mr. Evans, the piano-tuner from 328.

I yelled at him, "Mr. Evans! It's me! Aaron!"

He looked startled; then he squinted at my streetcar and I put my head out of the window and waved so he could see me. He nodded his head and put up his hand but not in a wave. More like he was taking an oath in court. The streetcar was pulling away from the Hooverville now, rising on the bridge tracks, and Mr. Evans got smaller and smaller as we rose up over the muddy waters of the Mississippi. I kept watching Mr. Evans till he disappeared.

When I got off the streetcar, I had to do a lot of walking and asking before I found the street Betty Haskins lived on. I had never been in East St. Louis before, and one look at it made me wonder why anyone lived there when they could live across the river in St. Louis proper. It was dirty and ugly and all the men you passed in the street looked like they were packing gats or had a disease. Of course, St. Louis was dirty and some mornings the black smoke shut out the sun and burned your eyes so bad it made you cry, but East St. Louis made you *feel* dirty, if you know what I mean. And it was even hotter than St. Louis.

This street Betty Haskins lived on was not paved and had holes and gullies in it. The houses all looked alike, with stoops of wooden stairs going up from the sidewalk. From the looks of the street and houses, I couldn't believe that this was where the rich ladies lived who could afford to buy my mother's silk things.

The building that Betty Haskins lived in had four flats in it, two downstairs and two upstairs. I pushed the button over her name and waited in the East St. Louis sun with flies buzzing at me off the screen. It was exactly three o'clock. Suddenly there was a click and a lady's voice said, "Hello, who's there?" I nearly fell down the steps. The door hadn't opened and there was no one around and here was some woman talking to me! "Hello? Somebody there?" the woman asked. Now I located the voice. It was coming out of a box above the bell, but I didn't know how to speak back at it. So I just said "Hello" to see what would happen.

"Yes?" the voice said.

"I'm here to see Betty Haskins," I said.

"Who are you?"

"I have some things for her from the Windy City Hosiery Company. My mother is sick and I've come to deliver them."

"Oh, sure, honey, whyn't you say so? Come on up."

There was a loud buzz that also scared the life out of me, but I caught on that that meant I could open the door. There was a long flight of narrow stairs going up to the second floor. I got a good grip on the Windy City box and started up the stairs. There was a very peculiar smell pouring down the stairs from above. By the time I got to the top, I remembered the smell. There was a gypsy lady around on Enright who had this fortune-telling parlor in the basement and I had smelled it there. I used to give out circulars for her, ten cents from after school to six o'clock, and she always had a thick stump of incense smoking away. Nobody much went to see her and she finally moved away. When people aren't eating regularly, I guess they don't believe much in fortune-tellers.

When I got to the top of the stairs, I could scarcely see where I was. There were these dim orange lights with fringed shades over them and lots of beaded curtains. I was in a sort of corridor with several closed doors, and down at one end was a lighted room. I could hear voices and music coming from that room. One of the doors opened and a woman came out.

"Why, aren't you cute!" she said to me. "Are you Annie's boy?"

"Yes, Ma'am."

"That's too bad that's she's sick. Just bring the package in here."

I carried the package into her room and she shut the door. There were more orange lights there but I could see better. The room was all full of silks and satins, and there was a big bed in the middle of it with a silk canopy over it and gold angels at the corners holding the silk. All the furniture was covered with satiny colors and plump pillows.

"Well, now, let's see what you've brought. Just open it up on this couch."

I had expected Betty Haskins to look like Mrs. Tyzzer or Mrs. Sebastian or somebody like that. Instead, she was a movie star. You never saw anybody so gorgeous. She had red hair and super white teeth and she was wearing a black silk kimono with red flowers on it. My opinion of East St. Louis suddenly improved, because if somebody that gorgeous who was rich chose to live there, there must be something to say for it.

I opened the box and she started to take out things and lay them on the bed. She picked up a silk sort of nightgown, I guess it was, with lacy junk in front, and held it up against her and looked at herself in the wall mirror. It was pretty embarrassing.

"I can wait out in the corridor," I said.

"Oh, you don't have to do that, honey," she said. "I'll just slip on this nightie to be sure it isn't too tight." She went behind a screen in the corner, and came out a second later wearing the nightie. I was sure embarrassed. "Now let's see," she said, and she went over to the bed and laid on it and stretched and rolled from side to side, testing out the nightie. I tried not to look at her, but I looked. Finally she got up. "Your mother sure has nice things," she said; then she went to the door, opened it, and stepped out into the corridor. "Rose!" she called out. "Are you busy? Theodora! You got a minute?"

In came two more movie stars. The one called Rose had a little too much rouge and lipstick on, but the Theodora one had black hair that hung all the way down her back and she looked 100 percent like Greta Garbo but with black hair. She reeked of perfume. She was wearing the shortest red satin shorts I ever saw and a bra to match and nothing else. Not even shoes. Rose had on a kimono like Betty Haskins', only white with pink flamingos.

"This is Annie's boy, isn't he cute?" Betty Haskins said to the others, and she pinched my cheek. Her hand had a lot of perfume on it. Rose said something on the q.t. to Theodora and they both giggled. They went through all the things in the box and looked at everything carefully. Rose tried on a few things behind the screen which she paraded out in to show the others.

A colored woman dressed in a maid's uniform, only the skirt was so short you could see she was wearing ruffled panties, came to the door. "Miss Theodora," she said, "your guest is here." Theodora took some money out from the center of her bra and so did Rose from inside her kimono, and they picked up their Windy City things and left. Betty Haskins looked at the bill and added some money of her own, and I counted it and it came to exactly the right amount. A bell tingled and she went over to the wall where there was an earpiece hanging on a hook. She put it against her ear and talked into a talk place in the wall. "Hello, who's there? . . . Oh, hello, honey, come right on up." She hung up and pushed a button and I could hear a buzzing far below. She thanked me for coming, said she hoped my mother would be better, and opened the door for me. She certainly had good manners.

I put the money in my pocket, first checking around with my fingers to be sure there weren't any holes in it, and I said goodbye and left. As I got to the stairs, there was a fat man mopping his head with a handkerchief just coming up. He took a look at me and his eyes popped open. As I started down the stairs, I heard him say hello to Betty Haskins and something about robbing the cradle and they both laughed. The music from the room at the end of the hall was louder, a woman singing to a banjo, and the incense was so strong it tickled my nose.

Going down those stairs, it suddenly dawned on me where I was. I had just read a book about a young woman named Nana by Emile Zola that was on the forbidden list at school, and also some absolutely forbidden stories by Guy de Maupassant, especially one about a woman who lived in a room with her little son, and when men would come up to visit her she would hide the little son in the closet. She would put him on a chair and tell him to sit there and not make a sound. But one night he fell asleep and fell off the chair, and the man visiting his mother yanked open the door and saw him and was furious and stormed away without giving his mother any money. The little boy felt terrible and cried, but his mother was nice and loving and tried to make him feel better. I thought it was an absolutely wonderful story, but until that moment it was something that happened in faraway France and not in East St. Louis, Illinois.

But now that I knew where I was, I had to have a look at that room at the end of the corridor. I went back up the stairs, carefully. All the other doors were closed. I tiptoed down the corridor toward the room where the music was. There was a beaded curtain over the door. I stayed close to the wall, then carefully peeked through the beads. It was a living room, with sofas and easy chairs and lights with fringed shades. Against one wall there was a bar with all kinds of bottles of whiskey on it, and the colored maid was pouring drinks. The girl who was singing and playing the banjo had on red pajamas and a red flower in her hair, and I'll bet she wasn't more than fifteen or sixteen. The fat guy was sitting in one of the chairs and Betty Haskins was sitting on his lap, with her arm around his fat neck. In another chair, Rose was sitting on the lap of a big guy with tattoos on his arms who was having a drink. The colored maid brought the drinks she had been mixing to the fat guy and Betty Haskins. The tattooed guy was rubbing his hand on Rose's leg, but she was singing along to the banjo and not paying any attention.

"You gonna spend the afternoon singin' or we gonna get down to business?" the tattooed guy asked.

"I thought you wanted to finish your drink," Rose said.

"Sure," said the tattooed guy, "but do I have to finish it here?" Rose got up and so did tattoo, and I turned and got away from there as fast as I could. As I reached the top of the stairs, I could hear the rattle of them coming through the beaded curtain. I went down two at a time and out the door and down the street, and my heart was really thumping when I got to the streetcar stop. There was a hot breeze blowing from the river but the incense was still strong in my nose. I could smell it all the next day.

Chapter Twenty-Six

All in all, there were now fifteen locks on the third floor and I was sure glad my father had paid in seventeen dollars before he left. The hallway looked like a prison, with all those locks hanging from the doors. I couldn't help the feeling I had there were people locked in, not out. The locks made the hallway very spooky to walk in, and as if that wasn't bad enough, this terrible thing happened with 342.

I was coming in the lobby from having had my supper of meatballs, turnips, and bread pudding at the Dew Drop Inn when I noticed this ambulance double-parked in front of the hotel. Just then, I heard some bustling as the hotel doors opened and two men in white jackets came out pushing a stretcher on wheels. They passed right under my nose. On the stretcher was a body all covered with a sheet except for the shoes, men's shoes, which stuck out from under one end. I watched them push the stretcher up to the back of the ambulance and slide it inside. One man closed the ambulance doors while the other went around and got behind the wheel. The man who closed the doors had a stethoscope sticking out of his pocket. He got in beside the driver and they drove away with their light flashing but no siren.

Arletta, the elevator girl, was standing in the doorway, watching them. "What happened, Arletta? Who was that?"

"You know that Mr. Barnaway or Borroway or whatever his name was in 342? The one who walked with a cane?"

I knew who she meant. He was the kind of man who looked at you but never smiled or said hello.

"Well, Ben locked him out this afternoon. I took him up about five o'clock and I guess that's when he discovered he was locked out."

"Didn't you tell him?"

"I don't tell nobody nothin'. This locking out is a sin and I have nothing to do with it, I just leave myself out of it. Anyway, about half an hour ago, Maggie went down to her broom closet at that end of the hall and she found Mr. Barnaway or Borroway hanging in front of his door. She come running down the hall and called me and I went around to have a look. He had cut the ropes that pull the hall curtains and tied them together and got up on the hall table and tied one end of the rope around the transom and the other end around his neck. Then he just stepped off the table, and he must have been hanging there with his tongue out and his eyes popped ever since I brought him up. Ben came up and cut him down but it was way too late. He fell to the floor like a sack of corn meal. This is his cane." She was holding his cane in her right hand. "I wonder what we should do with it? It don't seem right to lock it up."

Chapter Twenty-Seven

July came in so hot I had to get up during the night and pour water on the sheets so's I could sleep. The days were even hotter. Without school, life was very dull and lonesome. Billy Tyzzer had gone away to camp and Danny wasn't talking to me because the agate shooter had split when he plunked an ironie with it and he claimed it must have had a crack in it when I sold it to him, which it hadn't. You don't plunk an ironie with an agate shooter, that's all. But you couldn't tell Danny that. As for Lester, ever since he got his Marmon he was never around.

It was very boring to stay in the room and about the only excitement I had was this water-bug attack. The only steady bugs we had in the Avalon were roaches and water bugs. No lice, bed-bugs, or anything like that. There was a mouse once that used to run along the molding under the ceiling, but my father caught him by the tail in a trap and he was the only one. The roaches were always around, but the water bugs came in spasms. They were coal black and the hugest things you ever saw. The first time I saw one, I thought the mouse had come back. They had two giant feelers that sprouted out of their heads like lobster claws, and their legs had jagged points all over them. They were not as fast as roaches, but they were plenty fast for their size. Everyone said they were absolutely harmless, but you could never make me believe that anything that big and ugly was harmless.

Even though they scared the living daylight out of me, I always attacked them like they were vicious Martians. I kept my Water Bug Boomer all ready in the closet, and the minute I caught sight of a big black sinister water bug, I grabbed my Boomer and attacked. The Boomer was made of newspapers rolled and tied in such a way that it was flat on top and round on the bottom, which was the handle. Of course, I used it on roaches, too, but mostly it was there for water bugs. On spying a water bug, I'd sound the siren, dash to the closet, grab the old Boomer, and then wham! down I'd crash on that water bug like it was a Hun tank. Water bugs squashed white, roaches squashed yellow. Also, you didn't see many roaches except when it was dark and the lights went on, but water bugs were on the go night and day.

I hadn't seen a water bug in weeks, but now I was squashing six or seven with my Boomer every day. Having to be on the lookout for them all the time made me pretty nervous, but it also gave me something to do.

I hung around the tennis courts some, but I didn't have much luck finding kids to play with. Mostly when people go to a tennis court, they go with someone to play with, or with doubles.

So it was sure a welcome surprise when there was a rap on the door and there stood Sid Gutman with his chomped cigar in his laughing face. "Hey, there, Aaron, you rascal, come and give your Uncle Sid a big hug!" He had a high, raspy voice that somehow made you feel good just to hear it. No wonder he was such a good salesman. And what a laugh he had! His belly would shake and his breath would come out through his teeth in great puffs. He grabbed me and pulled me up against his full round belly and gave me a tremendous hug. Then in he came, talking a mile a minute and laughing and asking questions about how my mother was and what did I hear from my father. The thing about Sid Gutman that was so wonderful was that he was cheerful from the inside out.

He traveled a lot and wasn't around very much, but when he *was* around he made everything brighten up. He took off his jacket and went over to the sink and washed up. He wore a thin black belt around his large middle, with a big gold buckle on it that spelled "SID" in diamonds. Or what looked like diamonds. He had a gold ring with a purple stone in it on his tea finger, and a stickpin in his tie that was the gold head of an Arab, with diamonds as his eyes and a pearl as his turban. He kept talking even while he was washing his face, telling me to get ready, he was only in town for the day and we were going to put on the feedbag and then do a little important shopping. I put on my black shoes and number 1 white pants, and we went out of that door like it was Christmas.

Sid Gutman had his car outside, a Graham 8, and we drove downtown to Leonard's for a lunch of corned-beef sandwiches on poppy-seed rolls and cheesecake. Poor Arnie, I wondered what he would do with his surplus baloney.

"Now, you know what the date is?" Sid Gutman asked. "July 3rd. You got your firecrackers?"

When I said I didn't have any firecrackers, he put on this horrified act. "You don't have your fireworks? Call yourself a patriotic American? I'm ashamed of you. Let's have another piece of cheesecake, then off we go for fireworks!"

After lunch we got in the car and Sid Gutman drove hilariously, pretending like it was an emergency, our getting to the fireworks. He drove to a roadside stand that had a big sign in front, "AN ACRE OF FIREWORKS." He took a market basket from a pile at the entrance and hung it on my arm. Then he began to go up and down the aisles, piling firecrackers into the wicker basket, sparklers, rockets, pinwheels, fountains, torpedoes, flares, Chinese crackers, Roman candles, snakes, everything, and I began to put things in the basket, too, the beautiful pile mounting up and up, so exciting I began to giggle and I couldn't stop and Sid Gutman kept loading things in the basket and I was giggling so hard I could scarcely keep up with him as he hurried up and down the aisles, plucking those beautiful firecrackers from their heaps and tossing them in the basket, and at the end they filled two big brown paper bags and cost $7.65. Can you imagine, $7.65 worth of firecrackers? Nothing but firecrackers. It was the niftiest afternoon of my life.

On the way through the lobby, after Sid Gutman had dropped me off, Danny Desot saw me with those two paper bags, and right then and there he forgot about that agate shooter.

By the time it got dark the following night, everybody in the hotel had heard about my fireworks. I set them off in the middle of the parking lot and there was quite a crowd. Even the taxi men from the Yellow Cab Company came out and stood in the alley and watched. I let Danny be my assistant.

After the first rockets went up, kids from all over the neighborhood came running and scooted under and around the grownups to get in front. I filled the sky with colors, and there wasn't a rocket that didn't go up true. I loved the smell of the rocket powder and the after-smell of the pinwheels. Some of the rockets shot up dead straight overhead and their colors showered right down on us. Me and Danny crisscrossed the Roman candles so that the fireballs passed each other in the sky, and the crowd went "Ooh!" and "Ah!" and "Look at that!" and I felt like a master magician showing them tricks they had never seen before.

When it was over and all that was left was the cracked smoke that hung in the air, I went up alone to the roof of the hotel with a box of giant sparklers I had saved. I stuck them in a line into the soft tar of the roof and then I lighted all of them at once. I sat down on the roof close to them and watched them burn. Some of the brilliant white sparks leaped onto me. The red-hot stems glowed through the white shower and I was Captain Nemo on my way to Venus. We were climbing the Milky Way, using the stars as a ladder, and once I got there I'd never have to come back.

Chapter Twenty-Eight

How was I to know that that day with the fireworks was the last fun day there would be? After that it was like a mud slide, coming down on you one slide after another. I knew about mud slides, all right. When we had lived on Concordia Lane in South St. Louis, there was a mountain of clay nearby where a brick factory operated. Us kids played on the mountain and dug caves in it and climbed all over it. But one afternoon after school, when it had been raining for a couple of days, we were out on the mountain in our rain clothes playing King of the Hill when the gooey mud at the top got unstuck and started to slide down on top of us. We scrambled around and got out of the way of it, but another slide was coming right on top of the first one and then another, and two of the kids got buried in it. We tried to dig them out but the mud kept on sliding down from the top. The workmen at the brick factory were all gone home, so we had to do the best we could. There was one gigantic slide that buried all of us, which was more scary than anything you can imagine, but we dug ourselves out of it and kept on trying to find those first two kids. We finally found one, a skinny little seven-year-old who shouldn't have been playing with us nine-year-olds in the first place. He was more scared than anything else, and when we dug the clay out of his nose he was all right. But we couldn't find the other kid, and by the time help came and they found him and rushed him to the hospital, it was too late.

So you can see I know about mud slides.

The Avalon mud slide started with Maggie, of all people. Usually whenever I heard the scuffle of her slippers and the squeak of her carpet sweeper coming down the hall, I perked up because she was the only friend I'd get to talk to in the morning. She always came in so cheerful, and smiling her three teeth and asking about my health and discussing all the gossip in the hotel. But this particular morning I'm referring to, she didn't come in cheerful at all.

She slapped her dust rag around a little and shoved her carpet sweeper back and forth in one place, but you could tell her heart wasn't in it. "I have some terrible news for us," she said, finally. "Old Mrs. Heinson done died yestidday." That was terrible news, all right. "She done took to her bed the day that nephoo o' hers died an' she kep' the door locked an' wouldn't let a pusson in but me. I'd go in there with m'passkey an' bring her some tea an' she took that, but you could tell she'd been punkchured an' th' air was leakin' outta her, same as a rubber tire. They're buryin' her this afternoon at the Watkins & Brothers Fun'ral Pa'lor. I'm gonna go, I guess, if'n they'll let me in. But I doan think they have a colored section."

"Me, too, Maggie."

"Well, that's fine. I'll meetchu at the corner at four o'clock after work an' we'll go in together. I'll hold you by th' hand an' say I'm your guvruness an' thataway they'll let me in." She started to leave, "Oh, almost forgot, last time I seen her she gimme this for you." She took Old Lady Heinson's little Bible with the silver edges out of her big apron pocket and gave it to me.

"I wish I could've seen her before she died," I said.

"Wal, she was funny thataway, didn't like to show herself if'n she warn't fixed up pretty and all powdered with that special jasmine she used. But she liked you tolerable much, I know that f'sure. You're the only one I know she give a present to."

I rubbed the leather and silver of Old Lady Heinson's Bible between my two palms. Then I opened it. Inside the cover there were four entries, one below the other:

For my dear wife on her 30th birthday with love,

Raymond, 1799

For our son and his bride, may they prosper,

Mother & Father, 1828

For my daughter Dora on her 21st birthday, to help light her way.

Papa, 1870

Dear Aaron, I pass to you the dearest thing I own and hope it will sustain your life as well as it did mine.

Your affectionate friend,
Dora M. Heinson, 1933

We were the only Heinson people at the funeral parlor, me and Maggie, and we just sat there awhile in the little room where the casket was, and thought about Old Lady Heinson. The casket was closed and Maggie went over and put the little bunch of daisies she had brought on top of it. There weren't any other flowers. After a while, we got up and left. I asked the man at the door where she was going to be buried. He said she wasn't. She was going to be cremated.

Maggie took my hand and we walked the few blocks to her car stop. I felt all hollowed out. The palm of Maggie's hand on mine was smooth and hard, and it was much lighter in color than the back of her hand. I asked her about that. She smiled at me and looked at her palm like it belonged to somebody else.

"The black's plumb wore off there," she said. "I guess nothin' wears as hard as black people's hands." I stood with her in the car stop till the streetcar came, and then I went on back to the hotel.

So, Old Lady Heinson was mud slide number 1. I guess she died of a Creve Coeur.

I checked the 309 box to see if there was a letter from my father. My mother wrote to me every day and her letters came in the morning mail, but I thought there might be a letter from my father. Last time I had heard from him he was in Kansas.

There was a letter all right, but it wasn't from my father but addressed to him. It wasn't until I got to the room that I noticed it was in an Avalon Hotel envelope. I thought I better open it.

TO THE OCCUPANT OF ROOM 309

This is to inform you that unless we receive a payment of at least 50 percent of your arrears within the next five days, we will be forced to terminate your occupancy.

At the end of that period, if payment has not been received, in accordance with Section 19 of the Innkeepers' Ordinances of the State of Missouri, we are empowered to seize all possessions and property of yours contained in the aforementioned premises.

THE MANAGEMENT

Oh, that Desot! How could he? He took the seventeen dollars, didn't he? I grabbed my Feltie and tore out of there down to the lobby. Mr. Desot wasn't there. I didn't wait for the elevator but tore up the stairs to the fourth floor and knocked on his door. Mrs. Desot and Danny were there, but Mrs. Desot said that Mr. Desot was over at the bank. She invited me to sit down and wait for him. Right away she started to paw around with Danny and show me where he had come leaping out of her stomach, but I certainly wasn't in the mood for *that* so I excused myself and beat it out of there and back down to the lobby.

Mr. Desot arrived about a half hour later. I showed him the letter and he took me back to his tiny office at the rear of the lobby. He sat down behind his desk and I sat on an old wooden chair in front of him. His hair was just as slick as always, but his face was more worried and his eyes were all black underneath.

"Aaron, I want you to understand about this," he said. "The bank runs the hotel, not me. You see, I had a big loan of money from them and I couldn't repay it, so now they are in charge of the hotel. I'm just sort of their manager now. I have no say. They seem to want to get everybody off the third floor and just rent rooms on the second floor to the dance-hall girls and that sort of thing. That's where the money is—the dance hall. They're turning the hotel into a . . . well, a not very nice place."

"But *five days*, Mr. Desot! My father is in Kansas someplace, I don't even know where."

"I know," he said in a very understanding voice. "All I can say is you better make arrangements to stay with relatives. I have no power, nothing to say. I've been twenty-five years in this hotel— I started here as assistant manager—and now I just came from the bank and they told me I must fire Maggie and Arletta at the end of the week. No more cleaning service on the third floor and no more elevator. Maggie's been in this hotel since it was built."

"Maybe I should go over and talk to the bank and explain about my father being away and all."

"You can go, Aaron, but banks don't talk to twelve-year-old boys. They don't talk to anyone who doesn't have money. They only care about money. Not about people. You better call your relatives. I'm very sorry. So very sorry."

So, that was mud slide number 2.

I tore up to Lester's door praying he'd be there, but I didn't even knock since I could see the edges of the two notes I'd already left, sticking out from under the door. Well, there were five days and maybe he'd come back from wherever he was. God, he *had* to come back! Call relatives—what relatives? And even if I had relatives to stay with, the minute I left that room after the five days were up, Ben would slap his ugly lock on the door and everything we owned would be gone.

What could I do? Listen, I had to do *something!* But the McShanes were gone, Old Lady Heinson was dead, Lester wasn't around, Sid Gutman was away, traveling his territory, wherever that was. There was my aunt and uncle in Keokuk, but they had already written to my father about a hundred times saying that if he didn't pay up what he owed for my brother they would have to send him home. I think it came to fourteen dollars. My uncle said that even at two dollars a week they were losing money on feeding him and they couldn't afford it. My father said it was only a bluff, but what do you think they would say if I wrote to Keokuk and asked them for $77.50?

There was my grandfather (hah!), but his Chicago restaurant had just gone broke and he had moved his family to Columbus or somewhere, to try to open another one. When she had told me about this, my mother had said it was a good sign that my grandfather hadn't tried to burn down his Chicago restaurant. But I couldn't see the good sign in that.

Then there was Minnie, but I already told you how nutty she was about money. Still in all, I'd have to think about her. While I was turning all this around in my head, the music began to blare up from the Good Times Taxi Dance hall and it set me to thinking about what Mr. Desot had said about the dance hall making so much money. It suddenly occurred to me that since I lived in the hotel maybe I could get some kind of job there. Then I could tell the bank I'd give them all my wages, and maybe they'd settle for that. I could sell tickets or sweep up or anything. Maybe work behind the refreshment counter. After all, I had had my own Nehi stand.

My mother had always forbidden me to set foot in the Good Times basement, but this was different. I washed up and went on down there. The main entrance was on the Delmar side of the

Avalon, but there was also stairs to go down from the lobby. The music was twenty times louder when you got down there. It smelled of smoke and beer, and they sure didn't spend much money on lights.

The first thing I came to was the men's toilet. It had two sets of doors, which were propped open, and I could see right through to where they were dancing. So I went in the toilet and looked things over from there. It wasn't anything like I'd imagined. I mean, you think of a dance hall, you think of crystal chandeliers and gold ceilings and the orchestra in tuxes up on a little stage. If you've seen enough movies, you know about dance halls. Even in the Vampire Room, you got the feel of it. But this place was just a basement with pillars all over the place, covered with colored paper that was half peeled away, and a few light bulbs here and there, mostly red and blue. A clump of girls stood next to a ticket booth at the bottom of the stairs where the customers came in. The band was sitting on old chairs in back of where the girls were, and they were just dressed in shirts, with no ties, rolled up at the sleeves. They smoked cigarettes while they played, and drank from glasses they kept at their feet.

There was a bar down at one end, with a man drawing beer as fast as his hands could work, and some tables and chairs around the bar. What got me was that nobody was really dancing. They'd come down the stairs and buy some tickets and walk around the girls and choose one, and then hustle her into the gloom of those red and blue bulbs where they'd choose a pillar and sort of move around on each other. No wonder the paper was peeling. The pillars were the busiest part of the dance hall. The customers who came in and out of the men's room didn't pay any attention to me. They were all hopped up, mostly jabbering things I didn't understand, like one guy telling his friend to try the blonde in the red dress because "she'll get your rocks off like Buck Rogers going to the moon." Some of the men put a quarter in a machine on the wall and got out a little packet that they put in their pockets; then they'd go back to the dance floor and I'd see them leave with one of the girls and go up the stairs into the hotel lobby. A lot of the men came in to wipe off their laps where they had spilled beer or something. It was amazing how many men had spilled things on the front of their pants. On the wall machine it said, "3 Guaranteed Prophylactics, 25¢."

When there was a band rest, the saxophone player came in to pee and I asked him where I'd find the owner. He didn't answer me at first, but when he'd peed himself out and was leaving, he pointed to a man with a hat on and a dead cigar in his mouth who was standing next to the ticket booth. He looked about as cheerful as Ned Sparks. Everything in his face pointed down, like he just had a big suck of a lemon.

I walked across the dance floor and stood beside him for a while, but he didn't pay any attention to me. Finally, I gave him a tug and he looked down. He also looked surprised.

"Sir," I said, "I live in the hotel and I wondered if you had some kind of job for me."

"What?"

"I could draw beer, I had my own soda stand and I worked for the A. W. Brown root-beer stand. . . ."

"Who let this kid in here?"

"And I'm good at cleaning up or selling tickets. . . ."

"Hey, Lou, you let this kid in here?"

"Maybe you could use someone who would go around and steer customers here. I could give out handbills. I know this whole neighborhood, I really do."

"Now, listen, kid, you run on back upstairs."

"Sir, look, I need a job, I really do. I mean, it's not a kid thing. My family's in very bad shape."

The owner took the cigar stump out of his mouth and put his hand on my shoulder and started to walk me back to the hotel stairs. The band was back in action, so he had to yell, "You know something, I like your style, kid, coming down here like this, and

I'd give you something to do, I really would, but places like this ain't allowed minors. You know what a minor is? Chrise, the police are bad enough as it is. All they have to do is *see* a kid down here, it'd cost me another fifty a week. So be a good boy and go on back up to your ma. This ain't no place for you, believe me."

He left me at the bottom of the stairs. The band was really making a racket with "Hold That Tiger" and there wasn't an empty pillar. He wasn't such a bad guy, that owner, I really think he would have given me a job if I'da been older. I really do. Holding on to the banister, I slowly clumped up the stairs, being a good boy and going back on up to my ma.

Mud slide number 3.

Chapter Twenty-Nine

I tried Lester's door about a hundred times a day, but he still hadn't come back from wherever he was. Every day I had this feeling that Something Would Happen, I didn't know what, but Something that would take care of things, but the five days began to pass by and there was no sign of Something.

So on Friday, when I went to play rummy with Aunt Minnie, I decided I had better do whatever I could with her. I didn't have much hope. After all, Minnie was the kind of woman who knew that a boy's mother was in the sanatorium, his father was out salesmaning, his brother was boarded out in Keokuk, but she never looked in on him or cared about him from one Friday to the next. I would come for the weekly rummy game and she'd say, "How's your mother?" and I'd say, "Better," and she'd start to shuffle and that would be the end of it. So what kind of woman do you call that?

I let her win, as usual, but when she started to dig around in her purse to find my movie quarter, I stopped her and showed her the letter from the bank. Then I told her how things were. She got very nervous. She blinked her eyes behind her glasses a lot, and she began to twist the big diamond ring on her right hand around and around and around. Her fingernails were high and round like the back of turtles, and as I watched that ring nervousing around her finger, I thought, Criminy, that one ring, that silly thing she wears around her finger, could end all our troubles. Without warning, I grabbed her around the throat so she couldn't scream. She clawed at me with her turtlebacked nails as she struggled to breathe, but my hands pressed ever harder into her throat until finally she went limp and the dead weight of her tore her from my hands. I reached down and took the big diamond ring from her finger, not bothering with the other rings or the earrings or the bracelet or brooch. Who would suspect a twelve-year-old boy? I made sure the hallway was deserted, then I hurried back to my room.

"Aaron, we've just got to raise that money," Minnie was saying. "I don't have much cash, but I think we can raise it all right. Do you have the name of the bank?"

"No, Ma'am, but I can get it from Mr. Desot, I'm sure."

"All right, you get the name of the man to see at the bank, and tomorrow, first thing, we'll go talk to him. Your mother is a lovely person and we mustn't let this happen to her while she's away sick. I'll think all this over tonight, and by the time we go—"

The door suddenly slammed open. No knock, just slammed open, and a short, plump man in a gray suit came stomping into the room. Before I knew what was happening, he dashed over to Minnie and grabbed up her right hand which she was trying to hide under the table.

"Richard, what are you doing?"

"I'll tell you what I'm doing!" He yanked her hand up. I grabbed his arm and started to yank on it.

"Hey, you leave her alone!" I yelled.

He turned to look at me, sort of surprised, since I don't think he'd noticed me on the way in. "Who the hell's this?" he asked. He looked like he was going to sock me.

"Oh, Aaron, this is my brother Richard," Minnie said. She was fantastically nervous. Richard suddenly grabbed her wrist again.

"What do you think you're doing with that ring?" he yelled. Minnie had twisted off the diamond ring and she had it in the hand Richard had grabbed.

"Maybe you'd best go on back to your room, dear," Minnie said.

"Yeah, get your ass out of here," Richard said.

I took the hint and left. But after I closed the door, I stayed right there with my ear glued to it. "My own sister! To think I'd be robbed by my own sister!" Richard yelled.

"I wasn't robbing you. I was just wearing them. I wear things and then I bring them back."

"Oh, yeah? Well, we just went over your bookkeeping and there are a hell of a lot of things that didn't get back."

"Well, not of mine. What things? Are you accusing me. . . ."

"You're damn right I'm accusing you! You're a goddam *thief*, that's what you are! My own sister!" Whack! He hit her. Whack! He hit her again. "Now where are all those things? You going to tell me or do I have to slap you silly?"

"Oh, please, Richard, please! I don't know! I haven't taken any—" Whack! Whack! "Oh, no! Stop, oh, please stop, Richard! My glasses! Oh, my eye, you've hurt my eye!"

"I'll punch out your goddam eye! Stealing from your own brother! Now you tell me!" Whack! "You hear?"

Minnie was crying and moaning now and I could hear her running around the room trying to get away from him, knocking over the furniture, begging him, but he kept after her, socking her harder and harder, and finally I got so scared I ran down the hallway and down the steps to the lobby to get help. But when I came running into the lobby, all those bright lights and the lobby full of dance-hall guys and the desk all clogged up, I couldn't do anything, I don't know how to explain it exactly. But there suddenly wasn't anything I could do about Minnie and her brother. So I just went on out the door. All the chairs in front were sat in by people I didn't know. Two policemen, twirling their night sticks, came walking by, but there wasn't anything I could do. I walked down Delmar for a while and looked in the windows; then I went back to the hotel. I expected to see police cars and an ambulance, but nothing had happened. I went back upstairs and tiptoed down the hall to Minnie's door. I sure didn't want that brother to fling open the door and find me there. But there wasn't a sound. I put my ear on Minnie's door but I couldn't hear a thing except traffic noises coming in through the window. Very carefully, I tried the door. It was locked.

The next morning, on my way out, the door of Minnie's room was open. Everything of hers was gone. I went in and looked around. The room looked like she'd never been there. Somebody had even cleaned it up.

And that was mud slide number 4.

Chapter Thirty

The next morning I woke up early, but I couldn't get out of bed. I didn't know exactly how early because we didn't own a clock, but I was pretty good on judging time by how light it was and the sounds. Sounds like the night men bringing in the taxis and the day men coming to get them at the Yellow Cab Company. So it was about seven o'clock.

I had switched to sleep in my parents' bed because it was closer to the window. I opened my eyes and looked at that hot sky and heard the taxi men, and I had this attack I sometimes get in my breathing machinery. What happens is I begin to concentrate on my breathing, pulling it up every time it goes down, not trusting it to go up and down by itself. Not only did I have this breathing crisis, but both legs were paralyzed from the thighs down. And as if that wasn't enough, my voice was gone. So I couldn't even call for help. Thank God I could use my hands and move my head.

I had had some terrible nightmares with a lot of fire in them, everything getting burned up including my brother, who kept yelling for help from out of the flames but nobody could find him, and my tennis racket, which was burning in a circle around the frame. But I wasn't thinking too much about the dreams; what I was thinking about was Minnie. I felt really awful that I hadn't helped her. So what if it was her brother? Did he have the right to sock her all over the place? Even if those were his rings on her fingers? Those two cops, right there in front of the Avalon. All I had to do was open my mouth and I would have saved old Minnie. Aunt Minnie. I was having more and more trouble dragging my breath up from the bottom of my chest. I began to really work on that so's not to go on and on about Minnie. What had really got me was Minnie's room suddenly empty like that, without a sign of her. Do you think he killed her and carted her off? The way he was socking her, he probably did. She was such an old thing. Every time she stooped for something, it sounded like a Venetian blind being let down. What I was, about Minnie and her socking brother, was a coward. That's the word all right, *coward*. I had been a coward once or twice before in my life, but this was the first time I'd been a coward when I didn't have to.

I lay there looking at the ceiling and keeping my breaths going and thinking about how really rotten things were. This was the fifth and last day of the bank's notice, and even though it was a Saturday I decided I had better go out to Fee-Fee and try to see my mother, visitors' day or not. Because beginning tomorrow I'd have to sit in 309 until my father got back, God knows when. I had already done what I could about food. With what I had left from what my mother had given me from the Windy City Hosiery money, after putting aside the Creve Coeur trolley fare, I had bought seed and a cuttlebone for Skippy and food for me. Bread, peanut butter, sandwich spread, and Horlick's Malted Milk Tablets. Also, I had gone by Arnie's and he had given me two sandwiches in advance. I had said I was getting a little tired of baloney, so he had given me an American cheese and the heel end of a sandwich loaf.

Thinking about all that food, I decided that a little breakfast might cure my paralysis, so I got out of bed and made myself a peanut-butter sandwich and a glass of Horlick's. I had a way of grinding up the Horlick's tablet into powder and putting it in a jar with water and shaking it terrifically until it got all frothy. It cured the paralysis, all right.

I got dressed in my second-best white pants and this shirt I have that my mother made into a V-neck with short sleeves when the cuffs and collar wore out. Feltie, Keds, cigar-band blotters (you never can tell), and I was ready to go. That's when I saw Lester's note under the door. I grabbed at it like a life preserver.

"Dear A. Just got back, 2 a.m. See you in the Vampire Room tomorrow (tonight!) around six. Lester."

Lester back! It was like winning the Irish Sweepstakes! I didn't know just what he could do about the $77.50 I had to raise, probably nothing, but if I was going to be shut up there in 309 it gave me somebody on the outside, and when that somebody was Lester, that was all I needed. I went off to Fee-Fee feeling tons better, I can tell you.

Even though it was Saturday, no one ran me off the Fee-Fee lawn. I made up this story for my mother that Lester had got me on as a permanent caddie at the country club, so I didn't know just when I'd be coming to see her. She was disappointed, of course, but glad that I had found a job. I felt bad about having to lie to her but I couldn't worry her with the truth, could I?

But what worried *me* all the way back, sitting there at the end of the trolley thinking about it, was that my mother had developed a cough. And the fact that she was in bed and not allowed to walk around like a lot of the others. I decided my suspicions had been right, and that my parents hadn't told me the truth. She was going to die, that's what. I was so worried I almost missed the Delmar streetcar connection. But then again she did look better, and her voice was good and clear and she smiled a lot more than she used to. I don't know, it's tough to know what to believe when you've got the kind of parents who tell you that babies come from eggs.

I got off at Delmar and Kingshighway, keeping an eye out for Patrolman John L. Burns as I crossed the street. It was only five o'clock, but it was so awful hot I thought I'd go up and sponge off in cold water before meeting Lester. The heat of the sidewalk was burning my feet right through my Keds.

As I got to the hotel entrance, two policemen were coming out. At first I just saw the two policemen, big cops with their collars open, and then I saw Lester. He was sandwiched in between them and he was walking with his head down. I just stood there as Lester and the two cops walked by me; then I yelled, "Lester!"

He stopped and turned around, and the two cops stopped with him. Lester was handcuffed.

"Come on, get moving," one of the cops said, and he gave Lester a little push. There was a police wagon parked at the curb in the loading zone.

"Wait a minute," Lester said, not moving, "I've got something of his and I've got to give it to him."

"I said get moving," the cop said.

"Why can't I give it back to him?" Lester asked. "It's his, and I ought to be able to give it back to him."

"Okay, all right," the other cop said. "Hurry it up."

Lester managed to get one of his hands in his pocket and he brought out his pearl-handled knife. "Here, here's your knife, A. Thanks a lot." He flipped the knife to me, pitching both his hands forward to do it. I caught it on the fly. Lester looked me in the eyes, not smiling or anything, before he turned and walked over to the police wagon. The cops opened the doors, and Lester stepped up into the black insides of the wagon. One of the cops got in with him. The other cop shut the door and turned the handle. Then he walked around and got in the driver's seat and drove off.

I watched the police wagon until it turned at Cabanne; then I went in to the desk and asked Mr. Neville if he knew why they'd arrested Lester. He said he didn't know but that the cops had been there watching for Lester for the past four days. Just like the Repleviners watching for our Ford, I thought. I hadn't known before that that they replevined people the same as cars.

I put Lester's knife in my pocket and walked around to the stairs. The elevator was parked there with its doors closed and the lights off. I had said goodbye to Arletta, and to Maggie, the day before. I pulled myself up the stairs, the banister wood feeling smooth and cool under my hand. I started down the hallway, then remembered to go back and go to the toilet. My stomach felt funny, like it was being pinched from the inside. I walked on back down the hallway, passing all those doors—Mr. Able's and Lester's and Mr. Evans's and the door where Mr. Barnaway or Borroway hanged himself, and Sandoz's and Old Lady Heinson's and Minnie's and Ella McShane's and all those other doors, and when I got to the end of the hall, to 309, I suddenly got mad about those handcuffs on Lester. No matter what he had done, they didn't have to do that to him. God, that was the worst sight I ever saw, those handcuffs on Lester's wrists! And on the street like that for everyone to see! Making him a criminal like that, when all he was was just like me, trying to get by. I'll get them for that, I really will! They won't get me out of that room, I'll tell you that, but when I do leave, I'll find my pal Lester, I really will, and the two of us will make them awful sorry they put those handcuffs on Lester's wrists. Just wait and see! They'll be sorry! They will!

I grabbed the pearl-handled knife from my pocket and snapped open the blade and stabbed it right into the heart of the shade on the hallway window. Then I ripped the blade downward and it made a screaming sound as I cut the shade in two, right down the middle, leaving it hanging there in two pieces, ripped apart, the deadest shade you ever saw. I went into 309 and locked the door behind me. God knows how long I'd have to stay there, but I'll tell you one thing, they'd never get a chance to put a lock on *that* door. Not 309. Everything we owned in the whole world was there, and the only way they were going to get it would be over my dead body.

Chapter Thirty-One

It was one thing to just have to sleep in 309, and eat a couple of meals there when there were meals, but it was a whole other thing to have to stay there twenty-four hours a day. When I woke up in the morning, I got dressed as usual and cleaned Skippy's cage and fed him. Then I went to the window and watched the parking lot for a while. There was nothing to see.

I put on my Feltie and began to walk around the room. Around and around the room in a circle. I had taken out the five books on my library card that I was allowed, but I couldn't have sat down and read for anything. I was too itchy. None of the exposures was working and the room was already hot enough to bake biscuits. And to make it worse, the St. Louis sun didn't actually get to our parking-lot window until afternoon.

I finally sat myself down and wrote my mother a long letter. She had given me a lot of three-cent stamps, and I posted the letter in the chute beside the elevator. You should have seen my description of what a marvelous hot-shot caddie I was. Mr. Jules Verne would have been proud of me.

Then I went back to walking. The feeling I had was like a feeling I had had once before, but I couldn't remember what it was. I mean I remembered the *feeling* but not the thing that *made* the feeling. But it was something terrible, that much I remembered. But it really bothered me that I couldn't remember the thing itself. I kept poking around in all the corners of my brain and sometimes I almost had it but then it would slide off again. It was driving me loony.

The godsend was that I suddenly remembered I had this crystal set in the closet that I made in manual training when I was in sixth grade at DeMun. There was also a little box with three extra crystals. I had put it all away when my father got his Atwater Kent and I almost forgot it was there. Of course it wasn't a really good crystal set like you'd go out and buy, but it worked. Actually it was an old cigar box with a place set in it for the hunk of crystal to go. Attached to that place was this piece of very fine wire that you tickled ever so lightly and slowly over the bumps of the crystal, all the time listening with this ear receiver that was attached to the crystal with a piece of electric wire. Mostly what you got in your ear was a lot of scrunchy static, but if you kept on tickling with the wire you would finally touch a bump that was a radio station, and if you held the tickler wire real steady you heard pretty good. Of course it faded in and out a little but if you had patience and a hand that didn't quiver, you could hear France Laux broadcasting the Cardinal game. So in the afternoon I listened to the ball game, but in the last of the ninth inning, when the Cardinals loaded the bases with two outs and a run behind, I got so excited I moved my hand, and by the time I refound the bump where the game was it was all over and I never did find out who won.

After the game was over, all there was to do was walk around some more or look at the parking lot where absolutely nothing was happening. Martin, the janitor, lit the usual stink fire in the ashpit and that didn't help matters. I sat down on the windowsill and watched the black stink smoke curling up into the sun rays and tried to make my mind work. I tried to think forward to something ahead that would perk me up, but there was nothing I could fix on so I finally gave that up. But I couldn't stop watching the black stink smoke making its snaky designs against the hot orange sun rays. I even tried to be Captain Nemo on the brink of a volcano but it didn't work. Then I tried to be the Count of Monte Cristo, which I never had any trouble being, but that didn't work either. Nothing worked. It was just too awful for anything make-believe to work. So I just sat there, kind of numb. The smoke faded away as the ashpit fire burned itself out and it began to be night.

I went over and lay down on the bed. I picked up one of my library books, but my mind couldn't follow the words so I put it down and turned off the light. I thought about Lester. And my mother dying maybe. And Sullivan. I tried to think about Christina Sebastian but I couldn't. All the times I'd laid on the bed and thought about Christina, and now when I really *needed* to think about her I couldn't. It was too hot to breathe. I listened to the night men coming for their taxis. I just laid there, thinking about nothing but the night men and the taxis, and I guess I fell asleep because I came to with an awful start when bam! bam! bam! there was this loud rapping on the door. My blood froze. Again bam! bam! bam! Then a key was put in the door and turned, but the inside bolt held it fast. I had thought that as long as I was in the room they would just leave me be, but now I knew that they were *trying* to lock me out, and I got scared. My breath stuck and my heart began to hammer, and I never stopped being scared from that first bam! bam! bam! on. I could see Ben out there in the hallway with that big Yale lock in his hand plain as if there wasn't a door, and Christian rubbing around on his legs, smacking his lips and waiting to get at Skippy.

I pushed the table against the door, not making a sound, and carefully got up on it and peeked over the transom. No one was there. I climbed down and got a chair and stood it up on its hind legs and crammed it under the doorknob. I piled some stuff on top of the table to make it heavier and jammed the near bed against the table. From that night on, that's the way I kept the door barricaded.

Now that I knew Ben was lying in wait to lock me out, you can bet I'd only open the door when I absolutely had to. Certainly

I'd never open it for any person like a fake Western Union boy or somebody saying they had a parcel or anything like that. All they had to do, once that door opened, was grab me and yank me into the hall and slap that lock on the door. Also, I remembered what my father had said about how no one, once they got the notice, should do anything regularly (like Mr. Able going to dinner every Thursday), so I planned to go down the hall to the chute to mail my mother's letter at a different time every day. And I'd race there and back so fast that Ben would have to be half greyhound to catch me.

The only other thing I had to worry about in the days that followed was going to the toilet. I could pee all right in the sink. It was too high for me, but I pulled down the shade and got up on a chair and ran the water and it worked out all right. But having a bowel movement was my biggest problem. I could just see how I'd race down to the toilet, get on and off the pot as fast as I could, and race back to the room only to find that Ben had slapped his lousy lock on the door. And the one thing about me and the toilet was that I was like I had a clock in me. Every morning at the same time. So what I did sounds pretty icky but it was all I could think of. My father had a huge pile of *Post-Dispatches* in the back of the closet, and what I did was to use a spread-out section of the *Post-Dispatch* every morning and then fold it up and put it in the trash can in the broom closet, which was just a little way down the hall. So those were the only times I'd quietly remove the barricade and slip out—to mail letters to my mother and sometimes to my brother, and to go to the broom closet. I knew all the sounds of the Avalon by heart, inside and outside, so I could tell, by listening, what was going on here and there, but one thing was very mysterious and I was never able to figure it out for sure. Every morning when I got up, there was mail under the door. The daily letters from my mother and sometimes one from my father, and twice there were letters from Sullivan. Poor Sullivan. My aunt and uncle were not being very nice to him because of my father being so far behind in his two-dollar payments. There were letters from the Windy City Hosiery Company, which I sent on to my mother, and letters for my father from the Elgin Watch Company, and the WPA, which I put away in his drawer. Also I got two comic postcards from Sid Gutman. But I never found out who put those letters under the door. Maybe Mr. Desot. He must have felt bad about me being a prisoner in the room and so maybe he sneaked me those letters. Good thing the bank didn't catch him, if it *was* Mr. Desot. If I hadn't gotten those letters, I don't know what I would have done. Gone out of my mind, I guess. As it was, I almost did.

Ben hammered bam! bam! bam! on the door two or three times a day, and then tested the lock to see if the inside bolt was open. He came at all different times, and once he came in the night long after the dance-hall band had started. Every time he banged on the door, my heart stopped and I held my breath till I heard his feet going away. He never rammed the door or anything like that, just tested the bolt and left. I guess he figured that all he had to do was wait me out and sooner or later I'd give up. Well, not me! They'd never get me in that Hooverville with Mr. Evans! Not me! My father would be getting back one of these days and I'd sure as shootin' hold out until then. They just didn't know *me*. After all, my father wouldn't be on the road forever. I had looked up Iowa, Kansas, and Oklahoma on my geography map and they were big, all right, but my father's last letter had been from Oklahoma City, which meant he had finished Iowa and Kansas, so it wouldn't be all that long till he got back. I would just have to keep from going loony, that was all.

When the criminal lawyer and his friends were across the hall, I liked to listen to them in the early part of the night before they got too drunk. After that it was just babble and grunts. The way whiskey made them talk it sounded like a foreign language. Sort of Germanish. But even when the men got drunk like that, if the blond lady started to sing they'd quiet down. One evening she just kept singing "Jeanie with the Light Brown Hair" in that pretty voice of hers, over and over, and the words came floating through my transom like soap bubbles. I could've listened to her all night, but Dillinger finally yelled at her to shut up.

I rationed my food out to last as long as it could, but once it gave out, I began to get hungry like I'd never been hungry before. What I mean is, all the times I'd been hungry, there was always the chance of finding something to eat. Like, you know, if there was school I could always wolf something off the little kids. Or Lester would rustle up some water-catsup soup, or whatever. Not that I hadn't gone a few days at a time with nothing in my stomach, but I'd never been in a state of *permanent* hunger before, and now I was. I bloated up on water as much as I could, but that just sort of made me feel sick. It drove me a little batty to think about the meal waiting for me down at the Dew Drop Inn. I should have gone in and told Johnny Cafferetta about having to stay in the room. I had thought about it but I forgot. Nobody can remember everything. I had meant to do it that last day, that Saturday, but the shock of seeing Lester in those handcuffs had chased everything out of my mind. Maybe Johnny Cafferetta would have brought something up for me. But even if he had tried, they probably would've stopped him at the desk. I thought about some of those really lousy meals I had had at the Dew Drop Inn and it made me drool. I'd never turn up my nose at a piece of gristle again. I promise you that.

I tried every which way to get my mind off of food. I had read all my books, so I got out the pile of old *Woman's Home Companions* that my mother had stored in the back of the closet. Minnie had had a subscription, and every month when she finished with one, she had passed it on to my mother. Looking through the *Woman's Home Companion* was how I started to eat roast beef and chocolate cake. There was this absolutely gorgeous roast-beef-and-gravy ad with little potatoes and carrots a whole page high, and I took a scissors and cut it out and began to eat it. What was amazing was how the paper actually tasted like roast beef. The same with the chocolate cake. I cut that out and then found an ice-cream ad, and I put the ice cream on top of the chocolate cake and it really tasted chocolate.

Actually, eating paper was not all that bad. I took little nibbles and drank water with it and my stomach really did feel a little filled up afterward. Also, I could spend a lot of time hunting through the magazines to put together terrific lunches and dinners. I ate things I'd never even tasted before. Like artichokes. And avocados. And lamb chops. But it was best to eat things I knew the taste of. The first bites were sort of gummy but I'd keep chewing the paper until it came apart. I'd grind the bites between the points of my eyeteeth and the paper would get soft and sort of like oatmeal.

Eating paper a couple of times a day made me feel less hungry, and I guess I'd have been all right if I hadn't received that letter from my father from Stillwater, Oklahoma. It said that the Ford had broken down and my father was stuck there until he could raise the money to repair it. He said he had written to the Elgin Watch Company and was awaiting their reply, but he was not very hopeful they'd send him anything since he had not sent them enough orders even to pay back his drawing-account expenses. Of course, I could understand people not buying watches, because they didn't have to know what time it was to get to their jobs since they didn't have jobs, or to know when to eat since there was nothing to eat.

But what I couldn't understand was why my father had to go strand himself in Stillwater, Oklahoma, when I needed him so badly. Couldn't he do *anything* right? The more I thought about him the madder—yes, *madder*—I got. He didn't even put a return address on the letter so's I'd have known where to write to him. I was just as mad at him as the time he took the two dollars out of my pirate box, without asking me, to buy gas for the Ford. It was all I had left after the Students' Savings Bank had gone broke, and my father just went into my drawer and found my pirate box where I had it hidden in a book that didn't have any pages. Borrowed it, he said, and he would pay me back. Hah! I was so mad I went yelling out of the room and down to the bathroom, and I locked the door and picked up a wet towel somebody had left on the floor and I wadded it up and threw it against the wall with all my might, and every time I threw it I yelled a dirty word.

That's the only time I really yelled dirty words out loud, that time whanging that wet towel against the bathroom wall. I didn't know all that many dirty words and I had to repeat some of them, but I was just that mad now and I snatched my Feltie off my head and began throwing it around the room, yelling every terrible thing I could think of at my father. I really hated him for being broken down in Stillwater, Oklahoma, and I took everything out on him—Lester's being in jail and my mother dying and poor Sullivan with those mean relatives, everything! Now what would I do! Now what the *hell* would I do? Eat paper for the rest of my life?

Couldn't he do one decent father thing? Just once? I felt like pulling back that lock and throwing open the door and walking out of 309. Let them have his precious Atwater Kent and his winter overcoat and the umbrella with the bone handle that was his father's. It would just serve him right. I flung my Feltie around and yelled all the dirty words I knew, *yelled* them so he'd hear them in Stillwater, Oklahoma. My smiling Herbert Hoover button smacked against the wall, so did my Admiral Dewey Achievement button, but I didn't care. I just whanged my Feltie against the wall and cursed a blue streak. He could even *die* in Stillwater, Oklahoma, my father could, for all I cared, right next to his dead Ford. He knew I was all alone, didn't he, and he should have been there with *me* instead of looking after his damn Ford! The hell with fathers! The hell with all of them!

Two huge water bugs skudded across the floor right in front of me. I sounded the siren and grabbed my Boomer and really crashed one of those water bugs. The other one escaped down the radiator pipe, but the one I crashed got splatted into a big black-and-white pancake, the way I felt like splatting my father.

The water-bug attack calmed me down some. I picked up my poor Feltie and dusted it off and put it back on my head. Then I went over and laid down on the bed. I felt awful, really awful. Like I had had twenty twelve-year-old molars that had just been pulled. And I had sort of cramps in my stomach. I guess I shouldn't have had that second helping of macaroni and cheese in the Borden's ad.

I closed my eyes and tried to think about how I'd manage to hold out. And thinking about that, I suddenly remembered what it was that happened long ago that had given me the feeling I had now. It was the tornado.

I was six years old, in the second grade. It was lunchtime and we were in the basement of the school eating our lunches out of our lunch boxes. It was a warm fall day, hot sun, and I was sitting by myself eating cookies when I noticed the windows above were starting to get black. The sun was disappearing from them like someone was slowly pushing a piece of black cardboard across the windows until suddenly they all went black and there was a terrible howling noise. A terrific wind full of dust, pebbles, papers, tin cans, everything, began whooshing through the windows.

All the lights in the basement suddenly went out, and the kids began screaming and running around and heavy teacher-voices began yelling at them. The howling noise outside hurt my ears. Kids were bumping into me and falling down all over the place. I felt my way along the wall to where I knew the janitor's room was. I got up on a bench under the window in the janitor's room and I could see out. It was pitch black out there and yet I could see what was happening. The most unbelievable things began to pass by the window, like it was a movie and I was sitting in my seat and all that passed was on the screen. A garage came tumbling by, end over end, and I could see the automobile inside it turning somersaults. The play-yard turner with all its swings came spinning along, the swings zipping around faster than they ever did with us kids on them. Automobiles floated by right side up and upside down, some with people still in them. Everything was up in the air and spinning. The awfullest sight was this baby buggy that had a baby attached to it with a leather strap around its middle. The baby buggy was bouncing along the schoolyard like a rubber ball, with the baby hanging out of it all bloody and dead.

A whole river of rubbish came whooshing by and every garbage can in St. Louis clanging and banging across the yard. And there were lots of people blowing along, just off the ground, like kites that rise a little but don't really lift up. The people knocked up against other flying things and bounced around like they were made of straw.

Then, like somebody pushed a button, the whole thing turned off. The black wiped away and the howling faded off and everything turned still. The sun shone again and you'd never have known anything had happened except for the terrible sight in the schoolyard. I opened the janitor's door and went up the steps and looked around. Nothing stirred. And there wasn't a sound to hear. The streets around the school mostly didn't have any houses left on them. There were streetcars mashed against trees at crazy angles and water was gushing out of busted fire hydrants. There were electric lines hanging down everywhere like old vines in the winter, making sparks where they touched. I looked up and saw that the roof of our school was gone. So was everything in the schoolyard. I looked down into the school basement, but no one was there. (I didn't know it then, but the kids had all been taken down another level to the boiler room.) That moment, standing there alone in the schoolyard with the world all come to an end, that's the time I had the feeling that was like the feeling I now had in 309. Thank God I finally got it straightened out, where that feeling came from, because, as I told you, it had been driving me batty.

But in the days that followed after that letter from my father, other things began to drive me even battier. The worst thing was I started to feel like I might have a fit like Ella had. I began to get this strange feeling in my head and a ringing sound in my ears and my legs felt pretty numb. I remembered that Ella said she'd never had a fit until after her father died, so that proved it could start in on you at any time. I was really scared about having my first fit with no one there to watch my tongue. I cut a piece of wood out of an old cigar box with Lester's pearl-handled knife, for me to use on my tongue. But if I went all stiff and scary the way Ella did, how could I manage to fish out my tongue? It worried me a lot.

One of the other things I started doing was taking my pulse all the time. I really can't tell you why, but I just started to take my pulse all the time. Even though I didn't have a watch, I knew how to count in seconds, so I was able to tell how many beats I had to the minute. Every time I took my pulse, I kept track of the numbers on a piece of paper. Once my pulse beat was way up to eighty-six and I was sure it was a sign that I was about to get my first attack. So I grabbed my tongue stick and jumped in bed so as not to fall and hurt myself when the fit came. The ringing in my ears was worse and I felt nauseated. I had been feeling nauseated quite a lot. I closed my eyes and waited for the fit to start, but in the meantime I fell asleep.

When I awoke, it was night and the criminal lawyer was across the hall telling a long story about how he defended this plumber who was accused of having had a baby with his own daughter, who was fourteen years old. It was a very interesting story, especially the parts about how the criminal lawyer tricked the witnesses and what he told the jury and how the jury was locked up for ten hours before they came in and said the plumber was not guilty. The criminal lawyer didn't sound very drunk at all.

So I just decided right then and there to go across the hall and tell him what was happening to me. If he was all that good, getting a not-guilty for a plumber who had had a baby with his own daughter, he should be able to do something for someone twelve years old trying not to get locked out of his room.

Chapter Thirty-Two

The criminal lawyer's door was open. Over by the windows there was an electric fan wagging its face side to side. I knocked on the doorjamb and they all looked up. The blond lady, who was wearing a pink slip like my mother used to sell, and the criminal lawyer, who was sitting in front of the fan, and Dillinger, who was in his chair at the window.

"Well, well, if it isn't big A, little a, r-o-n!" the criminal lawyer boomed out. "Come in, little man, come in!" I went in.

The blond lady came over and mussed my hair. "Why aren't you asleep, Red?" she asked. "We making too much noise?"

Dillinger didn't say anything but he looked at me like I had leprosy or rickets or something.

"Offer the lad a ginger ale," the criminal lawyer said. "Here, sit down here and have a ginger ale." He leaned over to pat the seat of the chair next to him, but he missed and almost fell out of his own chair. I guess he was a lot drunker than he looked.

The blond lady brought me a glass of ginger ale, and in her other hand she had a platter that was heaped up with about a thousand corned-beef sandwiches on rye bread. "How about a sandwich to go with the ginger ale?" she asked. She wasn't holding the sandwich platter very steady, but I managed to spear one from the top.

"Yes, Ma'am. Thank you very much." There were pickle slices on the side of the platter and she put a few on my plate. Two or three missed and fell to the floor but nobody paid any attention to them.

I bit through the rye-smelling rye bread and into the corned beef, and I just let my teeth and tongue *feel* how it felt before I began to chew it.

"Do I get a drink or you gonna spend the rest of the night with that kid?" That was Dillinger growling at the blond lady. She took the sandwiches back to the table and started to make Dillinger his drink. I kept my eyes away from him, but I could feel him staring at me.

"Do you have brothers and sisters?" the criminal lawyer asked.

I was getting ready for my second bite but I took the sandwich back out of my mouth. "I have a brother. But he's not here."

"Give the little man some more ginger ale," the criminal lawyer said.

"You mind if I get my drink first?" Dillinger snarled.

"Oh, I beg your pardon," the criminal lawyer said. "I didn't realize you had not yet been served. I'd best have another, too, Lady Margaret."

Good God, *Lady* Margaret! Can you imagine, *royalty* serving me ginger ale? She didn't sound English, though. But then what did I really know about the English except for Ronald Colman?

I took another bite of my sandwich and my mouth felt like singing. Lady Margaret brought the drinks to Dillinger and the criminal lawyer, and then, with a drink of her own, she came over and sat down on the floor in front of me and the criminal lawyer, and she began to sing. It was "Titwillow," about the little bird who died of a broken heart. I'd heard it before but Lady Margaret really made me feel sorry for poor Titwillow sitting in that tree by the river and singing his heart out. I was dying to go on eating my sandwich, but I figured it would be rude to sit there chewing in her face while she was singing. Anyway, it was so beautiful, the way she sang, that I really liked just sitting there and listening. A couple of times, the criminal lawyer sagged up against me because he was falling asleep, but then, on touching, he'd pop awake and straighten up. I figured I'd better have my talk with him as soon as Lady Margaret was finished.

Which I did. "Sir," I began, "I wonder if you could give me some advice. I have this problem across the hall that they're trying to lock me out."

"Who's trying to lock you out?"

"The bank."

"What bank?"

"I dunno."

"Then how do you know it's a bank?"

"Well, Ben's trying to put the lock on the door but it's the bank gave him his orders. For the back rent."

"Why, that's terrible!" Lady Margaret said.

"You come over tomorrow afternoon," the criminal lawyer said, "and I'll phone Desot."

"Well, I'll tell you about that—Mr. Desot says it's the bank." I started to tell the criminal lawyer what Mr. Desot had said, but I was no sooner into it than he fell asleep with his chin down on his chest. His glass tilted in his hand and the whiskey ran out onto the carpet but he didn't drop the glass. Suddenly there was this grab on my arm. It was Dillinger. "Okay, kid," he said, "tell the truth—she sent you here, didn't she?"

"She? Who?" I was scared out of my wits.

"Don't give me any of that dumb stuff. You smart-ass kids."

"Oh, Jack," Lady Margaret said, "don't pick on him."

"You shut your tramp mouth," Dillinger said, and sort of pushed the flat of his hand against the side of her face. "That lousy wife of mine sent the kid here to spy on me, didn't she?"

I looked at the criminal lawyer for help but he was sound asleep. "No, sir, I don't even know—"

"You think I don't know what you're up to, spying on me? Don't lie." He was like whispering, hissing through his teeth.

"Listen, Mister, I'm not spying on anybody!"

"Well, you go back and tell her to keep her nose outta my business. Got that? *Keep her nose outta my business!* You got that?"

"But sir, I don't know your wife. . . ."

"And if I catch you sniffing around here again I'm gonna whip the holy Jesus outta you. Got that?"

I was too scared to say anything more. Besides hissing at me through his teeth, he had this really mad look with the veins all out on his forehead. Boy, was he drunk.

Lady Margaret was looking in the mirror above the sink. "You bruised my cheek, you bastard you," she said. "Wait till Lew wakes up."

"Shut up," Dillinger said. "I ain't finished with the kid."

"Leave him alone. How come you're only a tough guy with kids and women?"

Dillinger let go of my arm and went over and grabbed her wrists. "I told you to shut up."

"Okay. All right."

"I mean *shut up*."

"Well, just look at my cheek and now you're bruising my wrists."

"All you gotta do is shut up."

"All right. I'm shut up. Now let go of me."

"You just *shut up*, that's all."

Dillinger had his back to me now, so I quietly sneaked out of the room and back to 309. I bolted the door and pushed the barricade back into place. It could have been worse, I thought—Ben could've locked me out while I was over there.

I got undressed and laid down on the sheet which was so hot it burned my skin. I wished I had taken the rest of that corned-beef sandwich. Two bites were all I got. And some pickle. Maybe if the criminal lawyer hadn't fallen asleep it might have turned out better. But that Dillinger really scared me, I'll tell you that. The way he hissed at me. I could still feel his hand on my arm. Well, okay, now what? Now that I've used up the last piece of help I could think of? The way I felt, I wouldn't have minded going to sleep and not waking up. I pray the Lord my soul to take. That'd be perfectly okay with me. Imagine a twelve-year-old boy knowing anybody's wife. One thing you'd never catch me doing when I grew up would be to drink whiskey. I'd rather get drunk on ice-cream sundaes.

My mouth still burned from the pickle, so I got up and brushed my teeth. Then I filled a glass with water and poured it around on the sheet. When I got back in bed, the wet sheet was sticky but nice and cool on my skin. I looked up at the lights on the ceiling and listened to the Good Times band. There wasn't a sound from across the hall. Listening to the music made me think about Ella. For somebody I hadn't seen all that much, I missed Ella. I wondered if she was all right now. Then I thought about my mother. Her last letter she had sounded very cheerful because the doctors had said the spot on her lung was closing much faster than they had thought it would. But who knows if that's really what they said.

I took my pulse and it was eighty-four. After Dillinger it's a wonder it wasn't a hundred and fifty. I started to think about Danny Desot. A couple of times I had heard him firing his BBs at the rats so I knew he wasn't at camp or anything. I got angry thinking about Danny, because he must have known I was shut up and it wouldn't have killed him to drop by once in a while. But then maybe he didn't know, or maybe his father was too scared of the bank. Well, listen, even if he had come around I probably wouldn't have opened the door. How they'd work it would be that Danny would knock and Ben would jump out and pounce on me. No lousy trick like that was going to work on me. But Danny could have lowered the tin can with the paraffin string out of the turtle window and we could have talked secretly. He could have at least done that. Or lowered me an apple or something. But maybe nobody told him about me. I don't know. I felt so darn miserable I was feeling bad about everyone. And those bites of corned beef had *really* made me hungry. My stomach was making all kinds of wild sounds, like a radiator when heat comes up in the winter.

I wished I hadn't remembered about the tornado. I kept seeing that baby buggy with the baby dragging out of it. I checked my pulse again. Still eighty-four. The sheet was already dry. There was a giant fly pestering me but I was too miserable to go get my Boomer and go after him. I really meant that about my soul. I would have really liked to die before I waked. I got to thinking about my soul. I guess I'd never really thought about my soul before. I tried to picture it. If the Lord was going to *take* it, it had to *be* something, like if He was going to take my heart I had a picture of that. But I was having trouble with my soul. I knew it wasn't supposed to be real like my liver or gizzard or anything, but still it had to be *something*, didn't it? Maybe it was whatever made me do some of the goofy things I did. Like always wanting to win at things and get E-pluses, and maybe it was what made me stay in this smelly room dying of hunger! But how can the Lord take a soul? Well, maybe it's some little doodad that hangs in the lung or someplace, something useless like your appendix, and it just hangs there with your soul in it and sometimes when you die the Lord takes it, and sometimes He doesn't.

I thought I heard a knock on the door. I stopped breathing and strained my ears. If it was a knock, it certainly wasn't a Ben knock because there'd never be any trouble hearing *that*. I probably was just hearing things. I was letting my breath out when I heard it again. This time clearly. Tap-tap, tap-tap, tap. I leaped out of bed and snapped on the lights and tore the barricade away from the door. Only one person in the whole world knocked like that. Only one! I threw back the bolt and turned the safety lock and flung open the door.

I was right. It was my brother Sullivan. He was standing there with his cardboard suitcase in his hand and he was wearing a little snap-on bow tie.

"Uncle Nathan sent me back on the bus," he said. "He got mad because nobody paid for me." The Keokuk sun had given him some freckles on his nose. I hadn't seen him in months and months, and he was wonderful to look at. His chin was quivering and I knew what that meant, so I held out my arms to him. He dropped his suitcase and ran to me and threw his arms around my waist and started to cry. I guess he'd been holding it in all the way from Keokuk. He buried his face against my chest and I could feel his warm tears on my skin.

Then I started to cry. I never knew I had that many tears in me. I guess I'd been holding it in for a long time, too. I just cried and cried, and so did Sullivan. We held tight on to each other and I tried to stop but I couldn't. Neither of us was alone any more, you see, and that was a big thing to cry about.

Chapter Thirty-Three

My father returned the following week. He had had to sell the few remaining watch samples that had works to pay for fixing the Ford and to get home. It was lucky he did, because the WPA letter had a job in it. When my father opened the envelope and read that letter, he jumped from his chair, knocking it over, and grabbed me and Sullivan around the shoulders and danced us around in a circle yelling, "Oh-wah! Oh-wah! Oh-wah!" I thought sure his mind had jumped the tracks.

He finally simmered down and read us the letter, in a voice like he was Father Coughlin. He had been appointed Clerk, First Class in the new WPA administration offices on Pine Street at a salary of sixty-five dollars a month! Now it was our turn to whoop it up and dance around, and I guess that was the first time I had ever seen my father's face truly happy. When he got the Elgin Watch Company letter, he had felt good, all right, but he still looked worried, I guess because having to leave and sell watches all over Iowa, Kansas, and Oklahoma to people who couldn't buy watches. But now all the down-lines in his face were pointing up. I think the best part of the job was the First Class. If he had just been made a clerk, it wouldn't have been the same. It was that he could say "Clerk, *First Class* with the WPA" that really made him happy.

God knows he said it often enough. But I didn't mind. It was music to my ears, too.

My father went down to the corner Walgreen's to phone Fee-Fee and tell my mother the good news. My mother was so happy she cried, but then I told you about my mother crying. She cried last Mother's Day when I gave her a bunch of dandelions from Forest Park. Anyway, after her cry, my mother told my father she was now a walking patient, and she said that the doctors had just told her that she could go home if she took it easy.

"She can't come back to this dump," my father announced in his Clerk, First Class voice. "She's got to live in a proper place. I'm going to talk to the Harlan Court people."

My brother stayed in the room while me and my father went over to the Harlan Court Efficiency Apartments, which were six blocks over toward the park. There were "For Rent" signs in most of the Harlan Court windows. My father showed the owner his WPA letter, and you'd've thought it said he'd just bought the Ford Motor Company. The owner popped up from his desk and opened the door for us and showed us a two-room furnished apartment on the second floor with a kitchen and bath that he said we could have for thirty dollars a month, including heat and hot water. My father then went to work on him and wangled a three-month concession. I guess nobody wangled a concession better than my father. The other thing he was a wizard at was jumping the electricity. It was this way he invented not to pay for electricity. He'd take a piece of wire and attach it to the electric line in such a way that the electricity passed from the main line into the apartment without going through the meter. His friend Carl Klein always said my father would electrocute himself one day but he never did. When the man from the electric company was due to read the meter, my father would disconnect his wire and then put it back the minute the man was gone. A couple of times the electric company sent an inspector to see if something was wrong with our meter, but my father explained as how we only used candles at night and the inspector wrote that on his report.

This Harlan Court apartment we were getting had a Murphy bed in each room and windows everywhere except the kitchen. The living room had a sofa and soft chairs and a little balcony you could stand on. When I was in the kitchen, which had a gas stove with four burners and an icebox that could hold fifty pounds of ice, I called to my father, who was in the living room, and asked him to say something. It was quite a thrill hearing him talk all the way from another room.

My father drove out to get my mother in the Ford and he brought her right to the door of the Avalon. The Repleviners were lying in wait for him, but I guess he didn't care now that he was a Clerk, First Class and not a salesman any more. My father paid no attention to the Repleviners and just helped my mother from the Ford, and then left it right there at the curb as if the Repleviners were doormen at some fancy hotel who were going to park it.

We had a swell reunion—all four of us together again, and then my mother straightened up the room and put everything in order. She said that was the way it was when we moved in and that's the way she was going to leave it. She put her stockings and her underthings in her handbag but everything else was left in the closet. My father had worked out the scheme that my mother and brother would go on ahead to the Harlan Courts and that me and him would try to escape with the only things that mattered— Skippy, the radio, and my father's heirloom umbrella.

My father had taken all the cord out of his string-saving drawer and tied it together into one long piece. When it got dark, he left the room and walked around the block. That way he could enter the parking lot from the alley without anyone in the lobby seeing him. In the meantime, I tied one end of the escape cord around the radio, all around it crosswise and up and down till it was *really* tied on. Then when I saw my father sneaking across the parking lot, I started to slowly lower the radio out the window. I had to be careful not to bang it against the window on the second floor as it passed by. My father was standing directly below me, waiting.

He untied the radio and I hauled up the escape cord and tied on the umbrella and lowered that. So far so good, but now came the scary part, lowering Skippy, because if he started to make a racket, with all those open windows, he'd give away the whole thing. I tied the escape cord around the ring at the top of the cage, and then, after warning him to keep his beak shut, I put on the cage cover. I tied it around the bottom with a piece of cord. One peep out of him and Christian would have canary for dinner. Just the thought of losing Mr. Skippy, who had been such a good pal all through that awful shut-in time, made me feel a little dizzy.

I held the cage outside the window for a few seconds to let Skippy get used to it; then very, very gently I started to lower it. The radio and umbrella had been easy to hold away from the building, but it was hard to get my arm far enough out to keep the cage from touching. As it passed the second-floor window, it swung in a little and tapped against the glass. Skippy didn't say anything but there was a big flutter of wings, which probably meant he had been knocked off the perch. I froze the cage right there where it was and held my breath, but I guess there was no one in 209, or at least no one who happened to look up and see a canary cage go floating by the window. My father was hissing at me and waving, so I quickly lowered Skippy the rest of the way.

As soon as I saw that my father had his hands on the cage, I dropped the escape cord. The scheme was that my father would sneak away from the parking lot with the radio, umbrella, and cage the same way he had sneaked in, and that I would meet him at Aubert and Fountain to help him carry the things to the Harlan Courts. I was supposed to grab my bag of marbles and my cigar bands, leave the key on the table, and go right on out of there, but I just couldn't. All those terrible days and nights I had spent in that stinky room and now I was supposed to hand over everything I had suffered for. Well, I couldn't. That's all. I looked at all my things in my drawer and hanging there in the closet, and I *couldn't* leave them. All the bank would do was throw them in Ben's dirty storeroom where they'd rot along with everything else. Well, not *my* things. They had Sandoz's things and Mr. Evans's things and Mr. Able's and now they'd have my father's and my mother's things, but not mine.

I didn't have much time. I stripped off my shirt and pants, and first I put on all my underwear shorts, and my three pairs of socks. Then I put on my three shirts, all my pants, my school sweater, my raggedy play sweater, and Lester's blue coat. The black shoes were a little big, so I was able to squeeze into them with my three pairs of socks. I stuffed my handkerchiefs and baseball cards into my coat pockets, looped my bag of marbles through my belt so's it hung from my waist, and plinked my Feltie on my head. I took a look at myself in the mirror. A little fat, but I scrunched myself up inside the clothes to get as small as I could and it didn't look too bad.

I reached up under my coat and stuck my Keds side by side inside my belt at my back, then covered them over with the coat. You couldn't even see a bulge, which gives you an idea of how roomy Lester's coat was. Okay, *now* I was ready! I picked up my pirate box and my cigar bands and started out, but I suddenly remembered I'd forgotten all about my tennis racket. Criminy, I should have lowered it with the umbrella. Well, I couldn't leave *that*, could I? But what to do? I certainly didn't look like I was dressed for tennis, and besides it was night outside. They had stopped Mr. Evans with his piano-tuning bag, hadn't they, and if they stopped me because of the tennis racket, they'd probably spot everything else.

I unbuttoned my coat and put the head of the racket up under my left armpit, then I buttoned the coat and held my left arm close to my body. It worked fine, and all you could see was a little bit of the handle sticking out from under the coat.

I went out and closed the door and I thought to myself, I'm walking down the Avalon corridor for the last time. My heart was thumping to beat the band. I was wearing so much clothes I could barely bend my knees to walk, and when I started down the stairs my leg missed the step and I just caught the banister in time. That was all I needed, to come bouncing down the stairs into the lobby with everything flying out from all over me. So I went down the rest of the stairs carefully. When I got to the bottom, with the bright lights of the lobby and all the people in front of me, I felt this big panic feeling rise up in me. Mr. Desot was behind the desk with Mr. Neville. Ben was standing near the door, chewing on a matchstick. And I could see Mrs. Desot out on the sidewalk in front of the hotel. I wanted to die. Or at least go up and take everything off.

But I didn't. I just scrunched up and jammed my left arm tight against me, and started across the lobby. I was pretending to look at my cigar-band book, but out of the corner of my eye I could see Mr. Desot and Mr. Neville look at me, and when I passed Ben he took the matchstick out of his mouth and looked at me, too.

"Whatchu got there?" he asked. He meant the cigar bands.

I nearly fainted. "None of your business," I said, and just kept going. It was probably the best answer I ever gave anyone in my whole life.

I went on out the door, feeling his icy hand grab my shoulder as I dug Lester's pearl-handled knife up to its hilt into his stomach. "Aaron," Mrs. Desot said as I came out on the sidewalk. All my blood dried up.

"Yes, Ma'am?"

"Did Danny speak to you?"

"About what?"

"About tomorrow."

Ben had come out on the sidewalk with his matchstick back in his mouth and he was looking at me. I held the racket against me even tighter.

"No, Ma'am, what about tomorrow?"

"Oh, that boy, does he ever remember anything?" Ben was still looking at me. "The birthday party tomorrow. Four o'clock. Can you come?"

"Oh, yes, Ma'am, thank you very much!" Trying to lock me out and now they were inviting me to a birthday party, for crying out loud! She reached over and touched my forehead. "My but you're hot! Aren't you dressed a little warm for this time of the year?" The sweat was pouring off me like I was in a shower.

"Well, yes, Ma'am, uh, I guess so, but I've had this cold coming on and my mother wants me to stay warm."

"She's absolutely right! Nothing like a good sweat to kill a cold. Mothers are always right, remember that!"

"Yes, Ma'am. Well, uh, I have to be going."

"Tomorrow at four o'clock. Don't forget."

"Oh, no, Ma'am!"

I had to pass right under Ben's nose. He followed me with his eyes without moving his head. I just kept on going. Mr. Desot came out and started to talk to Ben, and although I couldn't turn my eyes back far enough to really see, I think the two of them were looking in my direction. Every stiff-legged step I could feel a hand grab me. This gun in my back. But I kept the top of my racket tight under my arm and tried not to hurry. From the front of the hotel to Aubert and Fountain was two hundred miles and it took about six hours to get there. When I turned the corner into Aubert out of view of the Avalon, I quickly ducked into a candy store and watched to see if I was being followed.

"What the hell you think you're doing?" the owner yelled at me. It gave me such a start I dropped my tennis racket. "You steal that somewhere?" he yelled at me. I got out of there. Running. I raced down Aubert to Fountain and it felt good. Running stiff-legged is not as hard as walking stiff-legged, I found out. Spinning around the corner into Fountain, one of the Keds fell out of the back of my pants and I had to go back to get it.

My father was sitting on an iron railing under a streetlight with the cage and the radio at his feet, and the umbrella over his arm. I came puffing up with my tennis racket in one hand and one Ked in the other. The cigar bands and pirate box were under my arm.

"All set," I said. I could barely see my father I had so much sweat in my eyes.

"You're drenched," my father said.

"These clothes are a little too hot," I said, and then because it was either take them off or faint, I started to undress. I took off Lester's blue coat and my father put it over his arm, and as I peeled off sweaters and shirts and socks and pants, my father began to laugh, and I began to laugh, too. Each time I took something off, we laughed a little harder, till finally I was laughing so hard I could scarcely get the clothes off and my father was doubled over. People across the street came out on their porch to have a look but we didn't care. We were having this wonderful laugh together.

I got to laughing so hard I began to cry, laughing and crying and taking off those layers of clothes and piling them on my father's arm. Laughing so hard with the tears running down our faces, I'll bet the people on the porch across the street couldn't figure out if we were laughing or crying.

Three years later,
Aaron and Sullivan
were still . . .

Looking for Miracles

Chapter One

Farewell to the Ice Wagon, But Hello to What?

My job on the ice wagon was just about the best summer job in St. Louis. I'd stand there among the cold-steaming burlap-covered ice chunks sucking on ice chips while the wagon rumbled down the street with Mr. Manuche yelling "Eyeee-ees!" in a voice that rose up and into every kitchen. Little kids would run along behind the wagon begging for ice slivers or trying to get their mouths under the steady stream of ice-cold water that dribbled from the rear corners of the wagon.

When the wagon stopped for a sale, I'd pluck the ice pick from where it was stuck in the wagon's side, flip back the burlap, and pick-pick-pick in a straight line down the cloudy center of the ice block, splitting it neatly into the size Mr. Manuche wanted. Then I'd grab the tongs and dig its points into the sides of the ice chunk and push it forward onto the pad of burlap on Mr. Manuche's shoulder.

It was maybe 120 degrees out there in the St. Louis sun, with the street tar half melted, but I'd be standing there in the wet dark cave of the wagon, my Keds soaking in the icy water. At seven dollars a week it was a great summer job, all right.

I had worked for Mr. Manuche the summer before and I was supposed to start work for him again the day after I graduated from Soldan High School. The previous summer I had given my mother six of my seven weekly dollars, but this summer I was going to save it all because I was starting college in the fall, on a scholarship, and I needed every cent I earned to pay for my books and supplies.

One Saturday morning in May, I went over to see Mr. Manuche, but above the icehouse where it had said V. MANUCHE ICE & COAL, it now said SCHULTZ & SON. There was a boy my age out in front harnessing up Mr. Manuche's horse, Prince.

"Where's Mr. Manuche?" I asked.

"Gone," he said.

"Gone where?"

"Dunno."

"He sell his business?"

"Yup."

A big man with a lot of hair and tattoos came out of the ice-house onto the platform, pushing a hundred-pound block in front of him.

"Are you Mr. Schultz?" I asked.

"Yeah."

"I worked for Mr. Manuche last summer. I know the routes and I thought maybe you could use me."

"I got my son there."

"Well, could you use the two of us? I really know the routes and all the customers."

"You want to split your salary, John?" Mr. Schultz asked the boy.

"What salary?" the boy asked.

Mr. Schultz got a big laugh out of that. The boy spat on the ground and that made Mr. Schultz laugh all the harder, pointing his forefinger at him while he roared away.

I walked away feeling everything in my stomach. I had taken it for granted that I had this job, but now, without it, there was no way I could go to Washington University in the fall.

The first thing I felt was anger, which was usually the way I reacted when anyone got me in a corner. All right, I said to myself, I'll just go tell them to give their old scholarship to some rich kid who has money to buy books and supplies and pay for lab fees and all that. How could I possibly manage? My mother, who made a meager income from her Bell Company job, was behind in the rent and we skipped more meals than we ate. My father was still recuperating from his heart attack and couldn't have worked if he had had a steady job, which he hadn't.

After fast-walking a couple of blocks, I began to cool down. Anger left, feeling-sorry-for-myself moved in. I didn't want to go home for two reasons: one was that whenever anything like this happened, my brother, Sullivan, had a million questions to ask and I didn't feel like explaining everything to him; the other was that this was Saturday and I always stayed away on Saturday morning. We lived in three rooms above Sorkin's delicatessen, and directly across the roof from us was the Beth Israel Synagogue, where they prayed on Saturday. I really didn't mind the cantor's singing and all the congregation noises, but what used to drive me batty was this one old man who all morning long would keep coming out on the porch of the synagogue, directly opposite our windows, to have a coughing fit. He had twenty, thirty fits a morning and it was the kind of coughing that made his throat rattle. He would choke and turn redder and redder, each cough grinding deeper, gasping for air until finally when he was just about to suffocate he would hack up an enormous clinker, rasp it out of his throat, rear back, and spit it out over the railing. You could hear it plop on the pavement below.

I thought about where else I could go and decided to see if Billy Tyzzer was home. Billy and I had been friends since grammar school when I taught him how to stop being a cunny-thumb and shoot marbles properly. Billy was rich and lived in a house with its own yard. He always had pretty good ideas about how to make money, like raising canaries. He had put me on to how to breed them, even lending me a female to mate with our bird, Skippy. It was a good marriage and they produced four babies that should have brought me three dollars apiece at the pet store, but when they were old enough to sell, the pet-store owner rejected them because they were all females. Canary females are worthless because they don't sing. But that certainly wasn't Billy's fault. His canaries produced babies at the same time as mine, six of them, and all six turned out to be males. Eighteen dollars.

Billy was up in his room working on his stamp collection. He put down his magnifying glass and gave me the hand grip we had used ever since we had that secret club in the eighth grade.

"You know something?" he said. "I heard about a job only yesterday from a guy I used to go to camp with. There's this new camp that the CCC just built in the Ozarks and they're looking for counselors."

"Are you going to apply?"

"No. I'm going to work on my uncle's ranch in Texas."

"Well, do you think they'll take someone like me? I don't have a lot of experience."

"Just go over and see the director. I have his name. The YMHA is running the camp and they pay ten dollars a week. When I think of some of the finky counselors I've had. . . . Just go on over."

I'd said I didn't have a lot of experience. I certainly didn't. If ever there was a city boy, I was it. Not only had I never been to camp, but I had barely been out of St. Louis. Except for the time when my mother was in the Fee-Fee Sanatorium and I went to see her on the Creve Coeur trolley. I'd never been on a hike, couldn't swim a stroke, never been in a rowboat or canoe, never been on a horse, didn't know fauna from flora.

But this was a job—J-O-B—and maybe the only job that would come my way. None of the kids I knew had been able to find jobs, and the same went for most of their fathers. My father, after a long wait, had finally landed a WPA job but lost it five months later when he had his heart attack.

I phoned the camp director, Mr. Arnold Berman, who called himself "Chief." After all, it was Camp Hiawatha. He gave me an appointment for the following Thursday, which meant I had less than a week to become an experienced camp counselor.

What I did was to spend all the time I could at the public library. Sullivan would come along and read Tom Swift and the Rover Boys while I read every book on camping that they had on the shelves, plus the Boy Scout manual, cover to cover. Not only read, but memorized. At school I had developed a trick of being able to read a book just before an exam, remember the stuff practically word-for-word for the test, then let it evaporate right out of my head the following day. The Boy Scouts of America could have quizzed me about any merit badge (on paper) and they would have thought they were dealing with an Eagle Scout. Of course there's a world of difference between knowing how to start a fire without matches and being able to do it. But I figured there was little likelihood that Chief Berman would ask for any demonstrations in his office.

But I did practice what I could. Like at night I would step out our bedroom window onto the delicatessen roof; Sullivan would follow me. With the Boy Scout diagrams in my hand, I'd try to identify the constellations. Of course, I already knew the few easy ones, like the two Dippers, but I never could spot things like the Little Bear, the Dragon, the Whale, and the Peacock. Sullivan claimed he could see all of them.

"You don't see it? There it is—right there alongside the Big Dipper." He'd point his finger at the million stars up there and of course I had no way of knowing if he really saw what I couldn't see. My brother had a super-active imagination and it was hard to know with him what was make-believe and what was real. He had had some pretty awful years, so I guess when the reality got very bad, the make-believe came in handy.

What had made Sullivan's life so wretched was being farmed out so often. My father, like many others, had been unable to cope with the Depression, and as a result we became urban migrants, moving from one place in St. Louis to another, a jump ahead of the process servers. I went to eleven different grammar schools. We finally wound up in one room in the Avalon, a seedy hotel at Kingshighway and Delmar. My mother earned what she could at a variety of odd jobs, ranging from typing to selling lingerie to the ladies in the whorehouses in East St. Louis. But she could not work and also look after my young brother, who was then five. Her solution was to ship Sullivan to various relatives; he mostly boarded with my aunt and uncle in Keokuk, Iowa, who had several children of their own. Theoretically, my father was supposed to pay two dollars a week for Sullivan's keep, but he rarely had the two dollars to send. This resulted in a growing resentment against poor Sullivan, who was constantly berated for our father's dereliction by whoever was keeping him. Sometimes the irate relative would suddenly pack up Sullivan's meager belongings in his cardboard suitcase and send him back to us on the bus.

On those occasions when Sullivan did return to our family group, he lived in the practical fear that at any time he would again be farmed out. My father frequently discussed Sullivan's status in his presence as if he weren't there, a child-commodity to be shipped around like the watches my father used to sell before the Depression. I felt Sullivan's reactions, his hurts, very keenly, and as a result I developed a kind of subconscious guilt over being the Chosen One to stay with the family. But in all honesty, although I'd miss him when he was gone, I did benefit from his absence since I'd get a bigger portion of whatever food we managed to scrounge, and I'd have the bed all to myself. There were two beds in the room when we lived at the Avalon, with a screen in between. There was one full-sized double bed which my parents shared, and a smaller bed which I shared with Sullivan. We constantly quarreled over who was crowding who and I was forever drawing indented marks down the center of the sheet to delineate our respective territories.

Then, suddenly, he wasn't there to fight with any more, for no sooner did Sullivan get settled into school than my mother would find a job and off he'd go with promises that it wouldn't be for long. Sullivan was certainly aware that he was a burden both to those who kept him and to those who had sent him away. From five years of age on, Sullivan fully knew that, practically speaking, he was not wanted anywhere.

When he was away my mother yearned for him; occasionally she had hysterics, laughing and crying uncontrollably at dinner when his name was mentioned—but this faraway yearning was of no value to Sullivan. My mother tried to scrimp together enough extra money to telephone Sullivan once a week. Sometimes, though, she had to miss a week. One time, on the phone, she told him how much she missed him, and Sullivan, who was not a cryer, began to cry. "How can I hug you, Mama," he asked, "when you're in the telephone?"

Sullivan finally came back for good, never to be farmed out again, when my mother got a regular job with the Western Union Company in May of 1936. The Western Union Company had a policy of not employing married women, but my mother had lied to get the job. I had just turned sixteen, and my brother was going on eleven. It was going to be our first summer under the same roof and I had promised to teach him to play tennis on the public courts in Forest Park.

But that's about the only way Sullivan figured in my summer plans. He had been away too long and too often for me to know much about him. Or, to be honest about it, to *care* much about him. We had very little in common. We didn't even look alike. I was predominantly freckles, wavy red hair, prominent nose. Except for a few dribbles on the tip of his nose, Sullivan was virtually unfreckled, straight dark hair, button nose. No resemblance. Nor in our personalities. I was aggressive, boisterous, verbal, tempestuous. Sullivan was placid, quiet, taciturn, introverted. He spent most of his time sitting in a chair in the front room reading adventure books about swashbuckling men in faraway places. Rafael Sabatini was his favorite author.

Curiously, the only times I had had a rise of brother feeling toward Sullivan was on those occasions when he had his bad earaches. Sullivan was susceptible to ear infections that caused excruciating pain and ultimately had to be relieved by an ear doctor who went inside his ear with a scalpel and lanced the infected area in order to drain the pus. The doctor gave no anesthetic for this and the pain was such that my mother and I had to hold Sullivan so the doctor could perform his surgery. My mother would hold Sullivan's legs and I would hold his head and arms, pinning his head against my chest, as the doctor maneuvered his forehead mirror for interior illumination. Sullivan would wail in anticipation of the knife's pain, and then scream and writhe as the scalpel pierced the infection. Once he bit my forearm rather severely. Holding him like that, as he suffered that barbaric pain, was when I came closest to feeling a sense of being his brother.

Sullivan had a strong attachment to me, a *dependence* on me, but not in a pushy way. For the most part, this dependence emerged as a strong identification with whatever I was doing; he virtually suffered as I suffered, shared my happinesses and triumphs, became depressed when I did, angry over the same things I got angry about, and the sports and hobbies (such as collecting cigar bands) that interested me interested him. So, naturally, he became all bound up in my seven-day crash program to become a camp counselor. He tried to read all the camp books after I read them, but he couldn't keep up with my voracious pace.

I also read a lot of Indian books. I figured that since they called it Camp Hiawatha and Berman called himself Chief, they would be bearing down pretty hard on the Injun motif. I memorized some Indian songs and tried to do the rain dance as described in one of the books. Sullivan said it looked more like the Big Apple. The day before the interview Sullivan gave me what he called an

Indian Surprise Box. Inside it was a headdress he had made, using chicken feathers that had been plucked from Sorkin's chickens. Sullivan had spent a lot of time painting the feathers and sewing little beads on the headband. He suggested I wear it at the interview to impress Chief Berman.

I got to the interview a half hour early, but walked around the block a few times so it wouldn't look like I was too eager for the job. I could have spared myself the effort. Chief Berman's waiting room was packed with boys. My heart dropped. The woman at the desk gave me a number and I waited my turn. Most of the boys were eighteen or nineteen and you could tell just by looking at them that they could swim, hike, and paddle canoes. I kept going over the list of knots, trail signs, constellations, first-aid instructions, bird names, tree names, and all that that I had in my pocket. But looking at the faces of the boys as they came out of Chief Berman's office, I was pretty sure that all the jobs would be filled by the time they got to me.

Chief Berman was stocky and muscular, with a thin straight mustache and hairy eyebrows. He was very well scrubbed and creased. He gave my fingernails a close look which made me glad I had remembered to scrape them with my pearl-handled penknife. I was pretty well scrubbed myself, but not creased. He asked me my age—I told him eighteen. He asked what experience I had had, and I said I had been a junior counselor and counselor at Camp Chickachuck in Oregon. (A name I picked out of the Camp Guide section of *Liberty* magazine.) I also said I had spent a couple of summers at my uncle's ranch in New Mexico. (My uncle actually ran a men's-clothing store in Keokuk, Iowa.) Chief Berman asked me what my special interests were. I was thinking about the stream of boys who had been in before me, so I decided to lay it on thick. If the Chief had recently read the Boy Scout manual he might have found that my interests had a familiar ring to them, but as it was he listened intently as I ticked off my newfound knowledge of earth and sky.

Chief Berman looked at me intently. "Are you a leader?" he asked. He spoke in a stentorian voice with a lot of enunciation that made his pencil mustache bob around.

"How do you mean?" I asked.

"Are you a take-charge type?"

"Well, it might sound like bragging. . . ."

"That's all right—I like a man who can blow his own horn."

"Yes, sir. Well, I was captain of most everything I did. Baseball team, basketball, debate team, dramatic society, tennis team, president of the senior class. . . ." (As a matter of fact, I *was* captain of the debate team.)

"I like secure men who know who they are and where they're going."

"Yes, sir." I was having a hard time keeping my eyes off his mustache.

"I've been a camp director for fifteen years and I've had good counselors and bad. I had this one counselor who got *homesick,* for God's sake, and one who was afraid of bugs. Why, I've even had a counselor who couldn't swim!"

"No!"

"Can you imagine anybody applying to be a counselor and they can't swim!"

"Unbelievable!"

"I kicked his bottom right out of there!"

"I should think so."

"Now, this camp is a real challenge. Brand new, carved out of the Ozark wilderness, a real challenge, wild animals, primitive, cut off from civilization. . . ." He sprang out of his seat and whisked around the desk. "This is no sissy camp. I don't want any country-club counselors, get me? I want rugged men who can meet the challenge!" For emphasis he banged me on the arm with his fist.

I snapped up out of my seat. "It's my kind of camp, Chief!" I said. I almost saluted.

"Send in the next boy," he said, returning to his seat.

He was watching me, so I tried to walk out of there with a tough swagger, but, skinny as I was, it probably only looked like I'd gone stiff in the joints.

My brother was waiting outside the Y. "How'd you do?" he asked.

"I don't know."

"He didn't hire you?"

"No. They let you know. There were a million guys being interviewed." I was feeling depressed. I'd laid it on too thick. I mean, captain of *everything* and all that.

"Boy, lemme tell you, they're loonies not to hire you. I seen those guys comin' out and they *couldn't* pass you up for creepers like that."

In my brother's eyes I was Tarzan, Jack Dempsey, and Franklin Roosevelt rolled into one. We walked along for a while, me worrying.

"What'll you do if you don't get the job?" Sullivan asked, joining my worry.

"Not go to college, I guess."

"You *gotta* go to college."

"Well, let's not talk about it."

"You gotta go," Sullivan said. "Listen, we won't let them do that to you!"

Chapter Two

There's a Little Indian in All of Us, But Is It Enough?

I don't want to give a false impression of how I truly was toward my brother. I liked him, as I've said, but I never went out of my way to do anything for him. I never gave much thought to him since I was pretty much interested only in myself. This conceit may have been peculiar to my own character, or common to all sixteen-year-olds, or a natural result of the pressures and fears of all those Depression years. I don't know which.

Whatever the cause, I was totally self-interested and self-possessed. Even before the Depression, when my father was out on the road with his samples and my mother worked as a secretary at Woodward-Tiernan Printing, I was on my own quite a lot. It was a good thing that I was, for I acquired a certain resiliency and inventiveness, a certain turn of imagination and fantasy, a certain shrewdness and belligerency that helped me enormously when, at the age of twelve, I had to live alone in that dreary room at the Avalon Hotel. My mother had been taken to the Fee-Fee Sanatorium for treatment of her consumption, and my father, after several years without a decent job, had gone out on the road on a drawing account for the Elgin Watch Company.

The highlight of that period at the Avalon when I lived alone, or I should say the lowlight, occurred when the management tried to put a lock on the door because we were so far behind with our rent. They couldn't padlock the door, however, as long as I was in the room, so I determined to stay there, despite the malevolent, sadistic bellhop who stalked the corridor, lock in hand, waiting to pounce on the door the moment I left the room. As the days of this siege passed, my hunger grew to the point where I started to eat the food ads that I cut out of old copies of the *Woman's Home Companion*. I would chew up a color page of a succulent roast beef surrounded by roasted potatoes and vegetables, drink a glass of water, and feel as bloated as if I had just had three actual helpings of that rotogravure roast beef.

But eventually this self-delusion began to fade, and with both my mind and my stomach at the snapping point, I was miraculously saved by the totally unexpected arrival of Sullivan, who had been once again shipped back from Keokuk for non-payment of his keep. When I unbolted the door and saw him there with his battered cardboard suitcase and his snap-on bow tie, I threw my arms around him and we had a good cry together.

I mark that siege at the Avalon as the beginning of my being so self-centered. That's not to say that I didn't care about my mother getting well, or that I wasn't terribly upset when they called me to the principal's office to tell me that my father had had a heart attack and to come to the hospital right away because he was not expected to live through the day. But these were all things that I carefully kept exterior to my innards. They touched my epidermis—I should say my derma—but not my lungs and heart. That's how Sullivan touched me: he was a prickle on my skin.

But for Sullivan I was something in the deepest part of him. I suppose I represented what he wanted to be. There was no one else to emulate. Even before his heart attack, our father was an ineffectual man who made no attempt to establish any kind of relationship with his sons. He was a man of sound instincts and a certain kindness, but he lacked fiber, and particularly did he lack any sense of being. So there was not much to pass on to us. His ambitions were petty and his angers were, in effect, tirades against his own inadequacies. There was nothing in him to emulate. He was neither physical nor intellectual, subtle nor overt, compassionate nor distant. He was a dozen streams that seemed to peter out in the foothills of the problems he had to face. He was concerned about feeding us, but there was only his worry as our provision; it was our mother who had the grit to scrounge whatever meager food, clothing, and shelter we came by.

So Sullivan, adrift, saw in me the only sign of strength and anchorage. I was physically strong, excelled in several sports, was rarely sick, and fought my own feisty battles. I never gave ground, instinctively using a belligerent offense as my basic defense against the appalling onslaughts we suffered, mostly from the Depression. Whereas Sullivan was pushed around, I pushed others around. Not that I was a bully—I don't mean that at all. I mean that I was motivated by a combination of fantasy and ability that made me truly believe I was able to do almost anything I undertook—and do it better than anyone else. I almost never put myself in situations where I could not persevere. When I did encounter an adverse situation I backed out of it quickly. Football, for instance. I played enough to know that no combination of fantasy (that I was Red Grange) plus the reality of my speed and balance was going to overcome my inability to endure being smacked. I simply had a totally negative response to deliberate contact, so I scuttled football even though I was second-string quarterback and the coach wanted me to stay on the team.

I did the same thing in studies. My early encounters with physics and chemistry convinced me that I was no better suited to them than football—as far as I was concerned, they were the contact studies on the curriculum. I was second in my high-school graduating class and president of the honorary Torchbearers Society, but my scholastic achievements were based solely on my strengths. I avoided tackling my weaknesses to see if I could overcome them. I simply basked in the glory of what I knew I did well.

Of course, Sullivan was not aware of how I had pruned my weaknesses. He saw only my secure strengths, which gave the false impression of omnipotence. I had triumphed only over triumphs, not over defeats. But in Sullivan's eyes I was the personification of Big Brother. In addition, I was the privileged one who remained with the family while he was shunted off. I was also his nemesis, an indelible shadow cast on him wherever he went. At school, teachers I'd once had would say to him:

"Aaron's brother? I hope you can do as well. He got the only E-plus I ever gave. You have a lot to live up to."

That's all Sullivan ever heard, especially around the house. My mother and father would look at his report card and explode at him: "Your brother never brought home grades like that! Aren't you ashamed of yourself? Always listening to the radio and reading those junky books. . . ."

"*Captain Blood* is not junky! You just oughta read it—"

"Don't you talk back to me!"

"You just oughta read it sometime—"

"Did you hear me?"

"And *Scaramouche*."

"It's no wonder you're failing."

"I'm not failing. Looka there—a B, two Cs, and a D."

"That's as good as failing. There's never been a D in this house."

In the days that followed my interview for the counselor job, Sullivan worried as much about my not hearing from Chief Berman as I did. Convinced that I would be rejected, every day after school I tramped around looking for some other summer job, and Sullivan tagged along, but whatever I heard about or saw in the paper, there was always a line of grown men applying and I couldn't blame an owner for hiring a father instead of a boy of sixteen. The beauty of the counselor job was that it needed a boy, not a man.

And ten dollars a week to be out in the open, playing games and having fun!

But as the days passed without word from Chief Berman, I got more and more discouraged. Sullivan tried to cheer me up with money-making suggestions: a wash-your-car-in-your-own-drive-way service, a running-errands company, collecting bottles for the two-cent refunds—suggestions like that. I tried to get rid of Sullivan, because when I was miserable I liked to be alone, but there was no way to do it without seriously hurting his feelings.

Finally I heard from Chief Berman. It took me a while to get up enough courage to open the envelope. I had known from the start that I was going to be turned down. But I wasn't. Nor was I accepted. Would I please come in at my earliest convenience?

Sullivan sat on the steps of the Y and waited while I went in for my appointment. Chief Berman was on the telephone and motioned me to sit down. My hands were clammy. Sullivan and I had been to the Varsity the night before and watched James Cagney as the jury filed in with the verdict. The way he suffered, wetting his lips, trying to swallow, his breath coming hard, that's how I suffered as I waited for Chief Berman to hang up the phone.

"Now, I have a problem with you," he said. "I was terribly impressed by your knowledge and camping know-how, but I don't think I can make you a regular counselor because you would simply be *too* knowledgeable for the head counselor of any group I put you into. It would undermine his authority with the other counselors, you see. On the other hand, you are really too young to be a head counselor—the other counselors would probably resent you."

My heart sank. Over-zealous salesmanship had done me in. "Oh, I don't know as much as I sound like I know," I said.

"You are very knowledgeable," Chief Berman said sternly.

"Yes, sir," I said, accepting the verdict.

"You have a positively brilliant grasp of astronomy."

"Yes, sir," I said, cursing the Boy Scout handbook.

"And Indian lore."

"Yes, sir."

"Do you think you can handle ten-year-olds?"

The lump that had been sinking in my throat suddenly halted. I blinked. "Do I think. . . Why, I have a brother who's ten years old. I have him and his friends around me all the time." Actually, Sullivan had no friends.

"Let me explain Camp Hiawatha to you. It's composed of four villages, each for a different age group. These four villages are self-contained except for eating—we have one main dining building. Now each of these villages is run by a chief counselor with a staff of two regular counselors and a junior counselor. I've been thinking of you for the ten-year-olds."

"Yes, sir." Lump in throat in the ascendancy.

"I have two counselors who are only eighteen, as you are, and a junior counselor who is seventeen, so it's possible, if you handle the situation correctly, that you could assert your authority as chief counselor."

Lump dropped in panic. "Chief. . . ?"

"It pays five dollars a week more. Now, what I want to know is, do you think you could handle it? This is a brand-new camp and there will be unusual problems—quite a challenge. What do you think?"

Fifteen dollars a week! For that amount of money I would have answered yes if he had asked me if I thought I could fly across the Pacific in *The Spirit of St. Louis*. "I enjoy leadership," I said.

"I warn you, it won't be easy. The campers are going to be a handful. Half of them will be coming from good homes and paying tuition. The other half will be here on scholarships—poor kids from tough neighborhoods. The haves against the have-nots."

"It doesn't bother me," I said. "I've been both."

When I emerged from the Y and saw Sullivan's worried face. I couldn't help bursting into loud laughter. The worry flew off his face and he did a little jig, running up and down the Y steps the way Bill Robinson did. "I knew it. I knew it. I knew it," he sang as he jigged up and down the steps.

"Me big chief counselor," I said, but suddenly I stopped exulting and felt very sad. I just stood there on the steps watching my happy brother. Happy over my good fortune. Happy that I was going to have a good summer and be able to go to college in the fall. Sullivan, who had never had a good summer in his life.

Until this moment I had never thought about *his* summer. I would be away at camp. My mother would be working every day at the telephone company, 8:30 to 5:30. And my father would make his daily abortive rounds of the downtown jewelry shops and department stores, trying to sell his watch straps. There was a firm in New York that sent him leather straps on consignment, and after each sale my father would pay them and take his small commission. But there weren't many sales since people who barely had money for bread certainly didn't have money for watches and watch straps. Also, the heart doctor had warned my father, after his miraculous recovery, that he had to take it very easy.

So standing there on the Y steps, I had one of those moments, rare for me, when I moved outside myself and realized what a grim summer was in store for Sullivan. In a way, looking at him that day, I was seeing him as I had not seen him before. His joyful dance had abated, but he was still smiling his big smile, two teeth missing.

"Look," I said, "I just thought of something. Wait here." I started back into the Y.

"Where you going?"

"Wait here."

I went back to Chief Berman's office and asked him whether my brother could qualify for one of the camp scholarships. He gave me an application blank.

"You won't favor him, will you?"

"He'll just be another camper to me," I said.

I didn't tell Sullivan what I had in mind. What he needed least in life was another disappointment. But whether he would be accepted at Camp Hiawatha or not, I had done something that startled me. In the past, I had always treated the members of my family as obstacles to be kept from my ambitious path. I asked for nothing, gave nothing. I lived under a family roof, but the atmosphere was contentious and the conditions depressing, so I spent as much time *not* under the family roof as possible. School and after-school sports were my worlds. I was a star at school, heaped with praise and recognition. I had closer ties to certain teachers than I did to my family. But now, this unlikely moment with my brother, I had felt something inside me, really *felt* it. But in all honesty I would have to admit that rather than giving me a positive feeling, it simply disturbed me. Although I didn't admit it to myself, I was probably secretly anticipating that Sullivan's application, which I signed for him, would be rejected. I could feel good, then, over what I had tried to do for him, but not be saddled with the responsibility of having done it.

My main concern, however, in the days that followed my appointment as chief counselor of Indian Mound Village, was how in God's name I was going to maintain this hoax. I who had scarcely been out of St. Louis, never seen a camp, couldn't swim, couldn't canoe, couldn't ride—in fact, name any camp activity, I hadn't done it.

"And what if, in the meantime, Big Chief Berman contacts Camp Chickachuck and finds out I'm an impostor?" Sullivan and I were sitting on the grass at the Forest Park tennis courts, waiting for the period bell to sound.

"He won't."

"And what if he checks on me with Soldan High and discovers I'm only sixteen—just *turned* sixteen?"

"Why would he?"

"Because that's what people do—they check on you."

"I'll betcha he won't."

"He will. You just don't know."

"I'll betcha the agate shooter I won from Chris Donohue against your knife."

"And even if he doesn't check, what do you think he'll do when we go into the water on the first day and I drown? . . . Oh, God, why did I ever get myself into this?"

"Stop worrying. You're gonna be super-colossal. You are at everything, aren't you?"

"I only do things I know I can do."

"Sure, but you can do everything."

"No I can't."

"Name me one thing you can't do."

"Swim."

"So, okay, you'll make yourself swim."

"I've tried. I can't."

"You mean that one time in the Mississippi?"

"I almost drowned. All I got out of that were leeches."

"One time don't count."

"Doesn't."

"Doesn't count. How about your telling me before the big game when you played McKinley for the championship that you couldn't hit curves?"

"I always flinched before the ball broke."

"You struck out the first three times, but the fourth time you socked a curve over the fence and won the game."

"Blind luck."

"Now me, I been trying all spring, but I still can't hit a curve."

"Hitting curves and swimming are different things."

"They know I strike out on curves, so that's all they throw me. I get scared and back away. They don't even choose me to play any more."

"I think it's because Mother's so afraid."

"Of curves?"

"I'm talking about swimming. What's curves got to do with this? She's so afraid of water."

"Did she ever go swimming with you?" I detected a slight edge of envy in his voice.

"Only one time. The Silvers had an outing at the Forest Park Highlands and we all went into the pool."

"You and Mom?"

"And the others. Mom stood in the two-foot wading section and held my hand and wouldn't let me splash around with the other kids."

"Why?"

"She said it was too dangerous for someone who didn't know how to swim."

"But how did she expect you to learn?"

"I don't know. But I was afraid of the water and didn't say a word in protest."

"I think I could learn to swim if I was around water."

"Did you ever try?"

"Once in Keokuk we all went down to the river, but there weren't enough tire tubes to go around and no one would share his with me. So I just sat on the bank and watched."

Chapter Three

If You Don't Want to Give Up Your Pearl-Handled Knife, It's Better to Leave Well Enough Alone

When I told Sullivan that he had been approved for a summer scholarship at Camp Hiawatha, he simply looked at me blankly; my words were so many darts that had not penetrated his protective armor. He had been sitting in the lopsided, sagged armchair in the front room, reading *Twenty Thousand Leagues Under the Sea* (I was trying to wean him away from Sabatini and on to Verne) when I came in with the letter of acceptance that had just come from the Y.

I had expected him to give a whoop and a holler, but, as I have pointed out, Sullivan was not conditioned for good news.

"Don't you get it?" I said. "You're going to be in my village! You're going to camp!"

"This summer? You mean—*now*?"

"That's right."

Sullivan looked worried. "I don't have anything for camp."

"Like what?"

"Like a knife."

"You don't need a knife."

"Oh, yes you do! A knife and a hatchet and a compass. But I'd settle for a knife."

"Believe me, you don't need all that."

"What if I got attacked by a bear or something?"

"There are no bears in the Ozarks."

"What are there?"

"Wildcats and snakes."

"I think I better not go."

"Now, Sullivan, you're being silly."

"All the other kids will have knives and hatchets. I know."

"How do you know?"

"I just know, that's all."

"But you've never been to camp in your life. . . ."

"Neither have you."

"What does that prove?"

"That you don't know any more'n I do. Those kids'll have canteens and hiking shoes and lariats. I've seen plenty a pictures."

"Sullivan, look, are you saying you don't want to go? After all the trouble I went to?"

"You shoulda asked me."

"But everybody likes going to camp!"

"Well, maybe I don't have any camp in my blood."

I took out my pearl-handled pocketknife. "Okay, here, now you've got a knife."

"But what'll *you* use?"

"Don't worry about me."

"You mean I can really have your pearl-handled knife?"

"For the summer."

He took the knife very carefully, handling it as if it were made of eggshells. "You know, I never had a knife."

"I know."

He opened the blade.

"Whatever you do, don't lose it," I said.

"Don't worry. It's my trusty old knife." He slashed at the air a few times. "Those snakes just better watch out."

I really didn't like lending him my knife. It had been given to me during that time at the Avalon Hotel by a friend of mine whom the cops had arrested for stealing. He had given it to me for a keep-sake as the cops were taking him away. I never saw him again.

Sullivan would probably lose it. Served me right for having meddled with his summer. I needed the knife more than he did. Who ever heard of a chief counselor without a knife?

Chapter Four

St. Aaron and His Trusty Hydrophobia Slay the Water Moccasin

Camp Hiawatha was located in a primitive, rather impenetrable section of the Ozark lake region, which lies in central Missouri about two hundred miles west of St. Louis. The narrow, long, winding Lake of the Ozarks dominates the area, and Camp Hiawatha had been built on land that had been cleared on the southeast edge of the lake. It was a CCC project and I suspect the government chose this jungle-like site for the camp because clearing it gave a long stretch of employment to a large number of Civilian Conservation Corps workers. The only access to the camp was over a new, primitive dirt road that had been hacked out of the miles of dense forest and underbrush that intervened between the nearest highway and the camp. Just hacking the road must have provided jobs for half the unemployed of Missouri.

The counselors went to Hiawatha three days before the campers were to arrive. We went by bus from in front of the Y. The three days were to be used by Chief Berman to organize the camp and allow us to get acquainted. I was so nervous, so apprehensive I might somehow be exposed for the impostor I was, that I virtually didn't sleep the night before departure. Also, it was my first trip by myself out of St. Louis and I was overexcited about that. I sat in the back of the bus to make myself as inconspicuous as possible.

The trip took about seven hours, and the counselors horsed around and sang camp songs most of the way. Of course I didn't know any of the songs, but I was pretty good at moving my mouth and pretending to sing. Besides, no one was paying any attention to me in the back of the bus. Chief Berman was sitting next to the driver and every once in a while he told everyone to stay in their seats, but no one paid any attention to him. They sang things like "Drunk last night, drunk the night before, gonna get drunk tonight like I never got drunk before. . . ."

We stopped in Loose Creek to eat and use the toilet. While I was waiting my turn to get into the men's room, a short squat fellow with a heavy neck came over to me.

"I'm Mo Brennan," he said, putting out his hand. "I'm in your cabin." His hand was so thick I could hardly get a grip on it. He got in line with me.

"I'm really pissed off," he said. "I was supposed to be the wrestling and boxing counselor, but now Big Chief Pain-in-the-Ass tells me I'm switched to volleyball. Keeee-rist! Volleyball! Emphasis on team sport, he says. Volleyball! Listen, I'll run a team sport for him—the gang bang. I hear there's a Girl Scout camp across the lake."

The muscles in his neck appeared to ripple. His voice was a baritone growl, with the ends of sentences descending precipitously into his barrel chest. "Now, you're our cabin leader, right? So you go to the Big Chief and tell him ol' Mo Brennan is here for wrestling and boxing and not for fagging around with volleyball. Volleyball! You go tell him. He's over there having a doughnut."

"Well, why don't we wait till we get to camp?"

"What for?"

"I just think it's better."

"Crap. Go tell him now."

"No, I think it's best to discuss it at camp—now he's got his mind on other things."

"Then just tell him what I said and he better think about it. Go ahead, tell him that. I'd tell him myself, but I have a tendency to lose my temper."

I had moved up to next in line for the urinal. I realized that before I went in there to pee I had to make Mo Brennan understand that I was not going to be told what to do. Yet, I had no feeling of authority—just the opposite. My mouth was dry, and as Mo Brennan's voice got lower, mine got higher.

"Leave it to me, Brennan," I said, trying to force my voice down. I opened the door and went into the men's room. "I'll take care of it," I said as the door closed.

As I stood there, trying to pee, I felt frightened. We had not even reached camp and already I felt totally inadequate and fearful of the role I had taken on. Once we got to camp, how long would it take somebody like Mo to find out I didn't know my behind from a campfire?

The four villages of Camp Hiawatha were little camps unto themselves. My village, Indian Mound, was completely removed from the rest of the camp and could only be reached by a crude, narrow path that wound through dense woods. The village consisted of seven cabins made of logs and screen, a recreation hall of fieldstone and timber, a four-seater outhouse, a bank of showerheads (cold water only), and a central drinking fountain and water dispenser. The cabins were designed for four occupants, which meant we would have twenty-four campers in Indian Mound, the seventh cabin to be shared by the four counselors.

In addition to Mo Brennan, my counselors were Paul Roth and Myron Barmowitz, who was the junior counselor—which meant he didn't get paid. Paul Roth was of the upper class. Paul Trimble Roth. I had seen pictures of Franklin Roosevelt as a teenager, and Paul Roth looked a lot like early Roosevelt. He was slightly obese and spoke with an Eastern prep-school accent. His clothes were very expensive but not new. Starting at age six, he had been going to the best summer camps in the country, but for the past two summers he had loafed around his family's estate in Ladue, which was the ritziest St. Louis suburb. His indolence, however, had irritated his father, who was a mover and a shaker, and this banishment to Camp Hiawatha had been devised as therapy. The terms of the banishment were that if Paul stuck it out for the summer, he would get a Marmon roadster on entering Yale in the fall. He smoked a lot and had a peculiar way of smiling at you that made you feel inferior. Mo Brennan and he loathed each other on sight.

Myron Barmowitz was skinny, hairy, and pimply. He had overlapped teeth and cracked his knuckles a lot. He was very quiet, rarely spoke, and had hiccups several times a day. He was interested in absolutely nothing but the horn he brought to camp, and he was passionate about that. It was a cornet that he kept in a state of high gleam. It nestled in a flannel bag inside its black leather case, and Corny, which of course was his immediate nickname, kept it under his pillow during the day and at the foot of his cot when he slept. He would sit on the edge of his cot by the hour, fingering the three valves while blowing silently into the cornet. But sometimes, especially during the afternoon rest period, he would put the mute in and play it. He would lie on his cot, the golden horn pointed to the ceiling, his pimply cheeks puffed out. his eyes closed, playing slow and mournful jazz tunes.

I didn't mind Corny's music, but when Mo Brennan was in the cabin he raised hell. We finally worked out a compromise: when Mo was in the cabin, Corny would either not play the horn or else go play it in the rec hall. Paul Roth, nicknamed Bugs because of his deftness with a flyswatter, didn't care one way or another about Corny's playing, for he spent most of his free time playing chess with Babe Halpern, the assistant director (we called him Little Big Chief).

Two things happened the very first day of camp that miraculously gave me some standing among my fellow counselors and helped overcome my fear of being inadequate. The first incident occurred right at the start of the counselors' conference. Big Chief Berman displayed a large board on which a number of Indian relics had been mounted. "Now, the reason we are called Camp Hiawatha," he explained, "is that these arrowheads, spear tips, pottery pieces, and whatnot were found here during construction, proving that this region had once been an Indian settlement. That's our motif, our theme, our *raison d'être*—Indian!—and we must plan everything with that in mind. Yet, none of you knows beans about Indians. I want powwows and rain dances and braves on the warpath. Indian sing-a-longs, loincloths, headdresses, and totem poles. The works! Peace pipes. Tomahawks and teepees. War paint. Tracking in the woods without a compass. Now, fortunately there is one counselor among you who is steeped in Indian knowledge. I will ask him to meet with you every morning at nine a.m. and cover as much Indian stuff in three days as he can. I am putting him in charge of Indianizing Camp Hiawatha."

Then he called on me to stand up and be recognized.

Which I did.

I should have been panicked by this unexpected and unwarranted assignment, but curiously I felt a surge of relief. Instead of having to perform some camp function that would reveal my ineptitude, I was being called upon to do something that no one there knew anything about. What's more, I had prudently brought the two library books (*All About Indians, The Indian Reader*) from which I had gleaned the information that had impressed Berman, and which I had anticipated using for my Indian Mound Village program.

In the afternoon of that first day, a second event occurred, even more unexpectedly, that helped give me an even better camp position. We were taken down to the lakefront to get acquainted with the water facilities. Before going, we were briefed by Bud Fischer, the nature counselor. He was a tall, lean, handsome man, twenty or so, who was a track star at the University of Missouri.

303

He told us what we might expect in the way of animal life in the area, but emphasized that the only creatures that would give us any real trouble were two snakes, the copperhead and the water moccasin.

"They both abound in large quantities here," he said, "and they are both deadly. The copperheads are all around the camp in the underbrush, and the water moccasins are pretty heavy along the lakefront." He showed us large pictures of each snake. "We don't have any snake serum yet, so I urge you to be doubly cautious. Try to avoid brush and tall grass, which is the copperhead's hangout. He's not very large—usually under two feet—and he blends in with his surroundings—good camouflage, pale chestnut or hazel color with a lot of inverted Y-shaped dark blotches. His head has some red on it with cream streaks down the sides. What makes him so dangerous is that unlike the rattlesnake—and he is just as deadly—the copperhead strikes without movement or warning. And he's very aggressive.

"The water moccasin is just as deadly—in fact, they're cousins. He'll be in the vegetation right along the lakefront, or hanging on tree limbs that jut out over the water. He looks like just another twig. He hangs out there watching the water and when he sees something edible he drops on it, sinks in his fangs, swims around it till it dies, and then swallows it. If he's in the water he'll most likely be underside some floating object like a piece of wood. I think as long as the kids are swimming in our cleared beachfront area where the crib is, or away from the shores, they'll be all right. Otherwise exercise extreme caution. I hope to be able to trap a copperhead and a moccasin by the time the campers arrive so they'll have a firsthand look at the enemy. What makes the situation here so tough is that this is a new camp and the adjacent area has not yet reacted to the change. As far as these snakes are concerned, this is still their territory."

All the way down the trail to the lake, my ankles tingled with the expectation of being struck by a copperhead. But I was less concerned with the copperhead peril than I was with the possibility that we would all be expected to jump in and swim. Thankfully, that wasn't the case. What we did do was to get in several rowboats that were tied to the dock, six of us to a boat, and take a tour of the immediate lake. We rowed along in file (I sat in the stern of our boat with Paul Roth) and I felt rather exhilarated by this, my first boat ride. The water was still and very clear and there were swarms of dragonflies that hovered and darted over the surface. Occasionally I could spot clusters of tiny fish wriggling near the surface. I breathed deeply, tasting air, filtered by the pines on shore, that St. Louis never knew.

At the end of the lake, where it curved, our file of rowboats turned and started back along the shore. Startled squirrels and rabbits broke for cover. I spotted a chipmunk (I didn't know it was a chipmunk until Paul identified it) sitting on a rock. Two big hawks appeared over the trees, soaring side by side, their wing tips almost touching, and as we were all looking up at them—that's when the snake dropped into the boat.

It fell with a thud at the feet of the two counselors who were rowing. They immediately dropped their oars and scuttled backward over their seat. The snake started to wriggle along the bottom of the boat. There was no doubt it was the water moccasin we had seen in Bud Fischer's photograph. The two counselors in the bow of the boat jumped overboard. They were immediately followed by the two counselors who had been rowing.

"Come on," Paul said, tugging on my arm, "let's go." He dived over the side. I sat there caught in the transfixes of my fear of the water and my fear of the snake. The counselors in the water were yelling at me to jump. The snake had stopped and raised his head to reconnoiter. I felt light-headed and weak. I didn't move, just sat there with my eyes fixed on the snake. The only desperate thought I had was that perhaps I could let myself over the side and hold on to the boat. But I realized that that would leave my hands vulnerable to the moccasin. And besides, what if I slipped? I was too terrified of the water even to try that. My mother was there in the boat with me—warning me, exhorting me about the water. I was terrified of the snake, but it was less menacing than the water. There was that time I had put my head in the water and water went up my nose. Suffocating, coughing, gasping—that was how it was to drown.

The snake suddenly lowered his head and began to move toward me. I could feel a rush of adrenalin. I grabbed one of the paddles and sprang up. I began shouting at the snake as I smashed at him with the paddle. Just a gibberish of words, angry words, as I tried to kill the snake. I missed him. The blade of the oar was too wide to be maneuverable. I grazed his tail and spun him onto his back, but he immediately righted and kept coming. The counselors were screaming for me to jump. One of the other rowboats was hurrying alongside. I reversed the oar, holding it now by the blade. The water moccasin had cleared the seat. I came down on him with all my might and crushed his head. If I had missed him I probably would not have had time for another shot at him. I pounded him again and again and again with the oar, squishing his insides all over the bottom of the boat. I was mad as hell. It was fear, of course, but it looked like anger. Two of the boats finally came alongside and I stopped. I sat down on the stern seat, breathless and exhausted. My hands began to shake. Big Chief Berman and Little Big Chief Halpern, who had been in the lead boat, stepped onto my boat. They looked at the dead, battered water moccasin. Chief Berman picked it up by the tail and held it up for everyone to see. They all applauded and cheered and whistled. Little Big Chief Halpern clapped me on the back. Fear had made me a hero.

Chapter Five

The Two-Handed Broom Swat as Administered on the Seat of Reason by the Enlightened Leader

My brother arrived on the first bus of campers, with all of his belongings in an old knapsack that my father had saved from the World War. My father had never actually been in uniform, but they had already issued some equipment to him at the induction center when his deferment came through.

Sullivan spotted me as he entered Indian Mound with his group, and the apprehension on his face changed into a self-conscious smile. We walked toward each other and suddenly he thrust out his hand and we shook hands. It occurred to me that we had never shaken hands before.

There were three categories of campers: (1) kids whose parents could afford to pay the sixty-dollar fee; (2) kids who came from "good homes" but who could not afford to pay because their fathers were unemployed; (3) kids who came from tough, slum homes, whose families had suffered about as much before the Depression as they did during it. It was this third group that caused the trouble in the beginning.

Only a few of the campers knew each other before coming to camp, but in a very short time groups were instinctively identified and formed. A big, swarthy boy with a husky voice, nicknamed Horse Face, assumed command of the tough group three. By the second day he had established a hold over all twenty-four boys.

He and his pal, Knuckles, a skinny, ratty boy with a broken front tooth, went on a tour of all six cabins to inspect what each camper had brought to camp. Horse Face helped himself to whatever he saw that he wanted. The few who put up protests were immediately silenced by having their arms jammed up behind them to their shoulder blades.

On the third day of camp, the peace and quiet of the afternoon rest period were suddenly pierced by a fierce commotion in one of the cabins. The intensity of the sound sent Mo Brennan and me on the run.

The ruckus was coming from my brother's cabin. There were seven or eight boys in there, several of whom were shouting at Horse Face, who, when we arrived, was circling a table in the center of the room with a rusty bayonet in his hand. Circling with him, trying to keep the table between them, was my brother, Sullivan, who was half his size.

Horse Face was shouting, "Give it to me or I'll stick you!" As I started into the cabin, Horse Face made a leap over the table to grab Sullivan, who made a simultaneous dive under the table to avoid Horse Face's leap.

Mo and I grabbed Horse Face, who yelled, "Let hold of me, you finks!" I had to bend his hand into his wrist to get him to drop the bayonet.

"What the hell's going on?" Mo growled.

"Gimme my shiv!" Horse Face yelled. "It's my property!"

"Why was he after you?" I asked Sullivan.

Sullivan didn't answer, but opened his hand and revealed the pearl-handled pocketknife that I had given him.

"Whose knife is that?" Mo demanded.

"It's mine," Sullivan said.

"He tried to take it off him," one of the boys in the cabin said, "the same way he took my key chain."

Mo grabbed Horse Face by the arm. "Who the hell do you think you are?"

"I'm a damn side more'n you are," Horse Face said.

I could see Mo's neck muscles thicken and rise, and I was afraid he was going to slug Horse Face, who stood around five feet and weighed maybe ninety vicious pounds. "All right, all of you get back to your own cabins," I said. "You, too," I said to Horse Face, pushing him out the door in front of us. We followed him back to his cabin. He stopped a couple of times and Mo gave him a shove in the back to get him going.

"You've got to let him know who's boss," Mo said to me in a voice Horse Face couldn't hear. "These kids'll run us ragged if you don't."

"What do you suggest?"

"Beat his ass off."

"Well, first I think I'll give him a good talking to."

"*Him?* Hell, talking is working on the wrong end of him. Beat his ass off, I tell you."

"If talking doesn't work, I'll report him to Berman."

"You're going to *what?* What kind of camps did you work at? You're the head counselor, aren't you? Christ, you go snitching to Berman and these kids'll be rooting for Horse Face."

"Maybe you're right. You see, I'll tell you, Mo, I've never been a head counselor before."

"You goddam well *run* this place. You're Mr. Big. These kids are chicken poop and they better believe it."

Horse Face kept his belongings in a thoroughly battered footlocker.

"Open it up," I said.

"Up yours," he said.

Mo gave me a look.

"You heard what I said."

"That's my private property!" Horse Face shouted. "You got no rights to look into it." He plopped himself on top of the footlocker.

"Get up," I said.

"Up yours," he said.

"I said, get up."

"And I said up yours. And up your baby brother's."

Mo Brennan put both his hands around Horse Face's neck and lifted him off the trunk, choking him some in the process.

"God damn you, you wait'll I tell my father!" Horse Face shouted in his raspy voice. An instant picture of his father flashed across my eyes.

Mo held Horse Face by the hair at the back of his head while I opened the footlocker. There were a few items of clothing, rumpled and soiled; all the rest were articles of war. Clubs, knives of every description, slingshots, two hatchets, a BB gun, lengths of chain, homemade spears, rusty handcuffs, boards with nails in them—an awesome arsenal.

"What's all this for?" I asked him.

"Protection, that's what."

"Yeah? And who's supposed to protect us against you?" Mo asked.

"Keep your dirty hands off my stuff."

I began to feel my anger rising. Horse Face's three cabin mates were sizing me up. So was Mo Brennan. This little gangster had to be put in his place if I was to run Indian Mound. My temper had risen to a boil. I grabbed a broom that was standing next to the door.

"Bring him outside," I said to Mo. Mo marched Horse Face through the door and into the clearing in front of the adjoining cabins. There would be a good audience.

"Bend over," I said to Horse Face.

"Up yours," he said.

Mo grabbed him by the hair, yanked his head down, and held him that way. I drew back the broom and began slamming Horse Face across the behind. It was a heavy broom and I was able to get a resounding thud out of it. Horse Face yelped, but Mo held him firm as I laid into him with that broom. Pieces of straw flew off it as I put my whole weight behind every wallop.

When I let up, Mo yanked Horse Face's hair up, straightening him up. Horse Face was half crying.

"You, you—you'll get it when I tell my old man!"

"You stay in line, Horse Face," I said, "and no more backtalk or I'll wear out every broom in camp on you."

"Yeah? You and who else?"

"All right!" I said, grabbing the broom. "Ten more!"

Mo grabbed his hair.

"No! No!" Horse Face shouted. "I didn't mean it. Honest!"

"Then apologize."

Mo released his hair.

"I said apologize."

"For what?"

"For that backtalk."

"What backtalk?"

"Ten more!"

"Okay! All right! I apologize. That suit you?"

We took Horse Face's trunk over to the rec hall and locked it up. At first I felt there was something Dickensian about what had happened, with me on the side of the *Oliver Twist* heavies. But then I recalled the birch-whipping headmaster in *Tom Brown's Schooldays* and felt better about it. Mo had taught me my first lesson as head counselor. In tough cases like this, one must deal with the seat of reason. But I would have felt better if I had been able to deal with Horse Face without the broom.

Chapter Six

Better to Lose Your Money and Your Friends Than to Lose Your Center of Gravity

To my dismay, Sullivan was not having a good time. He was the youngest and smallest boy in his cabin, and the activities of camp were even stranger to him than they were to me. I tried to spend a little time with him every day during the afternoon rest period. The rest period was not intended as rest, like bed rest; it was simply a quiet hour when the camper was on his own. Sullivan and I often took a walk down to the lake and back.

"If I just had a friend," Sullivan said, "it would be lots better. But every time I think I have one, somebody steals him."

"You'll find one."

"Maybe not. I never had a friend in Keokuk."

"Perhaps you didn't try. You didn't like Keokuk, remember, and you didn't know how long you'd be there."

"Oh, I *tried*. There was this one boy named Virgil, I came right out and asked him to be my friend, but he said he couldn't."

"Did you ask him why?"

"Uh-huh. He said because he hated me."

"He *hated* you? He said that? What had you done to him?"

"Nothing, I tell you. I actually thought he was my friend. That's the trouble with me—people I scarcely know hate me."

"Now, come on, Sullivan, that's silly."

"Then how come I haven't got a friend? Answer me that. The

three guys in my cabin pal around together, but not with me. You know, like when they go up for meals, they tell me to go walk with someone else."

"Would you like to switch to another cabin?"

"No, it'd be the same thing. I guess I just don't have any pal-ship in me. But I sure wish I did. I bet I could be pretty good at it if I had the chance."

I tried to say things to reassure him that he had as much pal-ship in him as anyone else, but his realistic appraisal of past events was stronger than my assessment of his potential.

"Look, if I had palship in me, I'd have a friend, wouldn't I?"

I didn't really have an answer for that.

There was one camp event that Sullivan did get excited about. If a camper had a birthday that occurred while camp was in ses-sion, the event was celebrated in the dining hall with a candled cake, a chorus of "Happy Birthday," and a gift from Big Chief Berman. The gift was invariably some useless object like a Boy Scout calendar, but Sullivan was looking toward his birthday with great anticipation. I don't want to sound maudlin, but the simple fact was that Sullivan had never had a birthday celebration. Nor had I. Our family was so poor that eating and paying the rent was a constant, all-consuming struggle, and there simply was no time, no money, no atmosphere for birthdays, Christmases, Thanksgiv-ings, or anything else. Sullivan had never had a birthday party, a birthday cake, a birthday present. I kept a five-year diary and every birthday and every Christmas, one entry on top of the other, there was a mournful notation to the effect that my birthday had not even been mentioned, and that Christmas had passed with no tree, no presents, no stockings hung. In a way it was better to treat these occasions as non-events, for if you have no way to celebrate something that calls for food and presents, it is perhaps better to ignore it altogether.

Not only had Sullivan never had a birthday party of his own, he had never been invited to one. Sullivan would say that this was because he didn't have a friend, but more likely it was because we moved around so much we were never anywhere long enough for him to get on anyone's list.

As for his imminent Camp Hiawatha birthday, what Sullivan mostly talked about was the cake. He knew I had made friends with Floyd, the cook, and he asked me to have him write on the cake: A MILLION HAPPY BIRTHDAYS. I said I would.

Floyd was a tall, bony man with a sunken chest who had hair coming out of his nose and ears. He wore a white under-shirt, white duck pants, and a white overseas-type cap that he kept cocked over one ear. His bottom teeth, from eyetooth to eyetooth, were missing. He had a heart tattooed on one arm that read, OH, ALICE! and a long wriggling snake on the other that ran from his shoulder to his elbow. He always had a cigarette hanging out of his mouth. He talked a lot and constantly sipped from a mug that had TEA written on it. I made it a point to spend a lot of time in the kitchen talking to him. After all our lean years, and all the meals we skipped for want of something to put on the table, just to look at all that food and watch Floyd work on it and smell it cooking was a great pleasure.

Besides, I loved to listen to Floyd, who told me about his life and travels and all the wonderful practical jokes he had played on people. Floyd loved practical jokes. He even pulled a few in camp. The best was the one he pulled on Big Chief Berman. Somehow Floyd got hold of a piece of stationery from the Girl Scout camp across the lake. He snuck into the camp office and typed out a letter on the Girl Scout stationery addressed to Big Chief Berman saying as how Miss Rosemary McMartin, who was the good-looking director of the Girl Scout camp, would like to come to see him for dinner on such-and-such a date to discuss the possibility of mutual activities. Floyd signed it Rosemary McMartin and put it in Berman's letter box.

The Big Chief got all excited when he read the letter, and came into the kitchen and told Floyd to cook a really special dinner and have it served in Berman's cabin. The evening Miss McMartin was supposed to arrive, the Chief had his cabin all fixed up with flowers and candles on the table. He finally telephoned across the lake, around nine o'clock. Miss McMartin said that she didn't know what he was talking about and, besides, the last thing she wanted was to mingle her girls with our boys. Floyd had let me in on the joke; I met him in the kitchen after lights out. He got me laughing so hard I almost choked as he and I ate up the special dinner he had fixed for Big Chief Berman and his lady visitor.

The only thing I didn't like about Floyd was how he was always complaining about his wife. My mother and father were at each other so much that I could do without any more man-woman beefs. Floyd didn't spend much time with his wife, since he always had cooking jobs on boats or at camps, but every time he got a letter from her he was full of complaints. "Another thing," he'd say to me, "this wife of mine has got a thing about bills. It's only the twenty-fifth of the month, I already got this letter giving me hell cause I ain't sent her money to pay the bills which she is going to receive—get that, *going to receive*—on the first of the month. You ever hear of anything like that? These times, if you get paid at all it's a miracle, she's having a heart attack because she can't pay out the bills twenty minutes after she gets 'em. It's the thirtieth of the month, she's already running up to the landlord's apartment. Hello, Mr. Grevenrood, I got your rent for you. I got patches in my pants, she pays off the furniture four months early. If she can't go to the electric company's office on the day she gets their bill, she starts crying. It's a very emotional thing with her. Ah, well, she was an orphan, and I guess she's afraid."

Horse Face went after my brother again. Not about the pocketknife, about something else that was never explained to me. He had it in for Sullivan, I suppose, because Sullivan was a way to get at me. When I remonstrated with him, it was the same feisty, hard-mouthed Horse Face, so we had to have another shellacking with the broom. In his rage, Horse Face called me a freckled fruit, and called Mo, Gorilla Ass. There was a cookout that night with hot dogs and marshmallows, so in addition to fifteen broom swats I banished Horse Face to his cabin. Deprivation of the hot dogs and marshmallows seemed to hurt him more than my wallops. I instructed Corny to find a heavier broom.

I'd thought I could handle Mo's gripe about volleyball by ignoring it, but Mo was not one to be ignored. "You go up and tell Big Chief Pain-in-the-Ass," he said, "or I do. Which is it?"

"Volleyball's not so bad, Mo—why don't you give it a try?"

"I gave it a try. In the sixth grade. Well?"

"Okay."

"You've said that before. Every time I mention it you say okay, but you don't do anything."

"Okay."

"Okay when?"

"Leave it to me."

I didn't talk to Berman, but to Little Big Chief, Babe Halpern. Babe was a senior at Mizzou who had played guard on the varsity football team until he tore up his knee. He was a tall, beefy fellow who was always cheerful—in fact, jovial. He had a full laugh that came from his belly and he got along with everyone. I envied him his personality. I even tried to imitate him, but I didn't have that kind of laugh. Also I just wasn't the type to get along with everybody. Mo Brennan told me he had been at the football game when Babe had been hurt and that Babe was holding his knee in agony and weeping as they carried him off the field. I couldn't imagine Babe shedding tears. He stood six three or four and weighed around 220. When he talked to someone he had a habit of putting his arm around him and leaning down to lessen the distance between them. Mo said that Babe was Phi Beta Kappa in psychology; you could tell that psychology was his dish from the way he handled problems. Like Mo's.

"You tell Mo I think he's absolutely correct about the wrestling. That's his specialty and that's why he was brought here. Tell him I'll arrange with Chief Berman that Mo will have both—volleyball in the morning and wrestling in the afternoon."

Mo grumbled about the compromise, but the next morning he strung up a volleyball net and held his first session. He sat on a stool beside the net and limited his participation to adjudicating squabbles, but when his wrestlers assembled in the afternoon he got right onto the mat with them to demonstrate the various holds and techniques.

To my surprise, Sullivan enrolled with the flyweight wrestlers. It was the first activity he had shown any interest in. I asked Mo to give him a little special attention.

"I already have," Mo said. "I was impressed with his equilibrium. First-rate center of gravity. Hard to pull off his feet. He'll be all right if he can take it. Can he take it?"

"I should think so," I said.

Chapter Seven

Corny in the Pit and Mo on the Pendulum and All the Rats on Me

In the eyes of the Indian Mound campers, I never really became head counselor until the night of the "Pit and the Pendulum" bonfire. I had no idea it would have the effect on the boys that it did.

What I had planned was for the campers to sit around a night-time bonfire while I recited and acted out an abridged version of a short story by Edgar Allan Poe called "The Pit and the Pendulum." I had selected a site in a clearing back of the rec hall. There was a slope there that ran down to a flat grassy place which is where we planned to build the fire. At the fringe of this grassy flat was a large sycamore tree whose heavy branches hung above the flat. The afternoon of the bonfire I sent Corny to dig a square four-foot hole beneath the branches.

It was good and dark when we led the campers by flashlight down to the bonfire. We seated them in a tight circle around the fire, which cast dancing colors and shadows on the surrounding slope. The fact that we were situated at the bottom of this slope, encased by it, markedly contributed to the atmosphere of the story I was about to tell them. When they first sat down, the boys were noisy and full of wisecracks, the loudest voice, of course, belonging to Horse Face, but my first line quickly shut them off:

"The sentence—the dread sentence of death—was the last of distinct accentuation which reached my ears. I saw the lips of the black-robed judges, but then the figures of the judges vanished, as if magically, from before me; the tall candles sank into nothingness; their flames went out utterly; the blackness of darkness supervened; all sensations appeared swallowed up in a mad rushing descent as of the soul into Hades. Then silence, and stillness, and night were the universe. I had swooned."

I fell to the ground, stretched out lifeless beside the bonfire for a full minute. There wasn't a sound from the campers. Then I stirred and continued my recitation from my supine position.

"When I recovered, I lay upon my back, unbound. I reached out my hand, and it fell heavily upon something damp and hard. I quickly opened my eyes. The blackness of eternal night encompassed me. I struggled for breath. The intensity of the darkness seemed to oppress and stifle me. I at once started to my feet . . ."

I carefully rose from the ground and proceeded to act out the story as I told it.

". . . trembling convulsively in every fiber. I thrust my arms wildly above and around me in all directions. I felt nothing, yet dreaded to move a step, lest I should be impeded by the walls of a tomb. Perspiration burst from every pore, and stood in cold big beads upon my forehead. I cautiously moved forward, with my arms extended, and my eyes straining from their sockets in the hope of catching some faint ray of light. My outstretched hands at length encountered some solid obstruction. It was a wall, seemingly of stone masonry—very smooth, slimy, and cold. I started to make a circuit of the walls, but I had not counted on the extent of the dungeon or upon my own weakness. The ground was moist and slippery. I staggered onward for some time, when I stumbled and fell. Sleep soon overtook me as I lay."

Before I lapsed into sleep, I crooked up my head and looked around me at the faces of the campers: they were white, intense, eyes wide, nails chewed, knuckles bit. As I had discovered in my

Soldan histrionics, a good audience inspires an actor's performance, and that's what was happening here. "When I awoke, I cautiously walked across the slimy stone floor of my cell, tripped, fell, discovered that my head was suspended out over a very deep, water-bottomed pit that occupied the center of the dungeon." There was a distinct murmur from my audience when they saw my head hung over the edge of Corny's pit. "Shaking in every limb, I groped my way back to the wall, where again, after a stretch of agony, I fell asleep.

"When I awoke, the dungeon was awash with light. The walls, which I had taken for masonry, I could now see were made of huge plates of iron jointed together. I now lay upon my back, and at full length, on a species of low framework of wood. To this I was securely bound by a long strap that passed in many convolutions about my limbs and body, leaving at liberty only my head, and my left arm to such extent that I could, by dint of much exertion, supply myself with food from an earthen dish which lay by my side on the floor."

I strained to get my left hand a few feet away from my body, and I let out an animal groan that elicited a nervous response from my audience. "Looking upward, I surveyed the ceiling of my prison. It was some thirty or forty feet overhead, and constructed much as the side walls. On one of these ceiling panels was the painted figure of Time as he is commonly represented, save that, in lieu of a scythe, he held what, at a casual glance, I supposed to be the pictured image of a huge pendulum, such as we see on antique clocks. It was situated directly above me, but as I gazed at it I realized that it was not a painting at all but that the pendulum was in motion. Its sweep was brief, and of course slow."

At this moment there appeared, from just below a bough of the sycamore tree, a gleaming, sharp-edged blade that slowly began to swing from side to side. This elicited a chorus of sucked breaths from the campers.

"A slight noise attracted my notice, and, looking to the floor,

I saw several enormous rats traversing it. They had issued from the well which lay just within view to my right. Even then, while I gazed, they came up in troops, hurriedly, with ravenous eyes, allured by the scent of the meat. It required much effort and attention to scare them away."

Several rat-like forms came hurtling out of the pit, moving about rapidly, in and out of the pit. The boys recoiled and shrieked and clung to one another. In the semi-darkness, the stuffed socks that Corny was pitching out of the pit and pulling back with erratic jerks by their strings could just as well have been sharp-fanged rats. Above me, Mo Brennan, completely hidden by the sycamore's foliage, was slowly lowering the sweeping pendulum, which was the grounds keeper's sickle attached to a broom handle.

"After a while I took my eyes off the rats and cast my eyes upward. What I then saw confounded and amazed me. The sweep of the pendulum had increased by nearly a yard, its velocity was much greater, and it had perceptibly descended. I now observed—with what horror it is needless to say—that its nether extremity was formed of a crescent of glittering steel, about a foot in length, the under edge as keen as that of a razor; it hissed as it swung through the air.

"I could no longer doubt the doom prepared for me by monkish ingenuity in torture. Having failed to plunge into their pit by the merest of accidents, they had now devised a different destruction for me. Inch by inch, down, down it came until it swept so closely over me as to fan me with its acrid breath. The odor of the sharp steel forced itself into my nostrils. I prayed—I wearied heaven with my prayer for its more speedy descent. I grew frantically mad, and struggled to force myself upward against the sweep of the fearful scimitar. And then I fell suddenly calm, and lay smiling at the glittering death, as a child at some rare bauble."

Mo had lowered the sickle to about an inch above my body and I began to get concerned that, from above, he might not have an accurate perspective on just how close to me he was pendulum-ing that blade. Corny kept the rats darting in and out of the pit and I could tell from the surrounding sounds that the boys were as concerned about that sickle blade as I was.

"Even amid the agonies of that period, the human nature craved food. With painful effort I outstretched my left arm as far as my bonds permitted, and took possession of the small remnant which had been spared me by the rats. As I put a portion of it within my lips, there rushed to my mind a half-formed thought of joy—of hope. Down—steadily down crept the blade. To the right—to the left—far and wide—with the shriek of a damned spirit! to my heart, with the stealthy pace of the tiger! I alternately laughed and howled. Down—certainly, relentlessly down! It vibrated within an inch of my bosom! I struggled violently—furiously—to free my left arm. Down—still unceasingly—still inevitably down! I gasped and struggled at each vibration. I shrunk convulsively at its every sweep.

"It was *hope* that prompted my nerves to quiver—the frame to shrink. It was *hope*—the hope that triumphs on the rack—that whispers to the death-condemned even in the dungeons of the Inquisition. I saw that some ten or twelve sweeps would bring the steel in actual contact with my robe—and with this observation there suddenly came over my spirit all the keen, collected calmness of despair. For the first time during many hours—or perhaps days—I *thought*. I proceeded at once, with the nervous energy of despair, to attempt the execution of my thought, and my thought had turned to the rats—wild, bold, ravenous, their red eyes glaring upon me as if they waited but for motionlessness on my part to make me their prey. I had been waving my free hand above the dish to keep them from devouring the last of its contents. In their voracity, the vermin frequently fastened their sharp fangs in my fingers. With the particles of the oily and spicy viand which now remained, I thoroughly rubbed my binding wherever I could reach it. Then I lay breathlessly still.

"One or two of the boldest rats leaped upon me and smelled at the binding."

Corny tossed a couple of socks right on me to the horror of my listeners.

"This seemed the signal for a general rush of the ravenous animals from the pit and they swarmed all over me."

Corny fired a salvo of rats upon me from the pit. Mo was now grazing my shirt with the blade of the sickle.

"The measured strokes of the pendulum disturbed them not at all. They pressed—they swarmed upon me; they writhed upon my throat; their cold lips sought my own as they busied themselves with the anointed binding. Disgust, for which the world has no name, swelled my bosom and chilled my heart. Yet one minute, and I felt that they would chew through the binding. It loosened. I lay still. I was *free*. The binding hung in ribands from my body. But the stroke of the pendulum already pressed upon my bosom. It had divided the serge of my robe. Twice again it swung, and a sharp sense of pain shot through every nerve. But the moment of escape had arrived. At a wave of my hand my deliverers hurried tumultuously away. With a steady movement—cautious, sidelong, shrinking, and slow—I slid from the embrace of the binding and beyond the reach of the scimitar. *I was free.*"

There was a great sigh of relief and a cheer from the boys as the rats all scurried back into the pit and the pendulum disappeared quickly into the sycamore tree. But the cheer had not even died away when I plunged into the penultimate peril.

"But wait! There came to my nostrils the breath of the vapor of heated iron! A suffocating odor pervaded the prison! I panted! I gasped for breath! There could be no doubt of the design of my tormenters—oh! most unrelenting! oh! most demoniac of men! I shrank from the glowing metal of the walls as they started to move toward the center of the cell. . . ."

There now advanced toward me a wall of fire, forcing me backward, as Paul Roth, hidden behind the tree, began to push the fiery wall in my direction. The pushing device was a rake affixed to the base of the wall. The wall was a six-foot square of limbs covered with rags that had been soaked in kerosene. The flaming rags gave off an intense heat and an acrid black smoke that pervaded the area.

"Amid the thought of the fiery destruction that impended, the idea of the coolness of the well came over my soul like balm. I rushed to its deadly brink. I buried my face in my hands—weeping bitterly. The heat rapidly increased, and once again I looked up. The cell had been square, but in an instant it had shifted its form into that of a lozenge as the fiery walls moved toward each other, destined to force me into the pit. I could have clasped the red walls to my bosom as a garment of eternal peace. 'Death,' I said, 'any death but that of the pit!' And now flatter and flatter grew the lozenge. . . ."

Paul had moved the burning wall so close to me I could feel my skin getting parched.

"I shrank back—but the closing walls pressed me resistlessly onward. At length for my seared and writhing body there was no longer an inch of foothold on the floor of the prison. I struggled no more, but the agony of my soul found vent in one loud, long, and final scream of despair. . . ."

I let loose with a scream that probably startled my mother in St. Louis.

"I felt that I tottered upon the brink—I averted my eyes. . . ."

I was indeed tottering on the brink of Corny's pit, the fire just about igniting me as Mo Brennan dropped out of the tree and landed beside the pit.

"There was a loud blast as of many trumpets! The fiery walls rushed back! An outstretched arm caught my own as I fell, fainting, into the abyss. It was that of General Lasalle. The French army had entered Toledo. The Inquisition was in the hands of its enemies."

I collapsed into Mo's arms as Paul quickly withdrew the fire wall. Corny and Paul then helped Mo lift my unconscious form and the three of them in solemn procession carried me back to the cabin as the boys huddled behind them for the walk back to their cabins in the dark.

It was a hard and fast camp rule that all lights had to be out by ten o'clock, but that night in Indian Mound Village *no* lights went out. All through the night there was a steady stream of boys coming to the counselors' cabin. Some reported strange inhuman sounds that they wanted investigated; several came running up because huge rats were in their cabins (it only took one boy to "see" a rat for all the boys in his cabin to have seen it too); still others were sure a monster was on the roof or prowling in the bushes; four boys woke screaming with nightmares, and two wet their beds.

The following morning the boys were already assembled in the rec area for the breakfast trek to the mess hall when I appeared with Mo. Immediately they fell silent. "Form a line of twos," I said. They quickly fell in. Mo and I led the way as they silently trudged along behind us. They didn't quite know what to make of me—whether I was a sorcerer or a madman—but they were clearly intent on staying in line and not taking any chances.

Chapter Eight

A Copperhead's Bite Is a Whole Lot Worse Than Its Bark

Bud Fischer, the nature counselor, had captured a copperhead, which he kept in a secure wire cage. Chief Berman assembled the entire camp at the lakefront to have a look at the snake and to hear Bud tell about its habits and characteristics. The campers all sat on the slope going down toward the lake and Bud stationed himself and his copperhead between them and the water.

Bud said that in no circumstance was anyone to try to capture a copperhead, as he had done, because they were very fast and deadly and only an expert should try to handle them. He assured everyone that the snakes were very unlikely to go into the cabins or assembly areas and would most likely keep to their own terrain. But, he said, copperheads were aggressive and unpredictable, and might attack a person who unwittingly came too near to them.

Bud wanted everyone to know what the procedure was if bitten by a copperhead. The wound had to be lanced immediately, the poison removed, and anti-toxin serum administered. Bud said that the serum was on order and should arrive within a few days. It would be kept in the icebox in the infirmary and the sooner it was administered, he said, the better.

"The most important thing you can do if bitten," Bud told us, "is to lie still, because the more your blood circulates, the more the poison is carried through your body. All counselors have first-aid kits that have scalpels and suction cups in them and they should immediately lance a cross through the bite marks, causing the wound to bleed, and then draw out the bloody poison with the suction cup. Of course, if you are on a hike or somewhere where the first-aid kit is not handy, then use a pocketknife to make the cuts and suck out the wound. But be careful—if you have a cut or sore in your mouth, it's possible you will get the poison into your system that way, so let someone else suck out the wound.

"Now I'm going to let this copperhead out of its box so that you can see what it looks like and how it moves."

There was a loud stir among the campers at the front of the assemblage.

"Don't be concerned," Bud said. "I'll have him under control and after you've all seen him, I'm going to whack his head off."

Bud picked up a long forked stick which he had leaned against the cage, and with his left hand he took hold of a rope which was attached to a snap lock on the front of the cage. He stationed himself beside the cage, pulled up on the rope which released the lock. As the cage door swung open, the snake wriggled a short distance out of the cage, then stopped to reconnoiter. Bud quickly and adroitly stabbed the fork of the stick just behind the snake's head, pinning him to the sand. The copperhead immediately lashed himself around in a violent attempt to get free, but Bud kept his head firmly pinned, only the snake's body being free to wriggle.

Bud said it was one of the biggest copperheads he had ever seen, and one of the strongest. He suggested that the campers line up and pass by in single file to get a good, close look at the snake so that they could readily identify it. The first campers in line passed by at a distance of ten or twelve feet, but by the time our group took its turn the distance had been reduced to an intrepid four feet.

It's hard to say exactly what happened, it happened so fast, but just as Mo Brennan approached the snake with his group, which included my brother, the copperhead wriggled free from

Bud's forked stick, whipped around, and struck Bud twice in his left ankle. Bud yelled out a warning. Mo picked up the two kids who were in the vicinity of the snake and literally threw them out of the way, then he pulled back his right foot and gave the copperhead a terrific kick that sent it flying toward the water. Mo then grabbed the stick and pinned the stunned snake to the ground while others of us rushed the cage over to him and helped get it back in.

All attention now turned to Bud Fischer, who was sitting on the ground. Chief Berman ordered all campers to return to their cabins immediately. Bud had taken out his pocketknife and now he made several rather deep cuts right through the bright red dots left by the snake's fangs. Blood came gushing out. Mo was all set to start sucking out the poison, but one of the counselors, whose cabin was nearby, came running down the incline with his first-aid kit. He gave the suction cup to Bud, who started to use it immediately. The nurse had not come to the demonstration, but someone had gone to fetch her. Bud told Babe Halpern to use his handkerchief and make a tourniquet at the calf of his leg to keep the poisoned blood from spreading.

"We've got to get some serum," Bud said to Chief Berman. "As soon as possible. I took an awfully big shot."

Chief Berman told Babe to take the small truck and get to Bagnell or Camdenton as fast as he could.

"Do you know anyone who's got it there?" Babe asked.

"No," the Chief said, "just ask around."

"What makes you think there is any?"

"Because this is copperhead country."

Bud suddenly lay back on the ground and put his arm over his eyes. Mo took the suction cup and began working it.

"I'm cold," Bud said.

Someone ran up for a blanket.

"I'm going over to the Girl Scout camp," Chief Berman said. "They just may have some." He ran down to where the camp's outboard was tied to the dock. It wouldn't start. Murphy, the swimming counselor, ran down to help.

I turned my attention to Bud Fischer. He was shivering, but there were drops of perspiration on him. Mo kept working the suction cup. We covered Bud securely with the blanket and tried to raise the upper portion of his body so he'd be lying on a slant toward his feet. The nurse, a husky, middle-aged, brusque woman, arrived with a black medical bag, but there wasn't much she could do besides paint around the wound with some antiseptic.

Bud's arm fell away from his face as he lapsed into unconsciousness. His face was very white and cold. The nurse took his pulse and listened to his heart and looked worried. Nobody said a word. There were eight of us there, but not a word was spoken.

The outboard started up with a roar, and, with Murphy at the controls, the boat sped away from the dock. I figured it would take them about twenty minutes to get to the Girl Scout camp. Bud looked like he was dying and I was very frightened. It seemed so unreal not to be able to do anything. I watched Bud's chest, but I could not detect any breathing.

I was the first one to speak. "Is he dead?" I asked the nurse.

"No," she said.

"How bad is he?"

"Bad."

There wasn't much blood coming out of the wound because of the tourniquet, so the nurse took it off. Right away the flow of blood increased.

"Won't that release the poison through his body?" Mo asked.

"Yes," the nurse answered, "but we've got a lot of the poison out by now."

"But some of it is in him, isn't it?"

"Yes."

"Isn't that serious?"

"Yes."

"Might he die?"

"We need the serum."

We could still hear the boat put-putting across the lake. It was a small outboard motor and although they were going as fast as they could, they weren't going very fast.

We got more blankets and tried to make Bud more comfortable. Every once in a while the nurse would raise one of Bud's eyelids and peer at his eye. She never changed her expression. Some campers came sneaking down to have a look and we ran them off. We learned that before leaving for Bagnell, Babe had telephoned the doctor there but he was on a case in Eldon.

I had not thought much about death. No member of my family had died, and only once had I been to a funeral. (When I was nine years old, two kids with whom I had been playing had been buried in a mud slide and one of them died, but I wasn't there when the firemen dug out his body.) Also, it seemed unreal that anyone as big and strong and athletic as Bud could suddenly be leveled like this from a mere snakebite. I felt sick to my stomach and very conscious of my own breathing.

The nurse took a hypodermic out of her bag, filled it with something, and gave Bud an injection in his arm. After a few minutes he moved his head a little and made some kind of sound. Then he opened his eyes, just briefly, and closed them again. The nurse slapped his cheek several times and tried to rouse him by calling his name, but he didn't open his eyes again.

Mo was the first one to hear the returning motorboat. All of us, except the nurse, went down to the dock. We stood there in a line on the dock watching the boat enlarge as it headed toward us. There was no way to know if they had the serum or not because they'd be coming back in just about the same length of time. I couldn't get rid of the sick feeling in my stomach.

The boat seemed to return much faster than it had departed, and now, as it neared the dock, we could see why. It was a larger boat with a more powerful outboard. There were three people on board, Murphy, Chief Berman, and the nurse from the Girl Scout camp.

The boat roared up to the dock. We helped the nurse onto the dock and, clutching her bag, she ran with us to where Bud was lying.

She opened her bag and began taking things out; the two nurses worked together without saying a word. From the careful way she was filling a hypodermic from a small bottle, I knew it had to be the serum. Our nurse was rubbing alcohol on the crook of Bud's right arm, preparing him for the injection. The Girl Scout nurse held the hypodermic up to the sky and squirted a little of the serum, then she slid the needle into Bud's arm and slowly emptied the contents of the chamber.

"You know something?" Chief Berman said. "They just received it this morning. A girl was bitten last week and they had to take her all the way back to St. Louis."

"He'd have never made it," our nurse said.

The Girl Scout nurse took Bud's pulse and his blood pressure and listened to his chest with her stethoscope.

"I think we can move him," she said. "But try to keep him as steady as possible."

We didn't have a stretcher in camp, but we made one out of two poles and a couple of jackets, putting the poles through the jacket sleeves. Then we lifted Bud very carefully and carried him up the incline to the infirmary. We went slowly and tried not to jiggle him. Once or twice he made a little sound, but he was still unconscious when we left him in the infirmary.

I didn't eat any dinner that night and I barely slept at all. It was just getting to be dawn when I quietly let myself out of the cabin and went up to the infirmary. The light was on. Through the window I could see Bud sitting up in bed. One of the nurses was sitting beside him. He was holding a cup and sipping something hot. I would have gone in and talked to him, but for some reason

I began to cry. It was maybe the third time in my life I had cried. I couldn't understand why.

I went back to my cabin and fell asleep immediately. As it turned out, that entire summer, the only person bit by a snake was Bud Fischer.

Chapter Nine

Whoa There, Dicky Boy! The Head Counselor Is Pulling the Reins. Whoa! Dammit, Whoa!

I was able to elude detection as a non-swimmer by staying away from the waterfront. Having established myself as the camp's Indian authority, I had such a full program involving Indian songs, makeup, costumes, dances, ritual, and crafts that I easily fobbed off waterfront activity onto the other counselors. I was even supervising teepee and totem pole projects. Of course, I knew absolutely nothing about any of these activities, but neither did anyone else. The combination of my imagination and the camp's gullibility made my life a heap big cinch.

For instance, I had never heard an Indian song in my life, but one of my Indian books contained a few lines of an Indian chant which I expanded by using the same rhythm and inventing some words which were in the vein of the ones in the book. This is what I came up with:

Kili, kili, kili, kili,
Watch, watch, watch, watch,
Kay you kim kum kaw-wah.
Kili, kili, kili, kili,
Watch, watch, watch, watch,

Kay you kim kum kaw-wah.
Hay, ha-a-cham-wah,
Hay cham-wah polly-wam-ba,
Hay ha-a-cham-wah,
Hay cham-wah,
Polly-wam!

I made up some music to go with the words, and asked Corny to write down the notes for me so that Blanche Marlies, who ran the camp's office, could play it on the piano. I claimed it was a song I had learned from a St. Louis Indian who had gone to Soldan High with me. I taught the song to the Indian Mound campers and when Chief Berman heard them sing it he immediately decreed it to be the official camp song.

But I could not generate much enthusiasm among the boys for my Indian program because of the truculent resistance of Horse Face. He wouldn't put on war paint, try to dance, wear a loincloth, or sing a note of "Kili, Kili, Kili." I tried to explain about Indian braves and how, if he'd let me, I'd make him up as the fiercest warrior in the tribe.

"Not me," he said. "I don't wanna go around singin' and dancin' with lipstick on my face and wearin' a diaper."

"It's not a diaper—it's a loincloth."

"Call it what you want, it's a diaper."

"If it's a diaper, how come I'm wearing one and all the other counselors?"

"Maybe you *need* diapers, how do I know?" That got a great laugh out of the campers.

"Take off your pants and put on this loincloth," I commanded.

"No, there's no one gets my pants off."

Mo made a move toward him.

"I'll write my old man that you fruits are trying to get my pants off."

"All right—tell you what," I said, "wear the loincloth over your pants."

He hesitated. "All right, but none of that girl stuff on my face. I got a bad enough puss without all that gunk smeared on me."

"It's not girl gunk," I said. "Look, it's paste from red berries—just like the Indians used."

Horse Face covered his face with his arms. "Get away with that! I don't wanna be no goddam Indian!"

As I said, Horse Face's vociferous opposition put a decided damper on my attempt to turn the rest of the campers into an Indian tribe. I tried to tempt Horse Face with a really lethal-looking tomahawk that Corny made in his crafts shop, but that didn't work either. There was no way we were going to get him to decorate his face and wear a loincloth. He had been called Horse Face all his life and he wasn't about to do anything that would call attention to his physiognomy.

I was brooding about this while thumbing through one of my Indian books when I came upon a section devoted to the medicine man. On the page was an illustration showing a medicine man in full regalia—ferocious-looking, bizarre mask with a huge bird beak, jutted teeth, and wild, disarrayed hair; he wore a brightly decorated robe that reached the ground, and he was brandishing a fur-covered mace with dangling feathers. A-ha, I thought, the perfect lure for Horse Face—a ferocious mask to cover his face, a long robe to cover his body, and a lethal weapon to attack evil spirits. If Horse Face basically does not like being Horse Face, I reasoned, then this should be the answer to his Indian conversion.

I gave the medicine-man picture to Corny, who made a papier-mâché mask even more ferocious and bizarre than the pictured one. My Indian crafts workshop created a robe out of burlap sacks which we painted and beaded, and we made a wooden mace that we covered with painted toweling and chicken feathers.

I sent for Horse Face, and when he entered the rec hall, there I was in the middle of the room, in the medicine-man regalia. I strode toward him with a deliberate stalking step, and Horse Face didn't know whether to run from this menacing monster or hold his ground. When I was a few feet away, emitting animal sounds, he bolted for the door.

"Horse Face!" I shouted. "Wait a minute!"

He stopped.

I took off the mask. "Come here."

He slowly walked back to me. I put the mask and robe on him, and handed him the mace. I then steered him over to the window where he could see his reflection.

"Gom! Gom!" he grunted, a perfect sound for his new face.

"You are Shwani, the medicine man, healer of arrow wounds and procurer of rain."

"Gom! Gom!" said Horse Face.

"You cook magic potions and send magic smoke into the air."

"Gom de gom!" said Horse Face, and my Indian program was off the ground.

After that, when we had our weekly all-camp fireside pow-wow, each camper wore a chicken feather on his brow affixed with a rubber band and sang "Kili, Kili, Kili" while shaking his fists to the rhythm. To crown this tribal rite, I taught ten of my campers, my brother being one of them, to do a dance that I invented to go along with the song. It consisted primarily of vertical hops and horizontal bends at the waist with the arms extended overhead. Of the ten, Sullivan was by far the best Kili dancer and it occurred to me that perhaps there was something hereditary about terpsichore. But on added reflection I realized that the closest my father got to dancing was tapping his foot when the rhythm got hot.

The Indian costumes we used consisted simply of loincloths (towels) held up by a piece of rope around the waist. But when it came to war paint, that's where I excelled. At the start, I copied face markings I found in one of my books, but soon I began to embellish those and became more and more creative as I discovered my flair for face decoration.

My success as the Indian expert from St. Louis gave me such a heady me-heap-big-brave-Indian illusion that I decided, one day, to mount the camp's one horse, Dicky Boy. I had never been on a horse before, but I had seen Dicky Boy trotting around the grounds with Chief Berman and others astride and there didn't seem to be anything to it. Attired in loincloth, feather, moccasins (made in the leathercraft shop), and full war paint, I got myself up on Dicky Boy, who realized, the minute I sat down in the saddle, that he had someone on his back who had never been on a horse before.

So Dicky Boy took off. Not terribly fast, but off. I pulled back on the reins, I jerked the reins, I shouted "Whoa!" and similar exhortations designed to make him stop, but he kept going at a steady pace, not very fast, just loping along, making a round of the four villages.

Since I did not want the whole camp to know about my predicament (and thereby lose my Indian standing), I stopped yelling "Whoa!" and "Ho there, you jerk!" and simply smiled as bravely as I could as we endlessly made round after round through the villages. At first no one paid much attention, since Dicky Boy was a common sight, but along about the eighth or ninth time I came clopping through the villages I could tell my tours were beginning to be eyed with some suspicion. I tried pulling Dicky Boy's ears, his mane, hitting him on the head with my fist, but nothing I could do or yell in his ear had any effect whatsoever on Dicky Boy's duly appointed rounds. On my eighth tour through Bear Village one of the counselors yelled, "Look out, here comes Paul Revere!"

I had considered sliding off, but I didn't quite have the guts to jump from that height at that speed. But that did seem to be the only reasonable solution even though it meant that Dicky Boy would run free, perhaps run away, and I'd be held accountable for that.

It was Sullivan who ultimately rescued me. He suddenly appeared, running alongside me.

"You stuck?"

"He won't stop."

"Pull the reins."

"I did. I am."

"He just keeps running?" Sullivan was having trouble keeping up.

"I've got to get down," I said desperately. "My can is awful sore."

"Put your hands over his eyes."

"Do what?"

"Get up on his neck and cover up his eyes."

I shinnied forward and, clamping my legs desperately, stuck the flats of my hands over Dicky Boy's eyes. He immediately jammed on the brakes. I slid down, holding on to the reins. Sullivan ran over and helped me walk the horse back to his stable.

"You ever been on a horse?" I asked him.

"Nope."

"Then how'd you know that about covering his eyes?"

"I read once that that's how they lead horses out of fires. I even saw it in a movie. I know I'd stop running if someone covered my eyes. Wouldn't you?"

Just because I was able to avoid swimming didn't mean I avoided it altogether. After dinner, just before it got dark, when there wasn't an evening program and the lakefront was deserted, I would sneak down to the water with Sullivan to teach myself how to swim.

There was a crib there, designed for beginners, that was made of wooden slats and set into the water at a depth of three feet. Sullivan stayed on shore as my lookout, to warn me if anyone approached, while I tried, night after night, to get my feet off the bottom of the crib. That was my problem. I would put my face in the water and pick up one foot, but to release *both* feet and execute a dead man's float was beyond me. Also, the second I immersed my face in the water, I began to get an anxiety about breathing. Holding my breath outside of water, I was right up there with the best of them (a bunch of us at the Forest Park tennis courts used to have breath-holding contests), but when I put my face in water, ten seconds was about my bursting point. Just the feel of the water on my face set off a terrible fear in me that somehow the water would seep up my nose and choke me.

I finally got to the point where I could hold on to the side of the crib with my face in the water and kick my feet, but that was because I had the security of holding on. When I tried the same thing in the center of the crib, away from the side, both feet just wouldn't come up.

Occasionally I tried to help Sullivan, whose swimming problems were similar to mine, only more so. I'd try holding him on the surface by putting both hands under his stomach, but I could never get him to put his face in the water. I'd hiss angry, deprecatory things in his ear, telling him he was a coward, chicken, a baby, but it didn't help. He would strain his neck as high up as he could, and with one hand he'd hold tight on to one of my arms. In the process, he'd thrash around considerably, and his breath came in short, whimperish huffs and puffs. Sullivan displayed more acute fear than I did, but as swimming duds we were equal.

On our trudge back from these abortive swims, we never spoke a word. Sullivan was usually pissed at me for the way I had spoken to him; I was invariably angry and depressed, for I had been thinking all day about how that night I was finally going to float on the surface, how I was going to get those legs up and stretch those arms forward and put my face in the water and *float*. No one could say that I did not think positive all day long, but it had no effect whatsoever on my legs. I'd hop around a little, but I had no confidence that if my feet left the security of the wooden planks on the bottom of the crib, my body would stay on the top of the water. I also lectured myself on how little risk there was of drowning, since even if I sank to the bottom I was only in three feet of water and could easily stand up, but that also did absolutely no good. I have previously described my phobia about water; no amount of practice and thinking was going to overcome its leadening effect.

341

One evening, after we had gloomily returned from still another frustrating crib attempt, my brother appeared at my cabin door and asked to speak to me. I stepped outside.

"It's about Horse Face," he said.

"Oh, not that again!" I was on my third broom with Horse Face and I was in no mood to take him on.

"That isn't what I mean," Sullivan said.

"What isn't what you mean?"

"It isn't about Horse Face and *me*, it's just about Horse Face."

"What about Horse Face?"

"I want to get his bayonet."

"Sure, that's all I need, for you to run around with a bayonet."

"Not for me—I want it for Horse Face."

"Are you nuts? With his temper? You want to get stuck through the gizzard?"

"No, listen, let me have it. He won't hurt me with it."

"Sullivan—what the hell is this all about?"

"Well, I was just walking back to my cabin and I heard this noise in the trees there that sounded like somebody was in there, so I snuck over and had a look and it was Horse Face leaning there against a tree and he was, well, kind of, you know, crying."

"Horse Face? You sure it was Horse Face?"

"I was gonna walk away because, you know, crying is private, but I sometimes get pretty sad. . . ."

"Do you go off and cry like that?"

"Sometimes. I *used* to more than now. Anyway, I went on over to Horse Face and asked him what was wrong. First he didn't want to tell me, but I just hung around and he finally stopped crying and then he told me. About his father. What he said was that his father was in the war and got hurt very bad when the Germans used gas. His father can't work. Sometimes he's in the soldiers' hospital and sometimes he's able to come home. He's in the hospital now and he's very sick again and, you see, that bayonet belonged to Horse Face's father. I really think it'd be nice if he could have it back. I think he just sort of wants to have it, you know, to sort of, well, *have* it."

I gave the bayonet to Sullivan to take back to Horse Face. I suddenly felt very bad about all those broomings. Wouldn't it be strange, I thought, if Horse Face was the one who would become Sullivan's friend? I wondered what a man was like who had been gassed. I had thought of gassing as inevitably fatal. It had never occurred to me that there could be permanently damaged survivors—blind, perhaps, mentally twisted, paralyzed. Of course, that explained Horse Face. Poor Horse Face. In a way, he and Sullivan had much in common. Yes, it would be funny if Horse Face turned out to be the friend that Sullivan was seeking.

Chapter Ten

Why Do They Give You a Shot Between the Eyes When What You Need Is One in the Arm?

One of the best things about the summer was being able to talk about college with those counselors who were already going to such places as Washington University, Missouri, St. Louis U., Rollins School of Mines, and Northwestern. I had been to the Washington U. campus only once, but that one visit had engendered a queasiness that had made me want to ask questions about this new, mysterious life every chance I could.

Washington U. is located in the heart of St. Louis, but, situated as it is on high ground that gradually rises up from Skinker Boulevard, it gives the illusion of being somewhere off by itself. When I got off the streetcar on Skinker and looked up the long, elevated walk toward the fieldstone building that stood majestically and gracefully atop the hill, I felt both uplifted by its beauty and comforted to discover that it was no bigger than Soldan High.

But when I reached the summit, which was an archway that transected the building, and looked beyond, I was disheartened to see that this first-glimpsed building was but one side of a quadrangle of buildings that enclosed a grassy expanse of shrubs and trees. And that beyond this quadrangle lay scores of other buildings, each one the size of Soldan High.

As I stood there, bewildered by this discovery, classes let out and an overwhelming flood of students was disgorged into the enclave of the quadrangle; this mass of students made me aware, for the first time, of how severe the competition for survival would be. Our home teacher at Soldan had told us what percentage of the university freshman class flunked out, and that was partly why I was disturbed (but only a small part, for I had too much confidence in myself to fear flunking out). What primarily bothered me was that with such an army of students, how could I achieve in college what had come so easily and effectively in high school?

At Soldan I had been an overachiever, in scholastics, sports, and such extracurricular activity as editing the newspaper, writing and performing in plays and musicals, playing in the school orchestra, captaining the debate team, representing the school in oratorical contests. These achievements, and the recognition that went with them, counterbalanced the squalid conditions of our home life and were, in a sense, necessities for me. But the sight of those hundreds of students pouring into the quad convinced me that I would be nothing more than a tadpole in this pond.

I was also disturbed by the students themselves. They were so well dressed and sophisticated. Many of the boys wore suits and neckties, pork-pie hats, saddle shoes, and tweed sports jackets. Soldan High wasn't in a suit-and-necktie district, and outside of graduation, I don't think I ever saw anyone my age wear a necktie. (If they had, someone would undoubtedly have snipped it off him.) The Washington U. girls were also much better dressed and prettier and worldlier than the Soldan girls, and their breasts were bigger. They wore pearls and cashmere sweaters and most of them walked across the campus with boys, whereas Soldan girls mainly walked with girls.

I never had a girl in high school, mostly because I didn't have money to go on dates. Or clothes. But to be perfectly honest, I also had a terrible inferiority about girls. I thought of them as having different feelings than I did; and I thought of myself as singularly unattractive. No girl had shown any aggressive interest in me that would have disabused me of this conception, so I submerged myself in schoolwork and let my lively fantasies take care of my yearnings for those girls whom I was attracted to but much too inhibited to approach.

My meeting, that day, with the Washington U. Scholarship Committee went very well. I was told that I would be granted a full scholarship, but the presiding dean warned me that such a grant would not include the additional money needed for books, supplies, laboratory fees, meals, etc., and that I would have to supplement the scholarship with a job that would provide the extra money. I figured that my Hiawatha earnings would get me started, and I had hopefully applied for an NYA job which, if I got it, would take care of me the rest of the way. The National Youth Administration was a new government organization set up by Franklin Roosevelt to assist college students with jobs that were to be created on campuses and paid for, at the rate of fifteen dollars a month, out of federal funds. That wasn't enough to buy clothes, but it was just about enough for everything else, providing I brought my lunch.

The more I talked with those counselors at Hiawatha who were going to college, however, the more my fears about Washington were allayed. Not that they made me feel I would have an easy time of it—to the contrary, they all warned me of the perils of the transition from high school to college, a transition from relatively small classes with teachers who knew your name to huge lecture halls presided over by professors who read you their gospel and would have no personal contact with you from one end of the semester to the other. But what Bud Fischer and Mo and Babe and the others did make me aware of was that each year the seniors, a fourth of the student body, departed and that there was inevitably room for those freshmen who were able to endure and advance.

I thought about college a great deal; all the time, really. For years—all of high school and even before that—I had feared that because of our poverty I would not be able to go beyond high school. From the time I was ten, our life had been a struggle to survive, to elude creditors, landlords, and social workers who came around periodically to investigate the status of my brother and myself. A family that cannot put eight cents' worth of gray-fatty hamburger on the table for dinner is not a family that can likely produce seven hundred dollars tuition for college.

But my fantasy about going to college had been undaunted by the hamburger realities, and in my heart I somehow knew that when the time came I'd make it.

I go into all this to help explain my reaction when Mo Brennan appeared as usual with the Indian Mound mail for the daily mail call. Outside of an every-other-day letter from my mother, and a postcard from a girl I used to play tennis with in Forest Park, I had received no mail until Mo handed me this letter from Washington University. It had been sent to my home address and forwarded. I turned it over to see if, as always, my father had opened the flap of the envelope and read the letter. My father and I had fought this letter-opening battle for a long time. No matter how I yelled and screamed at him, he was compulsively attracted to my mail—all mail—and all he would ever say in response was, "What have you got to hide from your own father?" To my surprise, it looked like for once he had resisted the impulse to jimmy open the flap on the Washington U. envelope. I sat down on my cot to read the letter:

Dear Sir:

We regret to inform you that in the apportionment of our funds for scholarship assistance in the oncoming scholastic year, we find that our funding is insufficient to include you in the 1936–1937 program.

However, if you wish to apply again for the following academic year, in the spring of 1937, we shall be pleased to give your application prompt consideration.

Yours sincerely,
Lionel R. Bunting, Registrar

348

I sat there on my cot like someone had drilled me between the eyes with a .22. I could feel the blood running from my veins; my mouth went dry, and I was sick to my stomach.

Mo said something, but I didn't hear him. He came over and poked his forefinger against my chest. "Hey, what's with you? You're white as a nun's ass."

I didn't have the strength to talk, or even to hand him the letter. He took it from my limp hands and read it.

"I'll be a son of a bitch! I'll be a no good son of a bitch! Listen, they can't do that! It's too late—you haven't got time to do anything now, for Christ sake!"

It was just "Dear Sir," a form letter—that seemed to bother me more than anything.

"You get a lawyer—my uncle's a lawyer."

Paul Roth had come into the cabin on his way to play chess with Babe Halpern. Mo gave Paul the letter.

"That's the trouble with having to depend on other people for money," Paul said. "Can't you get it from one of your relatives?"

"My father used up all our relatives by 1933," I said.

"Well, can't he borrow the money from the bank or someplace?"

I just said no. I couldn't explain to someone like Paul that no one will lend you money if you have no visible assets. Or invisible, for that matter.

For the rest of that day I just lay there on my cot, staring at the ceiling, not moving, not even my eyeballs. I had suffered a kind of total paralysis. I sent Corny to look after my activities.

Well, I thought, that's that. I'll try to get a job, but next year they'll write me again: "Dear Sir." I'll probably be getting that form letter every summer for the rest of my life.

I didn't go to dinner—I couldn't have eaten if they had paid me. Heavy knocks like this invariably hit me in the mid-section. I had so involved my future existence with going to Washington that I could not even imagine what life would be for me in the fall. I had no working experience or skill; and with most everyone unemployed I could not see anyone hiring me. My ambition, as far back as I could recall ambition ("And what do you want to be, little man?"), had always been to be a trial lawyer like Clarence Darrow. I had read everything about Mr. Darrow and sometimes I would look in the mirror and address the jury the way he did. When I debated for Soldan (we won the city championship) I was Clarence Darrow all the way. But to make it to the actual courts I had to have a law degree, and "Dear Sir" had put an end to that dream. There used to be ways of getting admitted to the Bar without going to law school, as Darrow himself had done when he was young, but those days were long gone. And so were my hopes now.

I don't think I slept much, if at all, that night, but with the dawn of the new day came a slim ray of hope in the person of Babe Halpern. He had heard about my scholarship knock and came to the cabin to tell me about a private organization in St. Louis that had helped him through Mizzou.

"It's too late for this year, of course," he said, "but you should call the head of the organization and make an appointment to see her."

He gave me her name, address, and phone number: Mrs. Irwin Bettman, Scholarship Foundation, St. Louis. I called her that morning from the phone in Big Chief Berman's office (he was out) and told her I was interested in trying to get one of her scholarships. She said to come and see her. I didn't tell her that I needed the scholarship immediately. I decided it was better to spring that on her in person. Also, I didn't ask for a specific appointment because I knew it would be too far off.

I found out that the truck was going into St. Louis for supplies that afternoon, so I told Berman I had to go along to pick out some vitally needed Indian materials. The minute we hit St. Louis, I jumped the truck and went straight to Mrs. Bettman's address on Waterman Avenue. A uniformed maid opened the door.

"May I see Mrs. Bettman, please?"

"Was she expecting you?"

"Well, sort of. She said to come see her."

"She is quite busy at the moment. . . ."

"I'll only be a few minutes. Just tell her and see if she has a few minutes."

The maid hesitated. I smiled at her and stood up as straight as I could.

"Who shall I say is calling?"

She went away with my name while I stood on the porch outside the open door. It was a lovely big house with gardener-tended flowers lining the steps and potted plants all along the balustrade of the porch.

The maid returned and led me into a small sitting room. She said Mrs. Bettman would see me in a short while. I hoped she would hurry because my confidence was waning fast in these surroundings. The bravado with which I had stormed these Waterman Avenue parapets was deserting me even before Mrs. Bettman's appearance. I was beginning to feel self-conscious and foolish for having barged in to see her.

Mrs. Bettman was a tall woman, handsome and elegant, with a gracious calmness in her manner. I apologized of course for having appeared without an appointment, but I explained as quickly as I could about the disaster that had befallen me.

"That is certainly unfair on the part of the university," Mrs. Bettman said.

"I was just wondering—why I came to see you—if maybe you had one scholarship left over—maybe somebody who got one decided not to use it, or something like that."

Mrs. Bettman smiled and shook her head. "No, I'm afraid all our scholarships were given out last March. But we can certainly consider your application for next year. . . ."

"But next year . . . is so far away. And this is . . . Listen, Mrs. Bettman, going to college is something awfully important for me. I've really counted on it. I mean, there's nothing to live for if I can't go *now*. I know that sounds pretty melodramatic, but I've worked so darn hard all these years and now the kids with money who didn't do nearly as well as I did all go to college and I don't. Sure, I can wait a year and I guess I'll have to, but then going to college won't be the same."

I was having trouble controlling my lips, so I got up to go. "I'm sorry I bothered you. I just had to try. . . ."

Mrs. Bettman put her hand on my arm. "Before you go," she said, "come with me for a moment—it can't do any harm."

I followed her through a hallway and into a large living room, where, to my amazement, there were three card tables with ladies sitting around them, playing bridge.

"It just so happens I'm having a bridge party for the executive committee of the foundation," Mrs. Bettman explained.

"Oh, my goodness—and I interrupted . . ."

"It's all right, I was dummy this hand."

The ladies had stopped playing and were looking in my direction. I wanted to crawl under the rug.

"Ladies," Mrs. Bettman said, "I've just had an emergency visit from this young man who had a scholarship from Washington U. that was retracted at this late hour because they've run out of funds."

There was a sympathetic murmur from the ladies.

"He's a head counselor at Camp Hiawatha and came all the way in to see me."

"Where did you stand scholastically, young man?" one lady asked.

"I was second in my class."

"What school?"

"Soldan."

"How old are you?" another lady asked.

"Sixteen."

"And you're a *head* counselor?"

"Yes, ma'am."

"Why is college so important to you?"

"Because . . . well, I don't want to sound immodest, but I want to go to law school because Clarence Darrow is getting old and we'll need someone to replace him."

"A commendable objective," Mrs. Bettman said. "I can promise you serious consideration when we give out our scholarships next year."

"I'm terribly sorry to have interrupted your bridge," I said. "I had no idea—but it was a pleasure meeting you. It makes me feel better knowing there's an organization like yours that helps out those of us who need help." I had had a lot of practice at getting on the good side of those whose favors I needed, and praise such as this fell from my lips as spittle from a baby's.

Before I left, Mrs. Bettman gave me an application form to take with me. On the way back to Hiawatha, jiggling around in the old truck, I did feel somewhat better even though college in the fall was as hopeless as it had been before I went to St. Louis.

Chapter Eleven

Your Eyes Are Getting Heavy and You Will Do As I Tell You! Won't You? *Please!*

After Bud Fischer was released from the infirmary, he was never allowed to be alone. Wherever he went, whatever he did, a counselor had to be with him because he was prone to sudden faints. The Bagnell doctor who finally came to examine him said that it might be months before all the traces of the copperhead poison were out of his system, and until then the effect of the poison was such that he might keel over in a faint at any time.

And he did. The faint never lasted for very long, but you'd be walking along with Bud and he would suddenly crumple and fall to the ground, out cold. We were instructed, when this happened, to stretch him out, elevate his feet, and make sure he hadn't swallowed his tongue. After a few minutes he would stir, arouse himself, get right up, and continue walking as if nothing had happened.

One evening after Bud had walked back to our cabin with Paul Roth and me, little Chief Babe Halpern dropped by to ask me to tell a ghost story at the next weekly powwow. Word of my success in scaring the wits out of the Indian Mound campers with "The Pit and the Pendulum" had traveled to Chief Berman, and this was to be a command performance for the entire camp.

"You should have heard him," Paul said. "As that pendulum with the blade on it got lower and lower, moving toward the center of the victim's body, I thought those kids would all pee in their pants. He had them absolutely hypnotized."

That's how we happened to get on the subject of hypnosis. Babe, as I previously mentioned, was a psychology major, and he had performed some experiments in hypnosis that he told us about. He told us how, under hypnosis, people could be made to perform intellectual feats and physical feats they otherwise would not have been capable of.

"You mean you can enlarge a guy's brain and his muscles?" Mo asked skeptically.

"No, it's not a matter of enlarging anything. Rather, it has to do with suspending some things—blocks, inhibitions, feelings. It's rather simple in hypnosis to suspend the feeling of pain or fear or addiction. And with post-hypnotic suggestion we can implant reactions which can last for years."

"Like what?"

"Well, any number of things. Biting fingernails, smoking, fear of height, nervous tics. . . . We have instructed subjects in deep hypnosis to do something on a certain day and at a certain time four months later and they have done exactly as directed."

"You say 'we'—you mean you're a hypnotist?"

"We've been doing these experiments in abnormal psych. The professor is there, of course, but we perform the hypnosis."

"Can you do it to one of us?"

"I guess so, but you'd be resistive because I've told you all this and it would be hard to establish a position with you. There are eight degrees of hypnotism and you only get really interesting responses when you get to five or beyond."

My brother appeared at the screen door. He wanted a penny to buy some jawbreakers at the canteen.

"What about Sullivan there?" Mo asked. "He doesn't know anything about it."

Babe said he thought that Sullivan would be a relatively easy subject if he was willing.

"Do you mind if Little Chief Halpern hypnotizes you?" I asked Sullivan.

"What you say?"

"If he puts you to sleep."

"Heck no, I don't want to go to sleep. I want to go up and get some jawbreakers."

"You can go up in a few minutes. This is kind of a test to see if he can make you sleepy."

"Well, I'm not—so he'll lose."

"I'll give you a quarter if I can't put you to sleep," Babe offered.

Sullivan thought that over. He didn't have a penny to his name. "All right," he said, "but hurry up before they close the canteen."

Babe had Sullivan lie down on one of the cots and told him to relax. Then Babe took a key ring with keys out of his pocket and, holding it by the chain, let it dangle in front of Sullivan's eyes.

"Now I want you to watch these keys very closely," Babe said, "just keep your eyes on these keys, keep watching them, and listen to me as you watch these keys moving back and forth, back and forth, watch the keys, back and forth, back and forth, now you're getting a little sleepy, watch the keys, your eyelids are beginning to get a little heavy. . . ."

Babe was talking in a low monotone, his inflections keeping rhythm with the moving keys. I knew, from the way I had seen Sullivan react to candles, that he would be easily hypnotized. If Sullivan was at a table on which a candle was burning, he couldn't take his eyes off the flame, and pretty soon he got glassy and if the flame wasn't extinguished Sullivan would close his eyes and fall asleep sitting at the table. It only took a few minutes of watching those keys for Sullivan's eyelids to begin to flicker and then drop shut.

"You are now asleep, fast, fast asleep," Babe said. "Your eyelids are stuck fast. You can't open them. Try. Try hard. You see? No matter how hard you try, you can't open your eyes."

Babe put away the keys. "He's hypnotized," he announced.

"Show us some tricks," Mo said.

"Don't think of this as tricks," Babe said. "I've simply induced an unconscious state, and now I will impose myself on that unconsciousness and exert my will."

Babe stood up. "Sullivan," he asked, "can you hear me?"

Sullivan nodded yes.

"Good. Now I want you to get up and stand on one leg with your arms outstretched."

Sullivan did as directed.

"Your legs and arms are made of wood," Babe said, "and you are perfectly comfortable like this. You have no desire to move your arms and legs. You can stay like this for hours. You have no desire to put your leg down. Your arms are not tired. They are not going to get tired."

"He could be faking all this," Mo said.

Babe asked if Mo had a pin. Mo opened a drawer, scrounged around in it, and found a needle.

"Now, Sullivan," Babe said, "I want you to open your eyes, but you will see only what I tell you to see. Open!"

Sullivan opened his eyes.

"Good! Now I want you to think about your right arm. When I count to three your right arm will not feel anything. Nothing. It is made of wood, don't forget, and so you will not feel anything. Ready? One—two—three!"

Babe took the needle and jabbed it into Sullivan's outstretched arm. Sullivan didn't react at all. A little round of blood appeared over the needle prick. Sullivan continued to keep his one-legged balance.

Babe took some matches from his pocket and lit one. He moved the flame closer and closer to Sullivan's eyes until it was virtually searing his eyelids, but Sullivan did not even blink.

"Here," Babe said to us, "pass this piece of paper around and put down a number—five or six digits—with letters, if you want."

We passed the paper around.

"Now, Sullivan," Babe said, "I want you to listen carefully. I'm going to read you some numbers that I want you to remember. Then I'm going to tell you some things I want you to do." Babe slowly read off the list of numbers we had written down. Mine was 264176AB4Z. There were ten such numbers on the list.

"Sullivan," Babe said in a commanding voice, "when I say go, I want you to put down your arms and leg, go outside, get some water in the pitcher, pick up six stones, run to the rec hall and back, bark like a dog, do three somersaults, come back in here, and sit down at this table."

Babe said "Go!" and Sullivan did everything precisely as directed. After he had returned to the cabin, Babe put a piece of paper in front of him. "Now write down those numbers I read to you," Babe said.

Without hesitating, Sullivan wrote down a list of numbers. We compared them against the original sheet and there was only one mistake.

"You said you could plant some things that the subject would do later," I said.

"Yes, post-hypnotic suggestion."

"How about swimming? Tell him he can swim."

Babe told Sullivan that when he went down to the water the following day, he must jump in and swim. He told him how he'd kick with his legs and move his arms and hold his breath when he jumped in the water. While he was telling him all this, Sullivan made faint, jerky motions with his arms and legs and held his breath.

"What if I gave him some commands?" Paul asked.

Babe told him to try. Sullivan didn't react at all. Babe told Sullivan to close his eyes and Sullivan obeyed. "You see, he hears only me. If I told him that after he wakes his brother was not in the room, he wouldn't, *couldn't* see you even if you went over and put your arm around him. I have a very deep hold on his subconscious. He is definitely in the deepest kind of hypnosis."

"Well, you've sure made a believer out of me," Mo said. "Listen, what about my next chemistry exam? I have a hell of a time with chemistry. What about I get hypnotized and have all the formulas and equations read to me?"

"It might work if you knew what to do with them."

"I'm gonna come see you just before next year's finals."

"Well, I better wake up Sleeping Beauty," Babe said. "Sullivan, I'm going to count to three, and when I say *three*, I want you to wake up. Ready?" Babe counted to three, but Sullivan did not wake up. Babe repeated his instructions, again counted to three, but Sullivan did not open his eyes. Babe got irritated. "Now, come on, Sullivan, snap out of it! When I clap my hands I want you to wake up. You're not sleepy anymore. Your eyelids are not heavy. You are waking up. Open your eyelids. Awake! Wake up!" He clapped his hands. Two times. Three. Right in front of Sullivan's face. No response.

"For Christ sake," Babe said. "What is this?"

I moved over to the cot and knelt down beside my brother. "What the hell?" I said to Babe.

"Listen, take it easy," Babe said, obviously worried. "I've done this a dozen times and they always wake up."

He started all over again with his litany about Sullivan opening his eyelids and counting to three, but Sullivan did not react at all.

I felt a rise of panic. When I was a sophomore in high school, one of the fraternities hazed a boy—just an initiation prank, something they made him drink, I believe, but the boy went into a coma and, after ten days, died. I knew the boy—he was on the debating team with me. My panic about Sullivan embraced this memory; I reached in front of Babe and took Sullivan by the shoulders and shook him, calling out his name. Shook him hard. Slapped his cheeks. Quite hard. Nothing disturbed his deep sleep.

"We better get the nurse," Mo said and he went running out the door.

Babe kept talking to Sullivan, trying to awaken him in any way he could think of, but to no avail. Sullivan's face was white and rigid; he looked dead. I could not swallow. I put my fingers on his pulse—it was faint and slow, very slow.

The nurse, Miss Collins, came bustling in, carrying her bag. Mo had already told her what had happened. She shoved Babe out of the way and sat down on the bed beside Sullivan. She pushed up his lids and looked at his eyes. Then she put her head on his chest and listened. Afterward she opened her bag and took out the blood-pressure equipment. She watched intently as she pumped the blood-pressure bulb. My insides felt like I was dropping in a runaway elevator.

"I don't know a damn thing about hypnosis!" Miss Collins exclaimed.

"Well, let me tell you—" Babe started to say.

"And neither do you!" she snapped. She took out a hypodermic and shot something into Sullivan's arm. Then she waited several minutes before taking his blood pressure again. It was a cool night, but Babe was perspiring heavily.

Miss Collins stood up. "All of this boy's vital signs are way down," she said. "He doesn't react to stimulus. We'd better rush him in to see Dr. Eggerton in Bagnell. Let's just hope *he* knows something about hypnosis. If not, we'll have to keep right on going to St. Louis."

We carried Sullivan up to the main building, where the camp car was parked. I got in the back with him and the nurse. Babe drove and Mo sat beside him. I put my arm around Sullivan's limp body and held him against me. He felt very small. Babe drove down the narrow road at a breakneck speed. Occasionally the nurse reached over and took Sullivan's pulse. Each time I asked if he was all right. She didn't answer me. She was furious, and her fury extended to all of us. She was right. It was Babe's doing, but we had all condoned it—more than that, encouraged it. We were as much to blame, willing, eager spectators, as the perpetrator himself. Especially me. His brother. If I didn't have the sense to protect a small boy against this guignol, then who would? Some brother! I encouraged him and then watched him being treated like Pavlov's dog. Only Pavlov didn't get his dog into this kind of terrible trouble.

My lips were close to Sullivan's ear. The engine of the old car, going at that speed, made a great noise. No one would hear me. "Sullivan," I said, "Sullivan! Oh, please wake up, please! Sullivan. Sullivan. Please. Please! *Please!*" I talked to him like that most of the way to Bagnell, but he didn't hear a thing.

Dr. Eggerton was having a late dinner, but he came down to his office the minute we carried Sullivan in.

"He's in a hypnotic coma," Miss Collins said. "This fellow put him into a deep trance and couldn't get him out."

Dr. Eggerton gave Babe a withering look and ordered all of us out of the office except Miss Collins. We went to sit in the small outer office. Babe put his head forward and buried his face in his hands. I was too nervous to sit. I began to fantasize how I would break the news to my mother. I didn't want to tell her on the telephone. Of course I'd have to take Sullivan's body back to St. Louis, but I couldn't just arrive with no notice; I'd have to let her know beforehand. Maybe I'd telephone my father and let him tell her—no, he was always so bad about delicate things.

I stood at the window and watched the flickering jets of the gas streetlamps. Our family didn't practice praying, so I just said, God, please help him. He had nothing to do with this, God, so please help him. He's a boy who's had no fun.

We waited in that little office for over an hour. Finally the door opened and the doctor came out.

"Where did you learn about hypnotism?" he asked Babe.

"At school," Babe said, standing up, "in abnormal psychology. I've done it ten or twelve times."

"In class? With your professor present?"

"Yes, sir."

"Practicing on other students?"

"Yes, sir."

"Superficial hypnosis. But when you deal with children—they're so vulnerable—don't you realize the deeper the hypnosis, the more difficult it is to handle the subject?"

"I do now."

"Well, you're not to practice any more of your hypnotism on anyone at Camp Hiawatha."

"Don't worry, Doctor."

"What about my brother?" I demanded. The hell with lecturing Babe when I didn't know about Sullivan.

"He's all right," Dr. Eggerton said. He opened the door and led us back into his office. Sullivan was sitting on a chair drinking hot tea. He gave me his big missing-teeth smile.

I knelt down beside him and put my hand on his arm. "Are you all right?"

"Sure—I'm fine."

"You know what happened?"

"The doctor told me. But all I know is I fell asleep."

"You don't remember learning some numbers and standing on one leg?"

"I did that?"

"Or having a needle stuck in you?"

"Really? Where?"

"I'll tell you all about it tomorrow."

"Show me where I got stuck."

I tried to show him, but there wasn't a mark. He finished his tea and we got up to go.

"Thank you with all my heart, Doctor," I said. "How much is your bill?"

"It gets charged to the camp," Miss Collins said.

"Goodbye, little man," the doctor said to Sullivan, putting his hand on top of his head.

"Goodbye, Mr. Doctor," Sullivan said. "And thank you for the tea."

The doctor smiled at him and we started to leave. Sullivan looked up at me, a worried look. "I guess I don't get that quarter, huh?" he asked.

Chapter Twelve

Chin Up, Pants Down, and the Mosquitoes Be Damned!

Mostly what the counselors talked about when they got together was girls. There was only one girl in the camp, Blanche Marlies, who was the secretary, but she had a boyfriend who came down weekends from Sedalia. I enjoyed listening to all the girl talk because, as I said previously, I myself had never had a real girlfriend. Nor had I ever had sex with one. I had played around with girls at parties and I daydreamed about sex a great deal, but the opportunity to get in bed with one had never presented itself.

At first I was amazed to hear the extent of the other counselors' sexual triumphs, but Mo, in his growly voice, put me straight: "You don't believe all this bullshit, do you? They're playing with themselves, that's all. That lunk in Mark Twain—what's his name?—Howley?—the one who spun out all that bullshit about spending the night with those two sisters—you can bet the only times he ever gets it out of his pants is to pee."

"You mean none of them has really laid a girl?"

"Oh, sure, *some* of them—but you can bet it's mostly the ones who don't talk. Like you. I don't hear you shooting off your mouth about all the dames you've bounced."

"Well, I haven't."

"Haven't what?"

"Bounced any."

"Not even one?"

"No, not really."

"What the hell you waiting for?"

"I just—well, haven't had the opportunity."

"Opportunity! You think they're going to come up and say, 'Please let's get in the back seat of your car and do it'?"

"Well, that's part of it—we don't have a car."

"I don't mean you *need* a car. Find yourself a bush or a back porch. Girls want to do it, but you got to push them into it."

"Do you do it a lot?"

"I used to—until I met Greta. Then I had eyes for no one else. Greta—well, she liked it, but it made her feel guilty and it would take her a month to get over it and ready to be persuaded again. But thank God that's over."

"Greta?"

"Yeah. We broke up the night before I left for camp. She was going off too, to be a counselor in a girls' camp, so I thought it was a good time to split up."

"What did Greta do?"

"What do you mean, what did she do? She went to school, like I do."

"Isn't that, uh, unusual?"

"What's unusual about going to school?"

"What I mean is, girls who do it are usually, well, waitresses or nurses or someone like that, aren't they?"

"What the hell are you talking about?"

"It's just that I hear nice girls from good families won't do it."

"Now listen, I'm a nice guy from a good family, right? I do it, it's okay, but if a girl has the same feelings I have and she does it, she's a scarlet woman, that it? The idiot American dream—to marry a virgin. Who the hell wants a virgin? Doesn't know anything, full of hang-ups, quotes her mother. The worst lay I ever had was a virgin. All she did was cry. Before, during, and after."

In the face of Mo's pique at my own virginal status, I was almost tempted, in justification, to divulge that I was really only sixteen, but then again I didn't know how he would react to having a head counselor above him who was his junior. But even at sixteen, based on the criteria of the other counselors, I should have long since made my sexual debut. I had come close a couple of times, but I knew that in Mo's eyes close was worse than total abstinence.

"Any guy who gets close," he had once expostulated to Corny, "and doesn't is either chicken or faggy."

Mo had received no letters (nor had he written any) until one arrived from Greta. It had been sent to his home address and forwarded to him. He was lying on his cot reading it during the rest period, when he suddenly shot upright. "Pin Oak! Listen, that Girl Scout camp across the lake, isn't that Pin Oak?"

"Pipe down, Brennan," Corny said. "I'm trying to practice." He was sitting on the edge of his cot, as usual, blowing silently into his horn.

"How do you like that? She's right across the lake!"

"Does she know you're here?" I asked.

"No, that spat we had, I didn't tell her anything."

"Is she trying to make up?"

Mo was too busy reading to answer. Corny accidentally blew a high note on his horn and we all jumped.

"I'm sorry! Sorry!" Corny recoiled at our stares. "I was just imagining this big riff and—"

"Right across the lake!" Mo exclaimed, jumping to his feet. He motioned to me to come outside; he led me toward the rec hall, beyond earshot of the cabin.

"Let's go over there tonight."

"Where? The Girl Scout camp?"

"Yeah."

"We'll never get permission—you know Berman."

"Screw Berman—we'll go on our own."

"You mean, not tell him?"

"What he doesn't know won't constipate him."

"But if he finds out, he'll can us."

"Not us. We're indispensable. Anyway, how's he going to find out?"

"You better go by yourself, Mo. I really need this job."

"I need you for the canoe. Besides, Greta may have a girl-friend and you'll finally get fixed up."

"You mean you're going to do it in a *Girl Scout* camp to *Girl Scouts?*"

"I'd do it in a church to nuns, for crying out loud! Anyway, once they take off those dumb uniforms they're not Girl Scouts—they're female potatoes like all the rest. I'm going up and sneak in a phone call to Greta, and tonight we'll paddle us over to Pin Oak."

"Now, wait a minute, Mo—I'm not much of a canoe pad-dler. . . ."

"Will you stop worrying? Cripes, no wonder you never get laid. Put your mind on what's important and everything else takes care of itself."

There was obviously no way I could turn Mo off. At eight o'clock he came to get me, and with a fearful sense of foreboding doom I followed him down to the lakefront, which was deserted. It was dusk. He put me in the bow of a canoe, showed me how to hold the paddle, untied the boat, stepped into the stern, and off we went.

Actually, paddling the canoe across the still, quiet lake in the dusk was a lovely experience. All I could hear were the shore birds settling in for the night and the sound of the paddles breaking the water. After a while I was able to stroke the paddle without splash-ing the surface. It was easy to navigate, since Pin Oak was the only installation on the opposite shore and its lights were clearly visible.

Mo had arranged with Greta to meet her on the shore a short distance away from the dock. As we neared the shore, a flashlight suddenly snapped alive and Mo headed for it. There was a clearing in the brush where it was easy to beach the canoe. Two girls were waiting there: the one with the flashlight was small, rather blond, with red cheeks and very white teeth. The other was, to put it quite simply, the most beautiful girl I had ever seen in my life—and that includes the movies. She had dark hair in a ponytail, violet almond-shaped eyes, and breasts that made a mockery of her Girl Scout blouse. The one with the flashlight was Greta.

"This is my friend Connie Firestone," Greta said to me after Mo had introduced us. Connie looked at me and smiled. I felt all my bones melt.

"We can't stay very long," Greta said, "because they may come looking for us."

"We brought a little snack," Connie said. She had a low voice with a whispery quality to it. They led us up the bank to a grassy spot where they had spread a blanket on which there were a cake and a thermos of lemonade. The gnats and mosquitoes were bad, but Greta passed around a bottle of citronella, which we rubbed on ourselves. Mo put his hand on Greta's thigh while he was eating his cake.

"I understand you're a head counselor," Connie said. She had long fingers with healthily pink nails bottomed with white arcs. The valley of her breasts showed above the top button of her Girl Scout blouse.

"He's our number-one Indian," Mo said, "and the best ghost man in camp. Sometime make him tell you 'The Pit and the Pendulum.' You won't sleep for a week."

"Oh, I absolutely adore ghost stories!" Connie exclaimed.

"Well, it's not really a ghost story—it's a horror story."

"Better still! Will you tell it?"

"Listen," Mo said, "Greta and I are going to take a little walk. You two make yourself comfortable on the blanket."

They left with the flashlight. "I'd feel pretty silly sitting here telling you a story," I said. I was having a little trouble breathing now that we were alone.

"Why did he want to take a walk?" Connie asked. "Just when we were all starting to have fun?"

"I guess they wanted to have—uh, to have a private talk."

Connie's violet eyes studied me. "Do you have a girl back home?"

"No, I . . . No."

"How come?"

"I wanted to keep the summer to myself." A pretty senseless remark, but I was having trouble keeping my head clear.

"I know what you mean!" Connie said, and I was grateful. "I did the same thing—cut off all my tangling alliances."

"Where do you go to school?"

"Stephens College in Columbia. I'm a sophomore. And you?"

"Washington University." What else could I say?

"Do you live in St. Louis?"

"Yes."

"I'll bet you never even *heard* of where I live—Chillicothe."

"I've *been* to Chillicothe."

"You haven't!"

"I went there once with my father when he had his jewelry line—to help him carry his samples."

"What did you think of it?"

"Prettiest main street I ever saw."

"Imagine your having been to Chillicothe! Do you think you'll come again?"

"No—my father lost his jewelry line."

"You know," Connie said, "it's chillier here by the water than I thought."

There wasn't a breath of air stirring, but I moved closer to her and put my arm around her. Just *barely* put it around her as if she wouldn't know it was there.

"I should have brought my jacket."

I put my arm around her more securely.

"Oh," she said, "I barely know you—but it does feel warmer."

If Mo had been sitting there instead of me, he would doubt-less have pushed her back onto the blanket and tried to make out. But I just kept on talking as we both faced out to the lake. I let my hand fall a little down from her shoulder so that my fingertips touched the side bulge of her breast. She didn't object. We kept on talking. She had a wonderful laugh. I put my other hand on top of hers. The smoothness of her skin and the scent of her neck were emboldening me. I looked her full in the face. She turned her violet eyes to mine.

"Are you feeling warmer?" I asked.

"I'm fine now," she said.

I put my lips forward to kiss her, but she rolled her lips away from me and all I got was hair. I could hear Mo growl, "Take her face in your hands and *assert* yourself!" But instead I took my arm from around her and clasped my hands across my knees.

"Oh, don't be hurt," she said.

"I'm not hurt," I said in a hurt tone.

"Yes you are."

"I'm not."

"Come here. . . ."

She had turned to face me. I put my arm around her again and she put her lips against mine. It was so powerful, so exciting, so beyond anything I had ever experienced with a girl before, that I felt myself ready to have an orgasm. Whether I would have had or not was to remain unresolved, for at that moment, with our lips locked and her soft billowy breasts pressed against me, there was a great stirring in the underbrush, a thumping, whirring sound, as Mo came pell-mell out of the vegetation, his pants half on, half off.

"Come on! Let's go! Let's go!" he shouted at me as he headed toward the canoe.

I unwound myself from Connie and sprinted after him.

"What's wrong?" Connie cried. "What happened?"

"Run!" I yelled to her. "Run!" She got up and ducked out of sight.

Mo literally picked up the canoe and pitched it onto the water. We scrambled aboard; as flashlight beams began to appear on shore, Mo propelled the canoe with mighty strokes toward Hiawatha.

"Keep low so they can't see our faces," he whispered.

It is very difficult, I discovered, to paddle a canoe and keep low at the same time. From the shore now a cacophony of female voices was coming at us. When we got to the center of the lake, we rested.

"What the hell did you do?" I asked. I was panting heavily from the canoe dash.

"They caught me with my pants down."

"Greta too?"

"No, she escaped."

"They know who you are?"

"No—my ass was bare, but I covered my face."

"But they know you're from Hiawatha?"

"They'll surmise that. Maybe they'll line all of us up for an ass inspection. 'You mean, Madam, that you can make positive identification of Counselor Brennan's ass?'" Mo suddenly thought of something: "Have you got freckles on your ass? I've never noticed."

"I don't think so."

"Did you score with that Connie?"

"I was just getting into it when you broke everything up."

"What a luscious piece *she* is!"

I didn't want him to speak of her in those terms. "We better get ourselves back to camp," I said.

"Yeah. What did you think of Greta?"

"Terrific."

"I got mosquito bites all over my ass."

"Now, *there's* how they'll identify you—you should have used the citronella."

Mo laughed. "Listen, buddy," he said, "when Greta's ready there's no time for citronella."

Berman never found out just who violated the virgin shores of Pin Oak, but after that night the canoes were all padlocked together. The day after our visit Mo broke out with a terrible case of poison ivy in the intimate places you can imagine. He was in constant misery, especially when he had to walk or go to the bathroom. "If I could only think of some way not to piss," he lamented. He kept himself painted with calamine lotion, but it didn't do much good.

Greta wrote him a letter, which he showed me, to say that she had poison ivy so bad she was running a fever of 103 degrees. It was a sad letter. There were tear splotches all over the ink. Of course, if Charlie Chan or Dick Tracy had been put on the case, Mo would have been easily collared, but lucky for Mo (and me) Big Chief Berman never got wind of the incriminating coincidence of the two poison ivies.

It took Mo about ten days to get rid of his affliction; I guess it taught him a lesson because afterward he never again mentioned going across to Pin Oak or even getting laid.

During the course of the summer Connie Firestone wrote me several letters that she signed "Love"; I reread all of them almost every day. I wrote to her much more than she wrote to me, but I didn't mind. I rekissed her a thousand times, and had a thousand fantasies about what might have been if Mo hadn't come charging out of the underbrush. I'd never known anyone like Connie. I think I would have married her right then and there if I'd had the chance. I asked her to send me a picture of herself, but she never did. We promised to find each other after school started in the fall, either in Columbia or St. Louis—after all, Columbia was only a couple of hours from St. Louis and I wrote how I'd hop down there on the weekends. I was so far gone I gave no thought to how I would finance even a single such expedition. The only reality that intruded on me was the pall of having lost my scholarship—and the status of being a college man.

But thanks to Connie, a rather dormant part of me had been inflamed; wonderment had shifted to desire. I couldn't get her out of my mind. One evening, in the middle of a chilling bonfire performance of "The Tell-Tale Heart," I began to think about Connie and me on the blanket that night, and I completely blanked out on the heart which was beating a lively tattoo (courtesy of Corny) under the ground at my feet. There were a couple of minutes there while I fumbled around, making up things as I tried to get back on the track, that must have made poor Poe wince in his tell-tale grave.

Chapter Thirteen

I'll Bet When I'm Dead and Gone, I *Still* Can't Do the Dead Man's Float

The camp did not hear about my brother's hypnotic coma because those of us who were party to it never mentioned it, and Miss Collins did not send a report to Big Chief Berman. We all liked Babe very much and we instinctively knew that if Chief Berman got wind of what Babe had done, he would fire him. Lucky for Babe, Berman had been across the lake at the Girl Scout camp when the ill-fated hypnotism had occurred. (Berman was visiting Rosemary McMartin, the Girl Scout directress, whom he had met that time he had gone for the snake serum.)

The day after the hypnotism Babe was full of concern about Sullivan, but there was nothing to worry about; Sullivan was in good fettle. In the morning wrestling session, he won his match, and Mo moved him up to number two on the flyweight ladder. Also, in the rec room that morning Sullivan found a Nehi bottle cap that had a winning twenty-five-cent mark under its inner lining. He came running into my Indian crafts room to show me his Nehi prize. The odds against finding a twenty-five-center were astronomical—in fact, finding *anything* under the Nehi bottle cap was pretty astronomical—and Sullivan was bubbling with excitement.

I asked him a few questions about the previous evening, but it was obvious that he recalled nothing; it was also obvious that he was none the worse for having endured the ordeal. Sullivan was beginning to enjoy camp and to shuck off the aura of morose detachment, of loneliness I guess you might say, that had always enveloped him. His unexpected prowess as a wrestler had given him a measure of confidence that he had never had before—albeit a tentative confidence, edged with a suspicion that it was not real—but without any element of cockiness.

My own feelings toward Sullivan were ambivalent: in one way I was happy to watch him beginning to respond to challenges he would never even have attempted before he came to camp. Sullivan was a non-participant who strenuously avoided any confrontation whenever he could. He had a ready excuse for not doing things, for not even *trying* to participate in any endeavor that involved competition. For instance, he did all right in school, studied just enough to get by, but he would never extend himself in a deliberate attempt to get a high grade for fear of not succeeding. If he only tried for a mediocre grade and received it, that satisfied him. Better to try for a little and achieve it than to try for a lot and fail.

When Sullivan started to wrestle, that was again his attitude, but Mo straightened him out right off the bat. For Mo, wrestling was a divine calling, and he inducted the campers into it like a holy order. From the moment they first set foot on the mat, Mo emphasized their assets rather than their shortcomings. He had a fine knack for making every boy feel that his quickness or his headlock or his body press was a remarkable achievement, and by the end of the first week there wasn't a boy in his class, Sullivan included, who didn't have dreams of becoming the new Strangler Lewis or Jimmy Londos. At the end of each session Mo would reward those boys who had done particularly well with a star which he glued on the back of the boy's left hand. For a camper to be able to walk around Indian Mound Village with one of Mo's stars on his hand was a swaggering achievement.

On the day after his hypnotic coma, not only did Sullivan find a twenty-five-cent Nehi cap and receive one of Mo's stars, but a much greater good fortune befell him. It happened in the evening when we went down to the lake for another of my fruitless attempts to get waterborne. As usual, Sullivan sat on the edge of the dock as my lookout while I lowered myself into the crib, full of the high resolve I had worked up during the day, determined that this time I would really *do it*. I had just started my pathetic attempts to fulfill that resolve when I heard Sullivan say, "Listen, I'm coming in."

I looked up and saw him standing on the ledge of the crib. Without hesitating, he jumped in and began swimming toward the far end of the crib. I couldn't believe what I was seeing. Sullivan's fear of water, as I previously explained, was as pronounced as mine, perhaps more so, but here he was splashing his way down the length of the crib, no anxiety, keeping himself nicely on the surface even though his strokes were clumsy. He splashed his way back to where I was and stood up smiling.

"Why didn't I do that before?" he asked. "There's nothing to it."

"When— How did you— Who taught you to—"

"Nobody. I mean, I dunno. I really dunno. I was just sitting here and I felt like trying to jump in and swim. So I did. Listen, A, it's nothing. Honest. Just stand up here and jump in and you'll swim."

Babe's post-hypnotic swimming instructions! Although I had seen it with my own eyes, I still found it hard to believe that anything so difficult as swimming could have been achieved with Babe's abracadabra. It certainly shattered my rationalization that it was some kind of physical deficiency in a person that rendered him incapable of swimming. The inner ear, something like that, that was probably hereditary and afflicted all the offspring of a family. Sullivan was proof positive that a non-swimmer's only obstacle was fear. If only I could be hypnotized and shuck off my fear as easily as Sullivan had. That wouldn't be possible now that Babe had been put out of the hypnotism business. But I am sure that if Babe had not promised to stop hypnotism, I would have taken the risk of a coma in order to get the same post-hypnotic natatorial results as Sullivan. I would have risked more than that, so desperate was I to get my feet off the bottom of that goddam crib and float freely on the surface. It seemed so easy, the way Sullivan had done it. Not to be able to swim was such a disgrace, so cowardly.

Angrily, I grabbed hold of the side of the crib, took an extravagant breath, put my face in the water, got my feet up, and tried to shove myself away. But no sooner had my hands left the security of the wooden railing of the crib than I panicked as I always panicked. My head jerked up; coughing, my feet plummeted to the bottom. Coward.

As we walked back up the trail toward the cabins, I felt dejected and depressed and, to be honest about it, resentful of Sullivan. I don't particularly mean jealous, although at that moment I certainly envied his sudden-found ability to swim, but my resentment was really beyond jealousy. It had to do with his very presence, the responsibility of caring for him, and caring about him. And that's what I meant when I said I was ambivalent about him. Since the beginning of the Depression, when I was ten, I had pretty much had to fend for myself, especially after we were reduced to living in that one room at the busted-down Avalon Hotel. I had to scrape and connive for everything I needed, from daily food to shoes for graduation from the Admiral Dewey grammar school. I even had to defend myself against my own father to keep him from unearthing my meager savings from their secret hiding place and plundering them.

In all this time, since Sullivan was mostly away with relatives, he was not an element in my life. Even on those brief occasions when he did return to live with us, I managed to exist around him, never involving myself in his existence at all. Out of necessity, I had learned to be self-sufficient, self-serving, and totally selfish. It was a way of life I had, by circumstance, been forced into, and it was comfortable, and in a real sense, this insecurity was my security.

But now Sullivan was no longer an itinerant who touched down for a moment without disturbing anyone or anything, only to disappear lightly without leaving any tracks. He was back for good and it was his home, such as it was, as well as mine, his hunger as well as my hunger, and if he was sad or sick I had to care, to get involved whether I wanted to or not. There was no longer any way to exist around him, to pretend he was some nameless boy from another country. I had been deeply moved and troubled when the nurse could not arouse Sullivan from that coma. During that drive to Bagnell when I held his limp body against my body, I had cared about him as much or more than I had ever cared about any of my own travails.

But I did not want to play this role. I had myself to look after, and that was enough. I did not want the additional responsibility and worry. I did not want to be big brother, although big brother I was. In name. And that's the way I wanted to keep it. Big brother in name only.

Chapter Fourteen

What It Comes Down to Is—the Only Pal You've Really Got Is Yourself, and Vice Versa

After my brother returned the bayonet, Horse Face quieted down. He didn't go so far as to be cooperative, but there was a precipitous drop in his obstreperousness level. As far as I could tell, his relationship with Sullivan was not that of a newfound buddy, but rather Horse Face adopted the role of a belligerent protector. Sullivan was kid stuff for Horse Face, but woe unto anyone who didn't treat Sullivan properly. Horse Face still preferred to do his palling around with his crony, Knuckles, but as far as Sullivan was concerned, starved as he was for a friend, Horse Face filled the bill. It didn't matter that Horse Face's partner in the mess-hall line was Knuckles or that in choosing up for baseball Horse Face selected several bigger kids before he chose Sullivan—what mattered was that he *chose* Sullivan. Also, on one occasion when Knuckles pushed Sullivan against a wall, Horse Face immediately popped Knuckles a good one between his shoulder blades.

I was walking along the trail from Blue Bird Village one afternoon when I heard voices in the adjoining woods and I stopped to investigate. A short distance off the trail I spotted Horse Face and Sullivan sitting with their backs against a tree, sharing a cigarette. Horse Face was obviously an old hand at smoking, but Sullivan was clearly making his debut.

"You ever drink any beer?" Horse Face was saying.

"No—not really."

"You never even *taste* any?"

"Oh, I *tasted* it."

"And?"

"Awful bitter."

"Bitter! Shows what you know! Beer is the most wonderful thing I ever drunk."

"You drink whole glasses?"

"Whole *bottles* is what I drink. Me and my old man. He taught me how you tilt the glass so's it don't foam all over. Sometimes we just sit out on the stoop nights and drink beer and watch everything."

"But don't you get drunk?"

"Naw—it just makes you feel good sittin' there drinkin' beer with your old man."

"I like the *idea* of beer. . . ."

"You ever been in the Budweiser plant and watch 'em mixing the hops and malt and molasses and honey and all the gunk that winds up in beer? That's some sight! And afterwards they give you free drinks."

"I didn't know they put honey in beer."

"Of course they do. That's what gives it the color."

"But then how come it's so bitter?"

"They use bitter honey."

"You sure know a lot of things."

"One thing I know about is beer."

"Now that I know it's got honey, maybe I could get to like it."

"Sure you could—nothin' like sittin' on the stoop with your old man with a good ol' beer and gettin' some drags off his cigarette."

"Don't your mother care?"

"She ain't around."

"Where is she?"

"She works nights at the laundry."

"All night?"

"Yeah—she goes in at six, until six in the a.m. A-course, some nights my old man don't feel good enough to sit outside, so then we don't drink beer." He sat silent for a while, looking up in the trees. "That's most of the time."

"My brother and me both tasted beer once and we didn't like it."

"Your brother don't drink beer?"

"No."

"Is he a creep?"

"Who? My brother?"

"Yeah. I can't make up my mind about him."

"You mean 'cause he don't like beer?"

"No, not just that. I mean everything. Like all that Indian shit—painting his face and hopping around and singing in that lousy voice of his."

"I think he's pretty neat."

"Yeah? What about gettin' us down there that night to watch him get eaten by rats? What's neat about that?"

"Was you scared?"

"Are you kidding?"

"Well, everybody else was."

"Anyway, what's so great about scaring a bunch of kids in the dark?"

"I thought it was terrific—the pit and the pendulum."

"How'd he do those rats? Did he tell you?"

"I didn't ask him."

"Ask him."

"You don't like him, do you?"

"I ain't made up my mind."

"But you said he was a creeper."

"I say that about a lot of people. That don't mean they maybe ain't all right. Your brother—the thing is he don't like *me*."

"He gave me the bayonet for you."

"Yeah, but he don't like me. That's my trouble. I ain't the kind of person anybody likes."

"I like you, Horse Face."

"No. I just think you want to stay on my good side."

"Listen, Horse Face, I'm your *friend!*"

"I don't know. My old man talks about it a lot. All those pals of his and how when he come back from the war and wasn't, well, okay, how they didn't have time to come around any more. My old man says you look out for yourself—that's the best friend you got."

"If something happened to you, Horse Face, I'd come around to see you. And bring you things."

"What things?"

"Oh, I dunno—things you wanted."

"Look, anything ever happens to me, you bring me some beer. Wherever I am, you smuggle in a couple bottles of cold Griesedieck under your sweater."

"You betcha."

"You'd do that?"

"I sure would."

"Even though you might get caught?"

"No difference."

"Well, I guess we got the last drag outa that." He rubbed out the cigarette butt on the ground. "How'd you like it?"

"It was swell."

"You feel all right? Not sick?"

"No, I feel okay."

"You'll make a good smoker."

Sullivan beamed with pride at this compliment.

"The trouble is that's the only cigarette I got, so you won't be able to practice."

"That's all right—I'll remember."

"That's what I don't like about gettin' stuck in a camp—you ain't got no way to go around and lift a package of cigarettes and a couple of beers."

"It's out of the way, all right."

"I hate to be stuck somewhere where I can't get my hands on things."

I quietly left them in the woods and returned to my cabin. I honestly couldn't tell whether Sullivan had a friend or not.

Chapter Fifteen

A Thousand Deaths, a Fellow Can Die, in Every Bottle of Rock 'n Rye

When I got back to my cabin, Babe was there waiting for me. He had organized an evening in Camdenton and he wanted to know if I would like to join in. Since I had never before been invited to participate in Babe's social plans, I figured his invitation was proffered as a token of his regret for the hypnotism debacle.

There were eight of us in Babe's party: Mo and Paul from my village, Bud Fischer, Floyd the cook, Babe, me, and two counselors from Blue Bird Village. On the way in, Floyd entertained us with stories about some of the practical jokes he had pulled on various people over the years. Floyd had a wonderful way of making a story come so alive you'd swear it was happening right then and there.

There was this one friend of Floyd's that he told us about whose doctor wanted him to go to the St. Mary's Hospital for some tests, but the man wouldn't go because of a terrible fear he had of hospitals. Finally Floyd talked him into going, but once he was in the hospital, the man was even more nervous and fearful and in a state of near-collapse. Meanwhile, Floyd had arranged for a streetwalker, who was an old friend of his, to dress up in a nun's hospital habit and go into the friend's room soon after he was admitted. The nun-streetwalker began to attend to the friend, straightening up his bed and all that, then she began to caress him and kiss him and finally she got in bed with him.

When Floyd came to visit his friend the following day, he found a changed man, a real hospital *aficionado*, and for the three days of his tests Floyd's friend couldn't have been more cheerful and cooperative, waiting for another visit from the obliging nurse-nun.

When it came time to leave, however, the friend refused to go and it was as difficult to get him to leave the hospital as it had been to get him to enter. Ever since then, Floyd said, his friend had been praying for some affliction that would hospitalize him again.

Floyd regaled us with stories like that all the way in.

Camdenton was a rather small Ozark town, but there was a CCC camp nearby, and also some of the men who worked on the Bagnell Dam lived in the town. There were two movie houses, three bars, a restaurant, a diner, and a taxi-dance hall called the Club Lido. The first thing we did when we got in was to go to the movies. One movie had *The Duke of West Point*, and the other movie had *Jeepers Creepers*. We decided on *The Duke of West Point*; halfway through it I was sorry we had not chosen *Jeepers Creepers*.

After the movie, we went to the diner for a hamburger and a shake. On our way there, Bud Fischer fainted, but Mo caught him before he fell to the sidewalk. It was a short faint and Mo just held Bud under the arms until he came to. None of the passersby paid much attention to Bud because there were so many CCC men in the town all the time getting drunk.

On our way out of the diner, Floyd suggested that we visit the Club Lido. I knew about taxi-dance halls from that time we lived at the Avalon. There was a taxi-dance in the basement, the Good Times, and there wasn't a night I didn't listen to the band music before I fell asleep, the sour wails of the saxophones coming up the narrow shaft that ran along one side of the building. Taxi-dance music was always slow and rhythmic, music to rub to.

I had actually been in the Good Times only once, when, in desperation, I went down there one night to see if I could get a job.

I was only twelve then, hardly an employable age to work behind the bar at a taxi-dance hall, but the owner was quite nice to me. I got a good look at the taxi-dance girls. I thought most of them looked like movie stars in their bright sparkly dresses in the twirling colored lights.

But the girls of the Club Lido were no movie stars. The only ones of our group who actually bought tickets and danced were Floyd and the two Blue Bird counselors. The rest of us stayed at the bar, which was located outside the low railing that demarked the dance area. Babe ordered Griesidieck beer for everyone, but I just let mine sit. As my brother had told Horse Face, I had tried beer once and found it had one of the worst tastes I had ever put in my mouth. Like soap.

Floyd spent five tickets on a pimply blonde with skinny legs who wore a ratty red dress that had a circle of wet where her customers had been rubbing against her all night. I never saw such ratty girls. If someone had given me a free ticket, I wouldn't have used it on any of them. The four men in the band were all drinking, tipping up their glasses while they were playing; it was hard to recognize the tunes they were trying to play. The piano player only played with one hand to keep his drinking hand free. There was a huge fat man who sat at a counter selling tickets. He kept calling over to those of us at the bar, urging us to "get a big dime's worth, come on, boys, your pick of our beauties, here you go, boys, three dances for a quarter." He even sent over one of his "beauties" to hustle us. She had oily hair that was parted in the middle and when she smiled at us I tried not to look at her teeth. She seemed to concentrate on Mo.

"How about it, big boy?" she said, rubbing her hand on the inside of his thigh. "Come over and Polly will show you a go-o-od time!"

"Get lost," Mo said.

She took her hand away like Mo's thigh had suddenly turned to flame. "Go screw yourself," she said.

"It would beat screwing you," Mo said.

Polly went on back to the fat man and said something to him. The fat man turned to look at Mo, and then he turned away and waved his hand at someone toward the back of the dance floor. A big, burly man with some teeth missing materialized out of the tinted darkness.

"We better move it on out of here," Babe said.

I didn't exactly follow what was happening. Babe put some money on the bar for our beers as the burly man started over toward us. As he got closer, I could see that his nose was twisted sideways and there was a heavy scar that ran along the corner of one eye. He was maybe thirty-five, maybe a little more. He walked in a slow way, sort of side to side, and he was looking straight at Mo. He came right up to Mo, very close.

"All right, punk," he said, "what'd you say to the lady?"

I felt a cold streak move up my back.

Mo didn't answer him, but he didn't back down; not an inch.

"I'm talkin' to you, punk."

"Look," Babe said placatingly, "I've paid up and we're going, so why don't you—"

"Keep your nose out of this," the bouncer said. "I'm talkin' to this punk here. We don't allow no punks like this to come in here and insult our ladies."

Babe said, "Come on, Mo."

Mo gave the bouncer one last look, then started to follow Babe, but the bouncer was not ready to let him go. He grabbed Mo by the arm in a tight grip. Mo took the bouncer's hand and threw it off his arm.

"You punks are all alike, aren't you?" the bouncer said.

"Stop calling me a punk."

"Aw, listen to that, he don't like to be called a punk. Well, I'll tell you what you really are—a fruit. Nobody but a fruit would come in here and not buy a ticket and bad-mouth one of our dancers. Well, I'm gonna let you in on what we do to fruits. We fix 'em so they don't come back. Not ever. Y'understand?"

He drew back his right arm and threw a heavy punch at Mo's head. Instead of trying to pull away or to duck, Mo lunged forward and as the bouncer's punch landed harmlessly over his shoulder, Mo wrapped his arms around the bouncer's waist in a fierce hug. The bouncer weighed much more than Mo, but Mo had him up off the floor in the circle vise of his arms, slowly increasing the pressure. Mo had his hands locked together behind the bouncer, who strenuously tried to extricate himself, but there was nothing he could do. The breath was being squeezed out of him. The bouncer tried to hit Mo with his fists, but, held as he was, all he could do was flail ineffectually at Mo's back. The bouncer's face changed color several times and he made an effort to say something, but all that came out were some gurgling sounds.

The fat ticket-seller, who I guess was the boss, came over to help the bouncer, but Babe and Bud stepped in his way and the ticket-seller didn't go any farther. The bartender was a small, bony man who pretended to be busy washing glasses.

Mo gave one crisp, sudden jerk with his arms and the bouncer passed out. Mo lowered him to the floor beside the bar and we all walked out. It had all happened so quietly and quickly in the dim light of the bar that no one on the dance floor seemed aware of it. But somehow Floyd had seen what was happening. He and the Blue Bird counselors had left and were outside the entrance in the truck with the motor running when we came out. Babe pushed in back of the wheel and we took off.

All the way back we were in a celebratory mood, laughing and recounting what Mo had done to the bouncer. In my fantasies I had often polished off bullies, but this was the first time I had ever seen a real villain get his comeuppance.

When the truck rolled into camp, Babe suggested we all go to his quarters, which were in back of the office. Blanche was in the office, working late, typing reports, so Babe invited her, too.

We crowded into Babe's small room, sitting on the bed and floor. Babe turned on the radio and started to get some things down from his shelf. Olives, sardines, crackers, peanut butter, and a large hunk of dry, granite-hard rat cheese. The last thing he brought out was a bottle that he had hidden in the bottom of his laundry bag. It had ROCK 'N RYE in big letters on its label. With the light behind it, the bottle was beautiful to look at, amber liquid with several white rocks on the bottom, coral in a saffron sea.

I had never tasted liquor, with the exception of that one drink of beer I mentioned previously, primarily because we never had any booze around the house. Not that my parents were teetotalers (I had seen them have a highball when offered one), but because there was never enough money for food, let alone booze. Also, I hated the smell of whiskey. I suppose that dislike stemmed from that time in the Avalon when the room across the hall was occupied, on a regular weekend basis, by a noted criminal lawyer, his blond woman friend, and another man, all of whom stayed in the room, drinking, from Friday afternoon to Sunday night. Their drunken sounds and the pungent smell of the whiskey floated into our room through the open transoms. After that, the very thought of whiskey disgusted me.

But the bottle of Rock 'n Rye which Babe passed around didn't seem like whiskey. Its color, its sweet taste, and honey smell resembled Coca-Cola more than booze. Blanche sat down on the floor beside me and began to fix peanut butter and crackers to go with the Rock 'n Rye. It tasted very good. One of the Blue Bird counselors tried to get Blanche's attention, but she seemed to prefer sitting with me. She was a tall girl, about nineteen, who didn't have a very good nose and wore a lot of bright red lipstick. I really didn't like girls with thick lipstick like that, and besides (a) my heart was in Pin Oak, and (b) Blanche had this steady boyfriend who came down every Saturday from Sedalia. But I had spent quite a lot of time the past couple of weeks working with Blanche on a camp show for Parents' Day and we had become pretty good friends. Blanche could play the piano and she was able to play the songs I made up for the show. I would write down some lyrics, the way I had composed for our high school shows, and then sing the words to some melody I invented. Blanche was able to listen to me sing the song and then right away play it on the piano. I had always been in awe of piano players. A couple of times Blanche pointed out how one of my new songs closely resembled some well-known tune, whereupon I would toss it away and make up another song.

The radio was tuned to a station in nearby Eldon that was bringing the music of Ben Bernie and his lads from the College Inn in Chicago. Blanche was a quiet, rather shy type who never talked much when we were working on the show, but as the Rock 'n Rye made its rounds, sipping it and nibbling the peanut-butter crackers, she began talking a blue streak. How much she liked my songs, and what fun she had when we got together. On and on. And about some uncle of hers who was with Tin Pan Alley in New York City and how she planned to send him some of my stuff to see if he would publish it.

Blanche began to sing along with Ben Bernie, who was singing, if you could call it that, "I'm in the Mood for Love." As Blanche was singing I found my eyes riveted on her lips, all that moving lipstick, and I began to giggle.

"I feel like dancing," Blanche said, putting her arm around mine.

"There's no room," I said.

She sat there holding my arm and humming along with Ben Bernie. "Oh, let's dance," she said, squeezing my arm against her breast. I was watching her moving lipstick and giggling.

"I know," she said. "Let's go across to my room. We can dance to my radio." She had a room in back of the other side of the office. She stood up, holding on to my arm, and pulled me to my feet.

"Where you two going?" Babe asked.

"We'll be right back," Blanche said.

They all made derisive noises of disbelief as we left the room.

Their voices sounded far away, coming from the distant end of a tunnel.

When we entered Blanche's room she immediately turned on the radio. Instead of Ben Bernie there was a woman singing,

When did you leave heaven,
How could they let you go?
How's everything in heaven?
I'd like to know.
Yes, I'd like to kno-ow. . . .

Blanche put her body against mine and started to dance, singing in my ear. She moved her body against mine in rhythm to the music, her breasts moving from side to side while her hips moved up and down. She was certainly well coordinated. I had never before danced like that. If the Club Lido girls charged a dime, Blanche was definitely worth two bits.

"You excite me," she said, and she moved her lips from my ear onto my mouth. I could feel the thick lipstick smearing off on me. It tasted like cherries. Blanche was getting very excited, but as she started to kiss me, I began to feel rather sick, a heavy, lumpish feeling in my stomach. I also felt a little guilty about being unfaithful to Connie. But what I mostly felt was that lump in my stomach.

"Listen, lock the door," she said.

My face felt hot and my forehead was quite damp. She turned out the light. I could hear her moving around in the dark.

"I'm over here," she said.

I followed her voice. She was in bed. She pulled me down beside her and put her lips on mine. She still had plenty of lipstick. My hand touched her back and to my surprise she had taken off her clothes. I had never been with a naked girl before, and certainly never been in bed with one. I touched around on her to be sure she was naked all over. She was. I should have been out of my head with excitement, for here was the moment I had so often thought about and fantasized, but my head felt funny now and the lump had moved up from my stomach to my chest. Blanche began to unbutton my shirt. Her breasts felt wonderfully soft and warm against my chest. She was terribly excited.

"Oh, oh," she said. "Please hurry, hurry and take me."

I started to unbutton my pants. The lump was in my throat now and my head was pounding. My mouth was flannel dry. Sweat was pouring off my forehead and running down the side of my face.

"Blanche, look . . . Blanche. . . ."

She was holding me for dear life and moaning and urging me to hurry. I was struggling to break her grip on me while trying to keep the lump down in my throat. My whole body was pouring sweat. I gave a mighty heave and rolled out of her grasp. I grabbed my shirt and headed for the door, bumping into everything in the room on my way.

"Where you going? Are you crazy?" Blanche was hissing at me. "How can you leave me like this? You bastard! Come back, oh, please come back."

I just made it through the door when the lump surged loose and I threw up. I'd never thrown up like that before. It seemed to come up from my socks, and my body heaved in great spasms. It came up through my nose. I had trouble breathing. I was terribly scared. I couldn't catch my breath between vomits. I wished to God my mother had been there. Somehow I managed to stagger over to the infirmary building, which was not far from the office. Although a dim light was burning, the room was deserted. In the middle of a table at the door was a sign: RING FOR EMERGENCY. I pushed the button; immediately I had to go outside to throw up again.

Miss Collins came into the infirmary, tying up her bathrobe. At first she didn't see me retching outside the door, but then she heard me. She gave me something white to drink, but I continued to vomit. She kept asking me what had I eaten, where did it hurt, but I was too sick to answer. I had never been so sick in my whole life. Miss Collins dug her fingers into my stomach to see if I had appendicitis. She studied my tongue. She probed for tender places in my abdomen. Through it all, I vomited.

From the shelf Miss Collins took down a large bottle labeled IPECAC and filled a shot glass with its contents.

"Drink it down," she commanded.

It looked awful. I shook my head. I wanted to ask her to phone my mother, but we didn't have a phone. Miss Collins put her left hand under my head and pushed it up while with her right hand she stuck the ipecac under my nose.

"Drink!" she bellowed. She started to tilt the glass, so it was either take it down the throat or up the nose. It was the foulest stuff I had ever had in my mouth. I howled.

"Shut up!" she commanded.

"Oh, God," I moaned.

"If you can keep that down you'll be all right."

I threw it up. She put another dose down me.

"I wish I had a stomach pump," she said. She asked me again and again if I had eaten anything or drunk anything, but I only moaned and groaned.

After the second dose of ipecac, I didn't throw up anymore, but I continued to gasp for air and exude sweat from every pore. Miss Collins gave me a pill that she said would make me sleep.

"I don't want to sleep," I said. "I want to die."

She bathed my face with a cold washcloth and after a while I passed out.

Sullivan was sitting beside my bed when I awoke. Hot sun rays slanted onto the sheet that covered me, but I had stopped sweating. Sullivan's close face was anxiously peering into mine. I felt like my insides had turned to plaster of Paris.

Sullivan shook my arm. "Wake up," he said. "Are you waked up?"

I grunted.

"How do you feel?"

"Like death," I mumbled.

Sullivan moved his face even closer, to get my ultimate attention. "No, listen, A, no dying, you hear? I'm counting on you . . . not to die." There were tears in the bottom of his eyes. I realized, looking at myself through Sullivan's eyes, what I currently represented in his uncertain world.

"Oh, I don't mean *really* die," I said, my vomit-sore stomach hurting with every syllable I spoke.

"Well, what do you mean?"

"Nothing. Just that I feel lousy. But I'll be all right."

"Promise?"

"Promise. Cross my heart and hope to die."

"There you go again."

"That's an expression."

"Just don't say die, all right?"

"All right."

"What was it, ptomaine?"

"Something like that."

"Well, you got to get better—it's my birthday tomorrow, remember?"

"Oh, sure." I hadn't remembered.

"You think Floyd will remember?"

"You bet. You're going to have the best camp birthday of all."

"A—listen, I was awful scared this morning." Only my mother and Sullivan called me A.

"Why?"

"When they came and said you were in the hospital. Somebody said you'd been poisoned."

"I'm okay."

"When I heard them say poison I thought maybe you'd croaked."

"Not me."

"And, you see, you're practically the only one who cares about me."

"What about Mother and—"

"Uh-uh. Nobody cares about you who sends you off to Keokuk."

"But we had to live in that lousy one room."

"They didn't send *you* away, did they?"

"I was bigger."

"But I was littler, so I took up less room and ate less."

"Now, Sullivan, Mother cares about you and you know it."

"Yes, but she don't care like you do."

"How can you tell I care?"

"You *do*, that's all. Like this birthday. You care that I have a big cake and all. Mother and Dad never—aw, you know about birthdays."

"Don't be too hard on them, Sullivan. They do their best."

"Oh, sure, listen, I 'preciate them. But I'd 'preciate them more if they. . . ." He suddenly didn't want to talk about it anymore. That was the way with Sullivan—he could only feel sorry for himself to a point, then he seemed to realize it was best to drop it and veer off into positive things. "But I'm glad you're not dead, hey! Can I do something for you? You need anything?"

"No. I'll be all right by this afternoon."

"You better be—I'm cutting you the biggest piece of my cake. You remember what I want wrote on it?"

I assured him that I did.

"You want to really know why I want a cake so much?"

"Yes, why do you?"

"Because I've got so many important wishes to make." With that he ran off so as not to be late for his beloved wrestling session.

I had indeed forgotten about Sullivan's all-important birthday. After he left, I gingerly sat up, tested my head and my stomach, and tentatively tried to stand up. My head felt disconnected, but I forced myself to get dressed and go to the dining hall. I thought about that bottle of Rock 'n Rye and I felt like throwing up again. Also, my misery induced despairing thoughts, never far from my surface, about having to pass up college in the fall. Floyd was busy at the stove. The food odors emanating from the kitchen almost forced me to turn back.

"Hello, hello," Floyd said. "You look terrible."

"Oh, I'm fine," I said. I didn't want him to know what Rock 'n Rye had done to me.

"You look like yesterday's scrambled eggs."

"Listen, Floyd, have you gotten a notice from the office that it's my brother's birthday tomorrow?"

He looked at some slips that were pinned to a chopping block with an ice pick.

"Yeah, here we are—Sullivan."

"Well, do me a favor, will you? It's a big birthday for him, so will you make a special cake and write A MILLION HAPPY BIRTHDAYS on it? Here, I've written it down."

Floyd told me to leave it to him.

On my way out of the dining hall I ran into Blanche, who looked right at me but didn't say hello or anything.

Chapter Sixteen

The Sun Broke Through and the Angel Flew in from Waterman Avenue

I trudged back to my cabin from the mess hall on legs made of old spaghetti. My head throbbed worse than ever. Life was as bleak as it had ever been. I could barely make it to my cot.

As I tenderly lowered my head I felt something on the pillow—it was a letter that my blurry eyes had not seen. I looked at the return address: The Scholarship Foundation of St. Louis. That reminded me of my dismal fate in the fall and I felt even worse. I opened the letter:

Dear Aaron:

I am really terribly pleased to inform you of one of those rare scholarship miracles that has befallen you.

As I told you, all of our scholarship money was allotted for the coming academic year, but last week a philanthropist who normally contributes to our funding, but who had been out of the country for the past year, returned to St. Louis and gave us a substantial contribution.

I convened the Committee for the express purpose of seeing if they wished to authorize a special scholarship for you out of this unexpected windfall. I'm happy to tell you that, having met you at my bridge party, they were unanimously in favor of granting you such aid. This means you will have a full scholarship for the entire school year 1936–1937.

When you return from camp, please come to see me so that we can execute the necessary papers. I must frankly say that it is moments like these that make all our arduous work worthwhile. I thought about you and your sad plight many times after your visit, and I don't know when any good turn of events has made me happier.

With all our good wishes,
Sincerely,
Mrs. I. Bettman

I started to cry. Just like that. I covered my face with the letter and let myself cry. Nothing better had ever happened to me, and it couldn't have come at a better time. A stranger, a woman I had seen once, barged in on, imposed myself on—for her to care so much, to give me such an enormous gift. The gift of being myself, of feeling equal; the light-hearted joy of looking forward; of feeling that someday I would be everything I had felt I could be.

All this from a stranger.

Chapter Seventeen

Why Put a Rose on the Grave If the Corpse Can't Smell It?

I was on the top of a ladder helping to hang an INDIAN MOUND sign over the entrance to our village, the letters made of branches, when a runner arrived summoning me to Big Chief Berman's office.

"You have a camper you call Horse Face."

"It's a name that came with him."

"Well, I just got a call—his father died. Have him pack all his things and the truck will take him to the bus in Jefferson City."

"I don't think he has any money."

"We'll get his bus ticket and give him carfare for when he gets to St. Louis."

Horse Face was in back of his cabin, throwing a knife into a tree trunk at ten paces—he was very good at it.

"That's pretty good, Horse Face."

"Okay—you came to crab about me not bein' at woodcraft, right?"

"No."

"Well, I'm sick o' that goddam totem pole. That's all we do is sandpaper that goddam totem pole."

"Listen, Horse Face, sit down here a minute—I want to talk to you."

He eyed me suspiciously, but sat down beside me.

"We've had our little differences, you and me, but I want you to know you've improved a hell of a lot."

"Maybe it's you who's improved."

"Maybe. I never thought of it that way."

"You were pretty pukey."

"Anyway, I just wanted to talk to you."

"I shouldn'ta skipped that goddam totem pole, I know, but I woked up this morning feelin' bad."

"In what way?"

"I woked up thinkin' about my old man and feelin' bad."

"What were you thinking?"

"Oh, I dunno—I just had a bad feelin' about him. You see, there's nobody to look after him when I'm away."

"I thought your mother and your Aunt Bernice—"

"Oh, yeah, but it's not the same for my old man as when it's me. A-course, sometimes when his head is funny he don't much know who I am, but then sometimes he knows all about me and we play casino and listen to the ballgames. I'm a Cardinal fan and he's strictly for the Browns, but it don't matter—I listen to his and he listens to mine. He likes to chew tobacco during the games. Other times too. He says it soothes him. But usually he ain't got none 'cause we ain't got the money to buy it. So when he runs out and really wants some I go out and lift it. I used to have to go into cigar stores and snatch it and run, and once I almost got caught— got knocked down and just barely got away—but now I figured out how to get into Christmeyer's tobacco shop at night and I only take a couple at a time and they ain't wised up yet."

"Horse Face, I really came to find you because I have something to tell you about him."

"My old man?"

"Yes."

"Something bad?"

"You know how sick he's been—how he suffers. . . ."

"He's dead, ain't he?"

"Yes. That's what I came to tell you."

"Oh, hell—and I wasn't there."

"I'm sure he was glad you were in camp."

"When I told him goodbye, it was one of his days he didn't know who I was."

"What you want to do now is remember all the good times you had. . . ."

"Sure, that's all he had—good times. What the hell you talkin' about, rememberin' good times?"

"But you said the ballgames—"

"You ever seen anybody'd been gassed? We'd be sittin' there, everything nice, and alla sudden he'd turn crazy—punchin' me and hollerin' and wettin' his pants, the spit comin' out of his mouth, hollerin' crazy sounds and knockin' over the furniture. Then when it was over, he'd . . . he'd cry. . . ." Horse Face started to cry. "He'd sit down on the floor and cry like he was three years old."

I put my arm around Horse Face's skinny shoulders. He bowed his head, his tears dropping onto the ground.

"I wish I coulda seen him like he was before—just once. My ma says he was the strongest man she ever knew." He turned his face to look at me, the tears running along his pointed nose. "What am I gonna do now? I really liked my old man."

"You're going to take his place. That's how it works—the fathers die and the sons grow up strong and fresh to take their place. You're going to be someone he'd be proud of."

"Crap. I'm gonna be another punk outa Dago Hill."

"When I get back to St. Louis, I'll be glad to see you, Horse Face. Sullivan, too."

"I won't be around."

"Where you going?"

"I dunno—somewheres."

"How about your mother?"

"She don't like me."

"Now, come on. . . ."

"Most of the time, she don't even talk to me."

"Well, *now* she will. Things will be different."

"You don't know my old lady."

"Promise me you'll wait till I get back to St. Louis."

"No, I'll go back and bury my old man and take off."

"It'll be tough for a kid your age to get along. You should stay in school."

"Yeah. Sure. My old man stayed in school—he was a high-school graduate—and look where it got him."

"But he had the bad luck of the war."

"Well, it's always somethin'. I ain't waitin' around for my bad luck."

Horse Face had stopped crying. He eased away from my arm and stood up. "How do I get back to St. Louis?"

"We're putting you on the Jefferson City bus."

"I better pack."

"You want help?"

"No."

"Your father would want you to stay put and go to school and make something of yourself."

"My father is dead. He don't want nothin'."

Chapter Eighteen

A Million Happy Birthdays, Count 'Em—But Don't Count This One

The dining hall was one vast rectangular room with screen on three sides. All of Camp Hiawatha ate at the same time, Indian Mound occupying four tables in the center of the hall.

Sullivan was so excited over the advent of his birthday festivities that he spent the whole meal alternately watching Big Chief Berman and the kitchen door, not touching his food. He knew that he was the only kid in camp with a birthday that day, which meant that he would have undivided attention. On our way into the dining room he had immediately checked to be sure that Big Chief Berman had a present beside his chair. I had already given Sullivan my presents, a bow and six arrows that Corny Barmowitz had made for me in his woodworking shop, and a pocketknife I had bought for thirty-five cents from Bud Fischer.

As the meal ended, Chief Berman tapped a knife against his water glass and stood up. "May I have your attention, please?" he said. "We have a birthday boy today, Sullivan Hotchner of Indian Mound Village, and it's number eleven for him."

There was a scatter of applause and a few whistles. Sullivan blushed.

"Congratulations, Sullivan, and here's a little something from all of us."

The Chief picked up the present and proffered it to Sullivan, who went over very self-consciously to receive it. He said thank you to the Chief and unwrapped the present, which was an American flag.

As soon as Sullivan got back to his seat, the kitchen door opened and in came Floyd carrying a huge birthday cake with eleven candles on it and a giant sparkler crackling in the center. It was three times bigger than any of the previous birthday cakes. Ornately covered with red and white icing, it had spun-sugar roses in bas-relief all along its perimeter. Floyd had certainly lived up to his promise. Sullivan's hands shot up to his cheeks as he jumped up from his seat. A pervasive *ooh!* and *wow!* swept the dining hall, and the campers gave the cake a much bigger hand than they had given Sullivan.

As Floyd put the cake in front of Sullivan, the sparkler anointing him with its flying sparks, everyone began to sing "Happy Birthday." Sullivan looked at his beautiful cake with its inscribed A MILLION HAPPY BIRTHDAYS FOR SULLIVAN, the birthday music filling his ears, and a smile of pure, unadulterated happiness came over his face. He stood over the cake, which was the size of a lady's hatbox and came up to his chin, closed his eyes, and made his wishes. Then he opened his eyes, took a couple of practice breaths, and with one giant effort blew out the twelve candles. The hot stem of the spent sparkler continued to glow. The campers gave Sullivan a nice hand.

Floyd handed Sullivan a large knife to cut the cake, and held a plate at the ready to receive the first piece. Sullivan carefully placed the knife so that the point was at dead center, then pushed down on it, but the knife did not make the cut. Now Sullivan put both hands on the handle and bore down hard, but he didn't make a dent in the cake. He picked up the blade and looked at it.

"I musta forgot to sharpen it," Floyd said.

Some of the campers, impatient to get at the cake, began to make fun of Sullivan for his lack of muscle. A third try also failed.

"Try cutting from the edge," Floyd suggested.

Sullivan put the blade against the edge of the cake and vigorously cut back and forth with it several times, but the knife stayed right on the surface. The campers were beginning to laugh and hoot now. I couldn't imagine why Sullivan could not cut his cake, no matter how dull the knife. Sullivan tried again and again, every which way, beginning to lose his temper, getting red in the face from his efforts.

I was just about to go over and help him, when Sullivan took the knife and scraped away some of the icing. Then he banged the blade against the heavy cardboard underneath. The room exploded with laughter at the cardboard cake, all the boys crowding forward to get a glimpse of Floyd's latest practical joke.

Through the tangle of the campers, I caught sight of Sullivan. There was a stricken look on his face and tears were running down his cheeks. The laughter was deafening. Sullivan threw down the knife and ran from the room.

"Wait, stop him!" Floyd yelled. "I got the real cake. . . ."

But Sullivan was gone.

Floyd came over to me. "Go get him," he said. "I've got a real cake for him. This was just a joke. Can't he take a joke?"

"No," I said, "he can't."

I took my time walking back to Indian Mound. I wanted to give Sullivan a little time to compose himself. I really wasn't mad at Floyd—how could he know what that cake meant to Sullivan? I tried desperately to think of something that I could say to Sullivan. He had again been betrayed, and I was party to it, albeit unwittingly.

I went to Sullivan's cabin and peered through the screen. He wasn't there. I went to my cabin, the rec hall, the waterfront, but he was nowhere I looked. I told one of the boys in Sullivan's cabin to alert me the minute he showed up, then I went back to my cabin to wait for him. Probably went for a walk, I thought.

That time of the year the Ozarks began to get dark around

seven thirty. By eight o'clock, when there still was no sign of Sullivan, I began to worry. I went up to the office and told Babe about him. He sent runners to the other villages in our camp, to find out if they had seen Sullivan or knew of his whereabouts. Word came back that he hadn't been seen.

At nine o'clock Babe and I went to see Chief Berman. The Chief became angry because we had not come to him sooner.

"Where do you think he would go?" Berman asked me.

"I don't know. He was so hurt and angry he might have gone anywhere."

"But where? Would he be more likely to follow a road or go plunging into the woods?"

"I don't know, but I'm going out to look for him."

"We're *all* going out, but we have to be coordinated."

"Do you think he'd do anything that involved the lake?" Babe asked. "Like taking a boat?"

"No," I said, "he just barely knows how to swim."

"Do you have a photograph of him?" the Chief asked.

"No."

"Well, let's wait an hour or so, and if he's not back by then I'll call the police."

In the next hour, Mo, Paul, and I went through the entire camp, but there was no sign of Sullivan. From the moment he left the dining hall, no one had laid eyes on him.

After Big Chief Berman alerted the state police, he organized two search parties, one to go north of the camp, the other to go south. I went with Babe's group, which headed south. We worked our way slowly over the dense terrain, using flashlights, calling, whistling, covering all but the totally impenetrable areas. But the region was so vast that by morning we had not gone very far.

We returned to Camp Hiawatha, covered with mosquito welts, hoping for good news from Chief Berman's contingent, but they had had no better luck. The police came with hound dogs, which sniffed Sullivan's clothes to establish a scent. All the local radio stations were called and given a bulletin with Sullivan's description, to broadcast every hour. Local police within a fifty-mile radius were alerted.

After breakfast, our group went back to continue the search: we worked all day long, but by five o'clock there was still no sign of Sullivan. All I felt was a kind of drained numbness. All night and day I had called his name and sounded my shrill two-fingered whistle that he would have recognized if he had heard it. It was stifling, humid hot as only the Ozarks can get. I had a sudden feeling that Sullivan was dead. A night in this thick undergrowth with all its perils, its mosquitoes and copperheads . . . I dropped in my tracks and leaned my back against the trunk of an old tree. Far off I could hear the hound dogs searching. I closed my eyes and tried to blot out the premonition that Sullivan was dead. I couldn't.

The other members of my group had probably moved on without me, not noticing that I had dropped out. A small plane flew low overhead, perhaps part of the search. I was too tired to think clearly about what had happened and what was happening. The event in the dining room had occurred with the swiftness of a street accident. Now, sitting there in the suffocating heat of the late afternoon, I tried to think of what I could have done or should have done while Sullivan was being made the butt of Floyd's crude joke. Even with hindsight's help, I could not think of anything. But what bothered me most was that I had done *nothing*, just sat there doing *nothing*, and certainly I could have done *something*. If only I had taken the knife from Sullivan and tried to cut the cake myself, then the joke would have been on *me*.

Where could Sullivan have gone? Oh, where? I could not hear the dogs any more. I felt utterly defeated. As I leaned my head against the tree and thought about Sullivan, what I remembered was the time we lived on Art Hill Place, just before the Depression. It was a nice apartment at the top of a steep hill overlooking Forest Park. My mother and father were both working then, and we had paid help to take care of us. There was this one girl, Thelma, who came to the apartment one day with a man who explained about her to my mother. The man was the placement counselor at a home for unwed mothers, and this girl, who had just become a mother, was living at the home with her baby. The home placed the girls in domestic jobs to help pay for their upkeep.

My mother hired Thelma, who was sixteen years old and very pretty. I was nine at the time and I remember asking my mother why Thelma always had two circles of wet on the front of her dress where her breasts were. My mother explained that that was milk for her new baby.

One of Thelma's duties was to take us to Forest Park to play. To get to the park, it was necessary to cross a wide expanse of streetcar tracks that ran along the bottom of Art Hill, parallel to the park. My mother had laid down a hard and fast rule that Sullivan and I were never to cross those tracks by ourselves. There had once been a serious accident there, and my mother, who was by nature a fearful woman, made us promise that we'd never, ever go across those tracks unless we were with a grownup.

One afternoon, a few days after Thelma had started work, she took us across the tracks into the park where there was a play area. After a little while she told me to look after Sullivan for a few minutes, that she'd be right back. For a while I played ball with some kids my age while Sullivan played tag, then he and I walked around looking at things. I spotted a couple of birds' nests and right away Sullivan had one of the great schemes he was always proposing. "Listen," he said excitedly, "why don't we get a lot of bird nests and put them all together in one tree with nails and a hammer and then they can all live together and be happy and eat clams like eagles do." For a four-year-old, he certainly had grandiose schemes.

It was early afternoon when Thelma left, but by four-thirty she had not returned. Sullivan and I stood at the park side of the tracks, looking for her, but she wasn't around.

I looked up and down the tracks. There was nothing coming.

"Come on," I said, "give me your hand."

"No," Sullivan said, putting his hand behind him.

"Look—there's nothing coming."

"No. Mom said no."

"But that dumb, stupid Thelma dumped us here."

"I wait."

Far away we could see a streetcar coming.

"What if she never comes back," I said, "you gonna spend your whole doggone life here?"

"Looka that streetcar," Sullivan said. "It could squish your guts all over."

"Okay, look, after it passes, we cross, okay?"

The streetcar went by with a rackety clatter, sending dust and sparks off the track.

"Now, come on," I said, "give me your hand."

"No."

"Then I'm going without you."

"I'll tell Mom."

"Go ahead. See if I care."

"I will."

"Come *on*, Sullivan!"

"No."

"I'll leave you—I mean it."

"No, no, no!"

I ran across the tracks, leaving Sullivan standing there. Across the tracks there was a row of stores—a cleaner's, a grocery store, a Greek luncheonette, a bar. As I passed the bar, I saw Thelma sitting there with a man. She was drinking and smoking a cigarette. At first I thought I'd yell in at her, but I didn't. I ran all the way up the hill to our apartment. It was after five by now and my mother was home.

"What! You left your brother there by himself? Next to those tracks?"

"He wouldn't come."

"That's a terrible, terrible thing to do!"

"What about Thelma? Don't get mad at *me!*"

We were hurrying down the hill.

"Never mind about Thelma. She'll get hers."

"Leaving two little boys like that," I said.

"I told you never to cross those tracks."

"But we were stuck there."

"I don't care—what if something happened to Sullivan?"

"Oh, he's all right. You'll see."

Sullivan was precisely where I had left him. My mother went across the tracks and picked him up. Then we all three went to the bar. My mother stood in the open door and called Thelma, who came out on the sidewalk.

My mother was in a rage. "How could you leave these little boys? I told you about the tracks!"

"I was just on my way back to get them," Thelma said.

"You tramp," my mother said. "Here you are full of baby's milk and you're picking up men at bars. Your kind should never be given a decent chance. I pity that baby of yours. Now, get up there and pack up your things."

"Who needs your stinkin' job? You and your stinkin' kids."

"You're not a nice lady," Sullivan said.

Thinking about Sullivan, who was four at the time, standing there on the other side of the tracks, sticking to the rules, patiently waiting, I felt a surge of hope that perhaps he wasn't dead. What was in his favor was that by nature he was a survivor. The Art Hill tracks. Keokuk. The ghastly ear abscesses. So maybe, wherever he was, he would survive this.

Chapter Nineteen

If You *Feel* Love, Even Though You Don't *Say* Love, Is That Enough?

As I suspected, I had lost contact with Babe's group, so I continued to search on my own. The dense woods I had been searching suddenly broke into a clearing beyond which there was a small town. All of the houses were on two streets, so it was easy to go from house to house, asking whoever answered if they had seen a small boy of Sullivan's description.

No one had. But when I went into the grocery store, the storekeeper told me that a boy who fitted that description had come into the store that morning to buy some crackers.

"Did he come from around here?"

"Nope—is why I mention him. Never seen him afore."

"Maybe I should ask the police."

"No police here. But up the road a piece in Harmonyville there's a sheriff."

I tried to hitch a ride, but only two cars and a truck went by and none stopped.

Harmonyville consisted of one street with houses and three stores. I asked someone where I'd find the sheriff and he directed me to the barbershop.

There was a man in the chair getting a haircut and a boy reading a Little Orphan Annie comic book. I asked the barber if he knew where I could find the sheriff. He looked up at me over his scissors.

"You're speakin' to him," he said.

"Oh, sir, I'm looking for my eleven-year-old brother who ran away from camp. I was told there was a boy around about here today who might be him. I thought maybe you might know something about him, this boy who was seen around here today."

"Yep. There he is." He pointed with his scissors at the boy with the comic book. "He run away from Eldenton. Waitin' for his pa to come git him." The sheriff went back to work on customer. "Lot o' boys runnin' away this time o' year."

I went on out of the barbershop, bitterly disappointed. I really thought, from the grocery man's description, that the boy he had seen was Sullivan. The rise and fall of my hopes had left me feeling more hopeless than before.

I walked along the dirt road of the town. The evening was getting darker. I was very tired, too tired to care about eating. I kept turning Art Hill Place and the car tracks over and over in my mind. I couldn't stop thinking about it. Sullivan at the tracks. Thelma. Art Hill Place, the last decent home we had had, the place we lived the longest during all those migratory years, going from one flat (in St. Louis an apartment for which you had to furnish your own heat was called a flat) to another, a jump ahead of the foreclosing landlord, getting a few months' concession (pay one month's rent, get three months free before the lease began to run) and then sneaking out at the end of the concession.

We'll, I'd have to face it: my mother had to be told. Berman had asked for her phone number, but I stalled him by saying we didn't have a phone—which was true. But we lived above Sorkin's delicatessen, and although Sorkin wasn't crazy about our getting calls there, it was possible to reach my mother on Sorkin's phone. If Sullivan didn't appear by morning, I'd have to telephone her. God, how I dreaded that. My mother had gone through enough— the depredations of the Depression, her confinement in the Fee-Fee Sanatorium for consumption, my father's heart attack, and now . . .

this. I felt terribly guilty about Sullivan's disappearance, for not having protected him, almost as if I myself had played the cake joke on him.

I had no idea how far I was from Camp Hiawatha. It was getting quite dark. I went into the general store. It didn't smell very good. More cat piss than soap and coffee. I asked the old lady behind the counter if there was a phone that I could use for an emergency call. She took me through a door back of the store where she lived.

The operator put the call right through. Babe answered the phone. He was very glad to hear from me. "I thought we'd lost both of you," he said.

I asked about Sullivan. No sign of him, Babe said. The police had followed several leads, but none led to Sullivan. Chief Berman had again asked how he could reach my mother. I said I would try to call her myself in the morning.

I paid the old woman for the phone, and bought a bag of pretzels, a pint bottle of milk, and an apple, for seven cents. Afterward I walked along the dirt highway until I found a field with a haystack. I got comfortable in the hay and started to eat my dinner, but I fell asleep before I could finish it.

I woke in the night feeling chilly and full of a dream about Sullivan that I tried to remember, but it was just beyond me. I dug deeper into the haystack for warmth. There were nearby animal noises, but the full moon's brilliant light counteracted them. I ate a few pretzels and fell asleep again.

When I next woke, the sun was up and the field dripped dew. I had been dreaming again, this time about the streetcar tracks; as I struggled to recollect the dream, I unexpectedly recalled something about Art Hill, something that startled me into sitting up abruptly; as the remembrance sharpened, I came fully to life. I jumped up, dusted the hay off me, and ran to the road. At that early hour, the sun just up, there wasn't much traffic, but the first truck that came along, a rickety Ford with some crates of chickens, I stepped out in the road and waved my arms. No time to be reticent about hitchhiking.

The driver was grumpy about having to stop, but he gave me a lift anyway. The chickens made a lot of noise and they smelled pretty bad.

The farmer dropped me off where the spur road to Camp Hiawatha transected the highway. I ran all the way to the camp. Of course, I could again be chasing a false lead, but not if I was right about connecting what had happened that time we moved from Art Hill to what had happened now.

The camp was not awake yet, so I encountered no one as I ran along the path that led to Indian Mound. I stopped for a moment in front of the rec hall, then ran around to the rear. There was a ladder lying on the ground. I propped it up against the building and began to climb up to the roof.

The moving van had been packed and ready to go when my mother discovered that Sullivan was missing. That's what I had suddenly recalled, that incident at Art Hill Place when we couldn't find Sullivan. I went up and down the block and my mother and father canvassed the neighbors, but Sullivan was nowhere to be found. Three or four hours of searching, my mother's anxiety mounting, and then Mrs. Harmon on the third floor came out to say that she'd thought she saw Sullivan going up to the roof.

I stepped off the ladder and onto the roof of the rec hall. There were two large galvanized ventilators at one end and a broad brick chimney at the other. I walked across the roof to the chimney, hoping against hope. At first look he wasn't there, and my heart dropped, but I walked around to the other side of the chimney and there, in the sheltered, hidden space between the buttress of the building and the chimney, was Sullivan. He sat with his back against the chimney, sound asleep. Beside him was the American flag he had received from Chief Berman.

As I sat down beside him, he awoke.

"Hi," I said. "How are you?"

He didn't answer. He bent his head forward and looked down at the roof between his legs.

"You must be hungry," I said. I still had a couple of pretzels in my pocket and I offered him one. Sullivan looked at it and hesitated before he took it. He took a bite, but he didn't eat hungrily.

"Can I go home?" he asked. "I don't want to stay here any more."

"Sure, if you want to. But what's there to do at home?"

"I just want to go home."

Home, those three rooms over Sorkin's delicatessen. Sullivan slowly munched his pretzel. We just sat there for a while, saying nothing.

"About the cake," he finally said, "does it mean I don't get my wishes?"

"Sure you do. You blew out all the candles, didn't you?"

"Yes, but you don't get wishes off a phony cake."

"Oh, I don't know about that."

I turned to look at him. He was so skinny and vulnerable. I had never told anyone that I loved them. Not my mother, not anyone. I loved her, all right, but I could never get the words out. Maybe it was a question of courage.

But now, feeling as I did about Sullivan, I felt I could tell him that I loved him; I felt I could actually say the words. I doubt that anyone had ever said that to him. Our family just didn't say that to one another. I put my hand on his arm and he turned his head sideways to look up at me.

"Sullivan, listen," I said; I really had it in my mouth to tell him that I loved him, the words were there, and I tried to say them, but I couldn't. I looked at him and I *felt* the love I had for him, but that's as far as it went.

He studied my faltering lips and worried face, and he managed a faint smile. I think at that moment he knew I loved him. He must have felt it. Certainly he knew that I cared, that I was not just his brother, but also his friend.

Sullivan picked up his flag, got up, and started to walk toward the ladder. So did I.

About the Author

A. E. HOTCHNER is the author of many books and plays, including *Papa Hemingway*; *Sophia, Living and Loving*; *The Day I Fired Alan Ladd*; and *The Good Life According to Hemingway* (2008). With friend Paul Newman, Hotchner cofounded Newman's Own, Inc., which has donated more than $200 million to charity from its line of foods.